Jesus Freaks

ALSO BY DON LATTIN:

Following Our Bliss: How the Spiritual Ideals of the Sixties Shape Our Lives Today

Shopping for Faith: American Religion in the New Millennium (with Richard Cimino)

Jesus Freaks

A True Story of Murder and Madness on the Evangelical Edge

Don Lattin

HarperOne
A Division of HarperCollinsPublishers

HarperOne

Photo Credits:
Introduction, Chapters 2–5, 8–9, and 11, photographs courtesy of
   The Family International.
Chapter 7, photograph courtesy of Shula Berg.
Chapter 10, photograph courtesy of Elixcia Munumel.
Chapters 12, 14, photographs courtesy of Davida Kelley.
Chapter 13, photograph courtesy of Rosemary Kanspedos.
Chapter 17, photograph by Don Lattin.
Conclusion, photograph courtesy of The Associated Press.

HarperCollins books may be purchased for educational, business, or sales
promotional use. For information please write: Special Markets Department,
HarperCollins Publishers, 10 East 53rd Street, New York, NY 10022.

HarperCollins Web site: http://www.harpercollins.com

HarperCollins®, ⚒®, and HarperOne™ are trademarks of HarperCollins
Publishers.

FIRST EDITION

Library of Congress Cataloging-in-Publication Data
Lattin, Don
Jesus freaks : a true story of murder and madness on the evangelical edge /
Don Lattin. — 1st ed.
    p. cm.
ISBN: 978-0-06-111804-3
1. Children of God (Movement) I. Title.
BP605.C38L38   2007
299—dc22   2007018381

07 08 09 10 11 RRD(H) 10 9 8 7 6 5 4 3 2 1

For the children

Davidito and Maria are going to be the Endtime witnesses.
They are going to have such power they can call down fire
from Heaven and devour their enemies.

—DAVID BRANDT BERG
MAY 2, 1978

Contents

Cast of Characters

(Note: Members of The Family International, which has called itself Teens for Christ, the Children of God, and the Family of Love over the past four decades, used numerous aliases. For purposes of clarity, this book uses one name for most characters, even though they may not have been using that name during that chapter of their lives.)

David Brandt Berg was the founder of The Family. He was known to his followers as "Uncle Dave," "Moses David," "Mo," "the Endtime Prophet," or simply "Dad."

Karen Elva Zerby took over The Family when Berg died in 1994. Originally one of David Berg's polygamous wives, she was later known as "Mama" or "Maria."

Richard Peter Rodriguez was the only son of Karen Zerby. He was raised as David Berg's spiritual son and proclaimed to be "Davidito." He was known in The Family during his teenage years as "Pete," but he called himself "Ricky" after he left the fold.

Susan Joy Kauten was Karen Zerby's longtime personal assistant and one of several young women who helped raise Ricky Rodriguez. During much of her time in The Family, she was known as "Sue" or "Joy." She legally changed her name in 1993 to Angela Marilyn Smith.

Merry Berg was the daughter of David Berg's eldest son, Aaron, and Aaron's second wife, Shula. Merry was known in The Family as "Mene."

Sara Kelley was the primary nanny of Ricky Rodriguez and author of *The Story of Davidito*. In The Family, she was called "Sara Davidito."

Davida Kelley was the daughter of Sara Kelley and Alfred Stickland. She was raised in David Berg's household and considered by Ricky to be a sister.

Elixcia Munumel was the widow of Ricky Rodriguez. She was known in The Family as "Nicole."

Peter Amsterdam was born Steven Douglas Kelly. He became Karen Zerby's second husband and the second highest-ranking member of The Family.

Jane Miller Berg was the first wife of David Berg. She mothered his four children: "Deborah" (born as Linda), "Aaron" (born as Paul), "Hosea" (born as Jonathan), and Faithy. Jane Berg was known in The Family as "Mother Eve."

Introduction

David Berg learned the tricks of the evangelical trade from his parents, shown here in a 1926 Miami handbill.

SOME CHRISTIANS MAY take issue with the title of this book, *Jesus Freaks: A True Story of Murder and Madness on the Evangelical Edge*. They may argue that the crazy cult chronicled in these pages has nothing to do with Jesus or the evangelical movement. They may say its founder was not a Christian—that he was a spiritualist or controlled by demonic forces. His sexual immorality, they may argue, is the very antithesis of moral values in the Judeo-Christian tradition.

That's an understandable reaction, but the odyssey of David Brandt Berg is deeply rooted in the Christian tradition. Berg, the founder of The Family, came straight out of American evangelicalism. His grandfather was a famous minister with the Methodist Church, and his father was ordained into another mainline Protestant church. His training as an itinerant evangelist was at his mother's side in the Christianity and

Missionary Alliance. And it was in the Alliance that Berg began his own late-blooming ministry.

During the spiritual counterculture of the late sixties, this previously unremarkable evangelist embraced a strange brew of Christian witness, radical politics, apocalyptic doom, and free love. His followers—known over the years as Teens for Christ, the Children of God, The Family of Love, and The Family International—survived Berg's 1994 death and continued to operate in 2007 as an international Christian ministry with thousands of devoted members living in cells and missionary communes around the world.

Berg's army of dedicated disciples emerged in the sixties as one of the earliest and most organized groups of "Jesus freaks" or "Jesus people," an evangelical movement fueled by two mighty spirits—Christian witness and counterculture zeal. During the sixties, calling someone with long hair a "freak" was not necessarily a putdown. Few "hippies" called themselves "hippies." Many used the word "freak" to describe themselves as a mark of separation from others who were not so enlightened. American pop culture glorified the Jesus people with stage productions and major motion pictures like *Godspell* and *Jesus Christ Superstar*. Billy Graham, the icon of American evangelicalism, gave the Jesus freaks his blessing. Maybe they had long hair and wore weird clothes, but at least they were following Jesus. At least they hadn't joined forces with the devil, or the Moonies, or the Hare Krishnas.

It wasn't long, however, before evangelical insiders heard rumors of strange and unorthodox happenings among Berg's flock. At first, the concerns revolved around the movement's overzealous recruitment of troubled teenagers and the extreme regimentation demanded in its ranks. But the greatest controversy would come when Berg started mixing free love and Christian prophecy. In the search for new converts Berg encouraged his female followers to expand the "law of love," a doctrine that promoted sexual "sharing" among members. Young women were sent forth into the world as sacred prostitutes to bring men to Christ and into Berg's fold. They called this witnessing tool "flirty fishing," after Jesus of Nazareth's call for his followers to become "fishers of men."

Berg was a prophet obsessed with sex. "We have a sexy God and a sexy religion with a very sexy leader with an extremely sexy young following," he wrote in one of his letters. "So if you don't like sex, you better get out while you can."[1]

At the height of the sexual revolution, the lustful prophet mocked traditional Judeo-Christian teachings on sexual morality, preaching that God blessed adults and children who fully expressed their sexuality. "Don't know what the hell age has got to do with it," Berg preached. "God made 'em able to enjoy it practically from the time they're born! But though God didn't count them as under age to have sexual feelings and sexual responses and sexual nerves and sexual orgasms from the time they're born, the System prohibits them from having them until they're eighteen to twenty-one years of age!"[2]

When it came to sex, Berg practiced what he preached. During the late seventies and well into the eighties, children in The Family grew up in a highly sexualized environment. Sexual play was encouraged among prepubescent children and practiced between adults and children and between adults and teenagers. In a 1973 letter originally intended for only his most trusted disciples, Berg wrote that "there's nothing in the world at all wrong with sex as long as it's practiced in love, whatever it is or whoever it's with, no matter who or what age or what relative or what manner! And you don't hardly dare even say these words in private! If the law ever got hold of this [letter], they'd try to string me up!"[3]

Berg even challenged one of society's greatest sexual taboos—the practice of incest. "There are also many Biblical exceptions to so-called incest, or the marriage of certain near relatives," he told his followers. "In fact, there would be no human race if Adam and Eve's two sons, Cain and Seth, had not married their sisters, because there was no one else to marry.... Marriages of brothers and sisters, mothers and sons and even fathers and daughters were very common in ancient times and were not even forbidden for the 2,600 years from the creation of Adam until the law of Moses!"[4]

Among those adult women who would later accuse Berg of child molestation were one of his daughters and two of his grandchildren.

My interest in this story began with children born into The Family. As a journalist, I'd been writing about new religious movements since the seventies. Back then, the story was one of worried parents trying to free their teenage or adult children from authoritarian religious cults. Those worries turned to hysteria following the horrific events of November 18, 1978, when more than 900 followers of the Reverend Jim Jones and his San Francisco–based People's Temple perished in a mass murder/suicide at Jonestown, a remote encampment deep in the South American jungle.

My fascination with new religious movements broadened into an interest in religious movements young and old. For the next twenty-five years, I covered the "God beat" for two San Francisco newspapers. Much of my time was spent writing about the Roman Catholic Church, the rise of the Christian Right, the battle over gay rights in American society, and the emergence of Islam as a force to be reckoned with at home and abroad. As anyone who reads a newspaper knows, rigid fundamentalism and righteous fanaticism are on the rise today among religious traditions young and old.

Fringe religion can be a harbinger of spiritual trends. Cults show us how religions are born. At first glance, the bizarre prophecies and sexual promiscuity among David Berg and his followers seem little more than circus sideshows. But the sexual abuse of children by religious leaders is hardly unique to this Christian sect. Over the past ten years, the American Catholic Church has been shaken by the scandal of priestly pedophilia and paid out over a billion dollars to adult victims of child sexual abuse. And in the aftermath of the terrorist attacks on September 11, 2001, who can argue against the need to better understand psychologically unbalanced zealots who twist scripture, exploit social unrest, and inspire an army of fanatics.

Sometimes it's hard to see the violent mythology in our own religious traditions. Berg and The Family came out of a modern Christian school of thought that puts great emphasis on the apocalyptic aspects of the faith—the Second Coming of Christ, the Rapture, and the Great Tribulation. This is the same Christian tradition on the rise in America today. It is the same Christian tradition that inspires millions of Americans to buy Reverend Tim LaHaye's *Left Behind* series of apocalyptic fiction and films. It is the same Christian tradition that uses fear to inspire and control—fear of eternal damnation, fear of not being one of the elect. It is the "the same revenge-seeking rhetoric that burns so hotly in the book of Revelation," observes Bible commentator and book critic Jonathan Kirsch.

"All the complexities of the modern world are swept away and replaced by the simple conflict between God and Satan," Kirsch writes. "Not coincidentally, the *Left Behind* series peaked at the very moment when the Western world awakened to the new peril that had replaced the 'evil empire' of the Reagan era—the challenge of militant Islam and, especially, the spectacle of religious terrorism on an unprecedented scale."[5]

Long before the first *Left Behind* book hit the best-seller list, David Berg saw himself as *the* Endtime Prophet—the anointed messenger of the coming apocalypse. It was no great leap for his followers to go from a belief in Jesus as the only way to salvation to a conviction that The Family was the only road to heaven. But for some, especially those closest to Berg, it was a deadly leap.

For more than thirty years, Berg controlled thousands of disciples by co-opting their most intimate relationships. He and his leaders would divide and conquer the emotional lives of their flock. On the surface, it looked like free love in The Family, but there was nothing free about it. Sex was used to control and divide. These Jesus freaks were not encouraged to maintain an exclusive emotional bond with one person. Spouses and children were shuffled around the world like playing cards, and Berg was the dealer.

Berg was the dealer, but he did not invent the game. A full century before he proclaimed the law of love, Christian Perfectionist John Humphrey Noyes (1811–1886) ruled over the flourishing Oneida Community in upstate New York, one of the nineteenth century's more successful experiments in sexual promiscuity and utopian living. Like Berg, Noyes was initially inspired to develop a divine justification for his own extramarital communion. Noyes's biographer Spencer Klaw cites "persuasive evidence that he was inspired less by theological considerations than by his own experience of the awesome power of sexual desire.

"Noyes was a man with powerful sexual drives, and for many years he was perhaps the most active participant in the sexual life of the community," Klaw writes. "He was a connoisseur of female sexuality, likening [one female] follower to 'a beautiful plant ... having no outward activity, yet throwing around a fragrance, pleasing our eyes and giving us delight for what she is, and not for what she does.'"

Like Berg, who offered detailed instructions in the art of seduction and insisted that his female followers "burn the bra," Noyes condemned the prudish fashions of his Victorian era. "Woman's dress is a standing lie," Noyes declared. "It proclaims that she is not a two-legged animal, but something like a churn standing on casters."[6]

David Berg also found a role model in Joseph Smith (1804–1844), the founder of the Mormon Church and the most famous polygamous prophet in American history. "The life of Joseph Smith and the Mormons was a great influence," Berg once confessed. "He was a very remarkable and admirable character in many ways."[7]

Joseph Smith, like David Berg, put great emphasis on the violence of the approaching Christian apocalypse. Both men bred generations of fanatics among their followers and among their enemies. Jon Krakauer said it well in his 2003 book on extremist Mormon sects in southern Utah: "The zealot may be outwardly motivated by the anticipation of a great reward at the other end—wealth, fame, eternal salvation—but the real recompense is probably the obsession itself," he writes. "Ambiguity vanishes from the fanatic's worldview; a narcissistic sense of self-assurance displaces all doubt. A delicious rage quickens his pulse, fueled by the sins and shortcomings of lesser mortals, who are soiling the world wherever he looks. His perspective narrows until the last remnants of proportion are shed from his life. Through immoderation, he experiences something akin to rapture."[8]

Like Berg, the Mormon prophet had a fondness for very young women. One exhaustive study of the thirty-three women who were Smith's well-documented wives reveals that a third of those partners were between fourteen and twenty years of age.[9] Like Berg, Smith married the already-married wives of his top male lieutenants, a practice anthropologists say can actually breed loyalty among the tribe.

Men who gave up their wives to Smith and Berg were offered spiritual rewards for their sacrifice.

Relatively little has been written about the children born to Joseph Smith's latter wives—a silence inspired by the secrecy and subterfuge surrounding the practice of polygamy in the early Mormon church. Smith and other Mormon leaders were publicly denying polygamy yet privately practicing it in 1844—the year the Mormon prophet was murdered during a shootout at a jail in Carthage, Illinois. Smith was imprisoned for ordering the destruction of the presses and all remaining copies of the June 7, 1844, edition of the *Expositor*, a newspaper published by a Mormon faction. Dissident Mormons at the newspaper were opposed to plural marriage and on that day printed a well-documented exposé of Smith's previously secret revelation on the taking of multiple wives.[10]

Like Smith, Noyes and Berg inaugurated plural marriage in secret and only among their inner circle. Noyes encouraged the members of his community to engage in nonejaculatory sex to avoid unwanted children. Berg, on the other hand, *outlawed* birth control, encouraging the production of babies to increase his flock and spread his message.

My fascination with this story began with these children—the children born into The Family. During the nineties, I began interviewing young adults who grew up in some of the most notorious cults to emerge from the spiritual turmoil of the sixties and seventies. Part of that research was published in February 2001 in a series of articles in the *San Francisco Chronicle* entitled "Children of a Lesser God" and in a later book, *Following Our Bliss*.[11] My research examined two generations in the Church of Scientology, the Unification Church (the Moonies), the International Society for Krishna Consciousness (the Hare Krishnas), and The Family.[12]

According to The Family's own statistics, there were more than 13,000 children born into The Family between 1971 and 2001. This book chronicles the short and tragic life of one of them—a young man named Richard Peter Rodriguez, who was raised to be the Prophet Prince in the coming Endtime. Ricky was born in the Canary Islands on January 25, 1975. He was the first child brought into the world from "flirty fishing," which could very well be the most unusual evangelical tool in modern Christian history.

Ricky grew up in the center of David Berg's sexual cyclone. He was born to Karen Zerby, a young convert who became sexually involved with Berg in 1969 and was later anointed as his heir apparent. His biological father was Carlos BelAir, a waiter Berg and Zerby befriended when they first came to the Canary Islands. Carlos was one of countless "fish" who swam through The Family during the flirty fishing years. He stuck around long enough to impregnate Zerby and get a glimpse of the child he fathered.

David Berg and Karen Zerby raised Ricky to be one of the heroes in their theological fantasy. In the gospel according to Berg, Ricky would be christened "Davidito." Ricky's mother would be crowned "Maria." They would be the "two witnesses" destined to sacrifice themselves and bring on the apocalyptic battles foretold in the Book of Revelation.

It was a self-fulfilling prophecy, but with a twist. Ricky would grow up, leave the fold, and denounce his estranged mother and spiritual father, making his own date with destiny. Consumed with rage, Ricky would become the reluctant martyr for an abused army of troubled souls—a lost generation that would return to haunt Karen Zerby and the rest of The Family.

1

Revenge of the Savior

NEAR THE ARIZONA/
CALIFORNIA STATE LINE
January 8, 2005 – Westbound
on Interstate 10

*Ricky Rodriguez in his Tucson
apartment on January 7, 2005.*

PREPARE TO STOP! *Prepare to
Stop! Prepare to Stop!* Ricky
eased off the accelerator
when he saw the flashing yel-
low signs. He'd been jamming it since he fled Tucson earlier that night
and headed out toward California on Interstate 10. Now, approaching
the state line, Ricky slowed down at the inspection gate, steering his
silver Chevy Cavalier toward two open lanes on the left. It looked like
easy passage for regular automobile traffic. Then he glanced down at
the bloodied pants crumpled on the floor by the front passenger seat.
Should he stop and stash the incriminating evidence? Would his Washington plates make his car more likely to be searched than vehicles
returning with California tags? What should he do? Stopping to hide
the bloody evidence might attract more attention than going with the
flow and taking his chances. None of the cars in the open lanes were
being checked. Ricky eased down on the brakes and slowed the four-
door sedan into the unmanned gate, stopping just long enough to read

a sign telling him there was "No Inspection Today" and to "Proceed with Caution."

It was too late for that—too late for caution. Ricky had already begun his crusade. Earlier that evening, back in Tucson, he'd slashed the throat of his first victim, Sue Kauten, who as a young woman had helped raise the Prophet Prince and was one of several adult women who engaged in sex play with the young boy.

That was decades ago. On this night, Ricky was just a few weeks shy of his thirtieth birthday. He'd been out of the cult for four years, but he couldn't shake his past—the sexual abuse, pressure to be perfect, and all the twisted prophecies of his messianic fate. No one but he could find his mother and bring her to justice. No one but he could make her pay for all the lives she and that other monster, David Brandt Berg, had destroyed over the past three decades. The hard part was finding his mother. Her whereabouts were the most closely guarded secret in The Family. There were recent rumors that his mother was back in the states—hiding out somewhere in New Mexico, or maybe California.

His mother, Karen Elva Zerby, grew up in Tucson and had been back to Arizona a couple times to visit her aging parents. In the past, in her role as his mother's personal secretary, Sue was part of an advance team sent ahead to make sure it was safe for Zerby to visit. Ricky knew his mother would be back someday, so he moved to the Arizona desert to wait for that day. His break came on Christmas Day 2004, when Ricky learned Sue would be visiting Tucson the first weekend in January. Sue would surely know how to find his mother, and Ricky was ready to do whatever it took to extract that information.

Crossing the border into California, Ricky glanced again at the bloodied pants on the floor of his car. It had been harder than he thought to kill another human being. It had been three hours since he left Sue Kauten's body on the floor of his Tucson apartment and ran out to his car. His mind was still racing, but his body was giving out. At least he'd made it to California. It was time to stop, time to polish off that case of Heineken and get up the courage to make his next move.

Proceeding west on the darkened freeway, Ricky saw that the next exit was "Lovekin Blvd/Blythe." From the highway, Blythe looks like any other pit stop on the way into southern California. There's a rise in the roadway just before the Lovekin Boulevard off-ramp, a gentle crest that reveals a new horizon. Filling the night sky above the town are the golden arches of McDonald's, the blue and yellow sphere of Motel 6, the red and yellow rectangle of Denny's, the orange and black Union-76 ball, a rotating bucket of the Colonel's chicken, and the latest logo to join this crowded field of corporate totems—the green goddess of Starbucks. These familiar symbols are stuck atop poles five stories tall, two to three times higher than any building in Blythe, a struggling farm town in the Palo Verde Valley, a patch of green on the edge of the Mojave Desert.

All Ricky wanted was a bath and those beers. He took the Lovekin Boulevard off-ramp and pulled into the Holiday Inn Express, which offered an indoor pool and free HBO.

Ricky loved movies, especially action flicks and martial arts films. His favorite movie was *Boondock Saints*, a notorious box office flop and cult favorite. Ricky's boss back in Tucson had recommended the film but had no idea how Ricky would take its violent, messianic message to heart.

Boondock Saints is the story of Connor and Murphy McManus, two Irish brothers living in a tough South Boston neighborhood. Fed up with a gang of sadistic Russian mobsters muscling into their part of town, the young men embark on a bloody crusade to rid their streets of this imported evil. In the opening scene, the McManus brothers kneel in a back pew of their parish church. It's St. Patrick's Day. While a young visiting priest recites the Lord's Prayer, urging forgiveness against those who trespass against us, the two brothers hear another voice of God, an Old Testament prayer calling out for righteous vengeance.

"Oh Lord, here's my flashing sword which mine hand will take hold in judgment," says the angry voice of God. "I will take vengeance upon mine enemies. Oh, Lord, raise me up to thy right hand and count me among thy saints."

Connor and Murphy (played by Sean Patrick Flanery and Norman Reedus) shock the congregation by marching up to the altar in the middle of the priest's homily. The sermon recounts the demise of a woman stabbed to death in the street nearly thirty years ago. "She cried out for help," the priest recalled, "time and time again, but no person answered her calls. Though many saw, no one so much as called the police. They all just watched as she was stabbed to death in broad daylight. They watched as her assailant walked away."

"Now, we must all fear evil men," the monsignor concludes, his voice rising. "But there is another form of evil we must fear most. And that is the *indifference of good men*."[1]

Like the brothers McManus, Ricky Rodriguez was on a violent mission—a righteous crusade inspired by crimes of the past and an even more maddening frustration with justice denied. Intellectually, Ricky had rejected the violent prophecies of his supposed destiny. Emotionally, he was still playing the misbegotten martyr.

Before driving to Blythe and checking into Room 109 of the Holiday Inn Express, on the night of January 7, 2005, Ricky set up a video camera in the kitchen of his Tucson apartment and shot his own movie. There were no special effects in Ricky's film—just a heartfelt video of a guy sitting at a table and talking about his weekend plans while loading Golden Saber bullets into a forty-caliber, semiautomatic pistol.

> Well, hey everyone, this is Ricky, and I'm making this video, um, well, for many reasons I guess. Ah, I suppose, the main reason is that I want there to be some record of the way I feel, um, my ideas, just who I was, really. I wanted to explain some of the things that I've been doing and thinking and some of the frustrations that I've had. Anyway, I don't know, just, I guess it's my, uh, sort of my last grasp at, uh, immortality. I know that I'm not immortal, and I know that this video is not going to make me so, but at the same time, I want to, uh, I want people to know that even though some of the things that I'm gonna try to do are rather shocking and, um, and maybe not right in a lot of people's books, I want to explain some of the reasons behind them. So anyway, I'm just loading some of my mags here. Uh, hope you guys don't mind if I do that while I talk.[2]

Ricky loaded the last bullet into the clip of his Glock 23 and set it down on a small table cluttered with other weaponry. There was one

Kydex sheath, a concealed holster ordered on the Internet; one Stun-Master, a device designed to incapacitate its victim with 775,000 volts of electricity; and a six-inch K-bar knife, sharp as a scalpel. There was also duct tape, gags, one barbecue fork, a soldering iron, and a large electric drill padded with duct tape for purposes of noise reduction.

Okay, so—I think I got thirteen in here. The cool thing about the Republicans is their love of guns. They just love their fuckin' guns, and now that the assault ban has expired, which I credit them for, we have high-capacity magazines. Now, I only have— this is my super cool Kydex sheath that I got from sidearmor. com. It's an in, I think they call it an in-belt, or in-waistband holder, so it doesn't actually stick out, it actually goes inside your belt so you pull your shirt over it, so it's very cool. Anyway, when you're carrying a loaded gun, the Glock is a very safe weapon, but there is no real safety on it, except for a little, um, button right on the trigger that has to be pressed for the gun to go off. So the idea of just sticking it in my pants with a clip or whatever just didn't really appeal to me. 'Cuz if you get into a fight or something, somebody stabs you or something, I don't know, er, but whatever, you're rolling around on the ground, you just don't want the fucking thing to go off. So this nice Ky-dex sheath worked very cool.

Ricky had been working out. He stood only five-foot-five and weighed less than 150 pounds, but he looked bigger on video. His biceps and chest muscles bulged beneath a sleeveless red T-shirt. He had shaved his head and his black stubble beard gave him a menacing look that mellowed when he smiled. His haircut made his ears seem to stick out and accentuated his long, thick eyebrows and large nose. On this night, his dark eyes conveyed a haunting mixture of levity, sadness, and resignation. His monologue—shot at two different angles in an unadorned kitchen—was punctuated with sudden outbursts of profanity and rage. His main props were his pistol and his knife. Ricky presented them to his audience with an almost pornographic passion.

I like my 23. It's small, compact. My high-capacity magazines went from a [capacity of] 10 to 13, so that's cool. I think I'm going a little, a little overboard. I bought a bunch of mags and all these fuckin' bullets. I went with a police round, the Golden Saber. It's a full load of powder. They don't, ah, they don't skimp. Some people say that the hollow points don't expand as they should because ballistic gelatin they use for their tests isn't really accurate. But, but I'll tell you if these go through somebody's skull, this fucker's gonna expand, so that's what I'm counting on. You see I'm counting on that because I have my Glock, all this fuckin' ammo, but the truth is this is my weapon of choice. The K-bar knife. Served Marines for many, many years. I changed the angle on mine. I learned a lot about knife sharpening recently. Um, they, they come with like a thirty-degree angle because these fuckers are abused. They're beat on, used for fuckin' everything. I only want it for one purpose, and that is taking out the scum, taking out the fuckin' trash.

Like the McManus brothers in *Boondock Saints,* Ricky was on a mission to rid the world of evil. His targets were not Russian gangsters in South Boston. Ricky's wrath was aimed at his own mother and her current consort, Peter Amsterdam, a loyal follower who rose to power following David Berg's death in 1994.

Now, more than ten years later, Amsterdam had taken the name "King Peter." Karen Zerby was "Queen Maria." Ricky had left the fold and was now the most dangerous member of a growing band of second-generation defectors. His alienated and emotionally damaged peers were his intended audience for the videotaped manifesto he shot that night in Tucson. Ricky, like many of them, had been struggling in the real world. There had been suicides in their ranks, lots of them. It was time for someone to strike back at The Family. It was time for revenge.

Ricky had married a girl he met in the cult. They left the fold and moved to Seattle. Ricky worked on a fishing boat in Alaska, got a job as an electrician, moved to San Diego, then to Tucson, but he couldn't shake his past, could never get rid of "Davidito" and the destiny laid upon him by David Berg.

I was really trying to fit in. I really was. Ah, it's something in the back of my mind, it's always like, I always felt like the resources that I had just weren't adequate and that no matter how much I did, how much I'd replenish those resources, it just wasn't happening. So I was just using my own power without replenishing it. Eventually it would be gone, which is kinda what I feel about it right now. I've been going nonfucking stop, like I'm sure everybody else has, um, since I, since I left that fucking cult...

But, anyway, getting back to suicide. That's what I wanted to do then. I would kill myself—and God how I want to do that—I want to follow that scenario. I just want to leave. Spend a few months and then end it. But you know what I feel is that would be the selfish thing to do. That would be the, the quitter's way out ... I'm trying to do something lasting. Something that I can look back at if I'm able to and know that—okay maybe I didn't technically do the right thing—but I tried to do something to help. I didn't just fade away, I didn't just turn tail and run and let those fuckers win, but I did what I could to make a difference. And I don't know how really far I'm gonna get, but I'm starting to think now that it's not gonna be that far. And that's gonna suck ass. Hmm, I might not, well I'll get one person, that's for sure—my source for information. Uh, the goal is to bring down those sick fuckers—Mama and Peter. My own mother! That evil little cunt. Goddamn! How can you do that to kids? How can you do that to kids and sleep at night? I don't fuckin' know. Anyway, that's my goal. But, I'm one person. I'm working under, eh, situations that aren't that great right now because I'll only have a small window of opportunity to, ah, get the information that I need out of this person.

That person was Sue Kauten. Sue was a trusted member of the Unit, the inner circle of Family leaders and a small group of children born into that elite fold. The whereabouts of the Unit had always been top secret. Most rank-and-file members of The Family never laid eyes on David Berg or Karen Zerby. The Unit traveled around the world, relocating every few years, teaching their far-flung flock through a constant stream of letters, prophecies, and other communiqués. The Unit was a cult within the cult. It was the testing ground for Berg's sexual, social, and spiritual experiments. Ricky was the primary experiment.

Ricky grew up in the surreal world of the Unit and remained a member of The Family through his early twenties. By 2001, Ricky was fed up and increasingly angry about all the child sexual abuse he had witnessed in the Unit. But he had lost track of the Unit's location since he'd defected and publicly denounced The Family.

Over the past year, however, Ricky sent a series of signals to his estranged mother that he wanted to reconcile. But his real goal was not reconciliation. It was extermination. Ricky had watched as other members of the second generation tried to redress their grievances and get justice through law enforcement, the courts, or the news media. Nothing seemed to work. Nobody seemed to care.

His videotape was a call to arms. Ricky was not just angry with those Family leaders who committed sexual, physical, and spiritual abuse upon the children of The Family. He was also fed up with the refusal of other second-generation critics to take direct action against the sect. Like the priest in *Boondock Saints*, Ricky was frustrated about that more insidious form of evil—the *indifference of good men*.

It happened right before me. It happened to all of you. Thousands of us, some worse than others. I had it good in many ways. I didn't get fucked in the ass, you know, I was a guy. A lot of you girls, phew, crap, I can't even compare my stories with yours. But that's not what this is about. We're not sitting here comparing, "Oh you got it worse than I did. You got it more times than I did." It's not about that. There's so many other kinds of abuse that went on, that to some of us was just as bad, to some of us it wasn't, and some of us didn't have it that bad. So I'm not gonna sit here and say, "Oh yeah, I had it the worst or I didn't" because it really doesn't matter. It should never have happened at all. To anybody. That's the point.

Ricky had been fine-tuning his plans for months. It was a time when much of the nation's attention had been directed at the 2004 presidential campaign between Republican incumbent George W. Bush and his Democrat challenger, Massachusetts Senator John Kerry. Both candidates spent a lot of time promising America that they would be tough on international terrorists. On this night, after the election but two weeks before the second Bush inauguration in January 2005, Ricky made a similar vow to his second-generation constituency of Family survivors.

I feel like we're in a war here. Uh, it's not necessarily a literal war—like I'm making it—but it's a war nonetheless. I feel like everyone of us who has left and in some way speaks out—in some way tries to help somebody—in some way tries to help ourselves—um, is a soldier in this war. It's a war on terror because these fuckers are the real terrorists. You know, Bush and Kerry get up there on their campaign platforms, and they both talk about how they're gonna hunt down Al-Qaeda terrorists and kill 'em. And kill 'em! That's what they said! "Hunt them down and kill 'em."

Well, you know, my question is, you know, what about these fuckin' perverts? You know—aren't they the real terrorists? Terrorizing little kids. Driving them to suicide. Isn't that like murdering them, basically? You fuck with their minds so much that they can't go on. They really can't go on.

Ricky's plan was to hunt down and kill as many of those terrorists as possible. He'd heard rumors that his mother and Peter Amsterdam had returned to the United States. He wasn't sure where they'd landed, but one place he could find at least some Family leaders was at a compound hidden in the woods outside Dulzura, California—just east of San Diego. That was the headquarters of The Family Care Foundation, one of the sect's front groups and one of the last places Ricky stayed before leaving the fold.

There was another reason to cross the Arizona border to hunt down more prey. Ricky thought—mistakenly, it turns out—that committing crimes in two states would draw the FBI into the case and finally get federal authorities to investigate the crimes of The Family. It's unclear where he got this idea, but one of the more memorable characters in *Boondock Saints* is Paul Smecker, a charismatic, almost mystical FBI agent played by actor Willem Dafoe. Ricky had gotten to know at least one federal agent, an officer with the U.S. Immigration and Naturalization Service who practiced at the Tucson firing range where Ricky took a gun safety course and got a concealed weapons permit. The last thing Ricky wanted was to have police caught in the crossfire when he gunned down his mother and her lover.

> Now—there is one problem though—and that is, that as I go on my merry way, I am not going to, ah, hurt, or try to hurt, any law enforcement. Now that's going to be really tough to do this without doing that. Um, but that's where I draw the line. I'm not gonna hurt them. I'm not gonna try to hurt them. I respect law enforcement. Um, the justice system has let us down. However, those cops are out there putting their lives on the line for us, and I must say, um, yeah there's some fucked-up cops out there, but I'm thankful for them, and I respect them.

On this first Saturday night in 2005, no agent of the state stopped Ricky at the state line. No one noticed his bloody pants on the floor and ordered him out of the car. He made it to California.

Ricky would have gotten there sooner if he hadn't roared past the junction of Interstate 10 and Interstate 8, missing the most direct route from Tucson to San Diego. But the avenging prophet had blood on his hands and a lot on his mind. His own Battle of Armageddon had begun, and the ghosts of his life and those of his spiritual father were already too much to take. He had missed the Interstate 8 turnoff in Casa Grande, Arizona, which just happens to be where the story begins.

2

Mama Berg

Virginia Brandt Berg, 1885–1969.

PIMA COUNTY, ARIZONA
December 1948 – Casa Grande
Valley Farms

DAVID BERG WAS a preacher's kid.

His mother, Virginia Brandt Berg, was a radio evangelist and itinerant preacher. Mama Berg made her name in the Pentecostal revival that began in a little church in Los Angeles and swept across the United States in the first decades of the twentieth century. Virginia rode the great revival from northern California to southern Florida, where she billed herself as the "Miracle Woman" and packed thousands into her most successful church operation—the Gospel Tabernacle of Miami.

Virginia was a preacher's kid herself. She was the daughter of the Reverend John Lincoln Brandt, a wealthy Methodist preacher. Brandt joined the Campbellites, a Christian restoration movement that sought a return to the perceived purity of the church described in the New Testament. The teachings of Alexander Campbell (1788–1866) and his distrust of church government inspired the movement and can be seen a century later in David Berg's condemnation of organized Christianity, something he and his mother called "churchianity."

Religious purity inspired David and Virginia's ancestors—three brothers named Adam, Isaac, and Jacob Brandt—to sail to the American colonies in 1745. They were Jews from Stuttgart, Germany, who to their parents' horror converted to the Christian faith. Disowned by their clan, Adam, Isaac, and Jacob brought their new faith to the New World as farmers in Pennsylvania and Ohio. They were part of a Mennonite sect known as the Brethren or "the Dunkers," so named because of their insistence on total immersion during the rite of baptism.

John Lincoln Brandt, a descendent of Isaac Brandt, was born in 1860 in Somerset, Ohio. David Brandt Berg would later write that his grandfather "was always a fighter, too, and I guess that's where I get a little bit of it. He was always fighting the Catholics or the Mormons, or in politics or something."

The Catholics burnt down his house in Toledo; the Mormons shot at him in Utah; and he was always right up in the thick of it somewhere, fighting something. But I never heard that he ever accomplished much with all that fighting. I don't know that that's any great advantage. I think he'd accomplished more by just loving them. But that was his way of loving them. He was trying to fight off the System that they were in and trying to keep the sheep in, and he packed the people in. He was colorful and dramatic and he really packed 'em in by the thousands in his church. He was also a gambler; he loved to gamble, and he had a stock market tickertape right in the office of his church, so he could keep up with the stock market. That's the way he made his three million dollars, and in those days, that was worth about ten times as much as it would be today.

So my grandfather became very rich as a result of his investments in the stock market, his books, his travels and tours. He could think of more ways of making money than a dog has fleas. It was just born in him, he was Jewish to the core. And even as a preacher he figured out ways of makin' money.[1]

John Lincoln Brandt married Nina Marquis, who came from an old Indiana family that claimed Daniel Boone as one of its ancestors.

John and Nina had five children, including David's mother, Virginia, who was born on May 27, 1886, in Ronceverte, West Virginia.

Virginia Brandt Berg's own ministry began with the Florence Crittenton Mission, a national network of homes for wayward girls. That's also how she met her husband, Hjalmer Berg, a striking Swedish tenor who had come to perform at a Crittenton Home social event held in Virginia's honor in Ogden, Utah.

Hjalmer was born into a large, poor family in southern Sweden. His father was a shoe cobbler. Before they immigrated to America, his family made extra money during the summer in Sweden as wandering minstrels putting on musical and acrobatic shows. Hjalmer kept up that tradition in the United States, where he got a job as a bookkeeper for the Southern Pacific Railroad but earned additional income as a concert singer on summer tours.

Inspired by his famous father-in-law, the Reverend John L. Brandt, Hjalmer Berg interrupted his railroad job, went to a seminary in Iowa, and was ordained a minister in the Disciples of Christ, a Protestant denomination that grew out of the antidenominationalism of the Campbellites. He and Virginia moved to northern California when Hjalmer landed a job as the pastor of a Disciples of Christ congregation in Ukiah, a lumber and farming community north of San Francisco.

David was the youngest of Virginia and Hjalmer's three children, and as his mother tells the story, he should never have been born.

On Christmas morning, 1911, his mother was on her way home from the hospital with her first son, Hjalmer Berg Jr. Christmas had always been her favorite day of the year, and this day seemed no different as she rode home in the morning light. Then, without warning, tragedy stuck. Virginia was thrown from her carriage onto a curbstone, breaking her back in two places. "How strangely God works," she would later write in her most famous sermon. "How swiftly, unexpectedly, tragedy can walk across life's path."[2]

Her next five years, or so the story goes, were full of agony, pain, suffering, and despair. She was paralyzed from the waist down, lying on rubber cushions, her face gaunt, her body emaciated. She and her husband had long prayed for her suffering to end, and then, on a Saturday morning in 1916, Virginia woke up in the bedroom of their home. "At that very moment I was healed! The paralysis had gone from my body! I felt cool and rested and sat upright in bed."

On the following Sunday morning, to the amazement of the Ukiah congregation, Virginia Brandt Berg walked into the sanctuary of her husband's church. It was a journey she would later describe in her sermon, "From Deathbed to Pulpit," a story that would launch Virginia's career as one of the nation's first woman evangelists and host of a pioneering Gospel radio show called "Meditation Moments."

David would learn the tricks of the traveling evangelists at his mother's side. Tricks, or at least a few lies, had found their way into Virginia's famous sermon. Deborah Berg, Virginia's granddaughter and David's oldest child, would later point out that the famous lady evangelist had been attending graduate school at Texas Christian University and having her second child during the five years she claimed to have been a bedridden invalid in Ukiah. That child, the couple's only daughter, ran away from home and eloped at age sixteen. Hjalmer Jr. turned away from the church and became an atheist. That left young David as the only child to continue Virginia's evangelical career.

David Brandt Berg was born in Oakland, California, on February 18, 1919.

"At first he was a fat and robust little fellow," his mother wrote in a letter to a friend. "But I overfed him [breast milk]—I had such a quantity—and he developed bowel trouble. Day and night he had the colic too, and I was just worn out! I had no one to relieve me."[3]

Her letter, written in the spring of 1919, credits a local faith healer for the baby's recovery. "At last I carried the little fellow to a mission in the city where an elder I knew prayed for him," she wrote. "The next morning he had the first natural bowel movement since his sickness began, and he has been alright ever since."

At the time, Virginia was on her own. There had been a falling out with the Disciples of Christ in Ukiah. Many of its members were wary of the miracle stories and faith healing testimonies that had become the center of Virginia and Hjalmer's ministry. They lost the pulpit in Ukiah, and Hjalmer was back out on the road working for the Southern Pacific Railroad. There had been some possible church jobs back east, but he and Virginia were quickly losing faith in the established churches.

"The old-line church will not accept our message," she wrote.

Virginia and her husband were caught up in the fiery spirit of the early Pentecostal movement, which had been sweeping the nation since a series of revival meetings held in Los Angeles between 1906 and 1909. It all started in the City of Angels in a little church on Azusa Street. Today, more than a century later, the Pentecostal movement counts more than 580 million adherents around the world and has come to see the Azusa Street revival as the spark that set the Holy Spirit ablaze.

Established church leaders in mainline Protestant denominations like the Methodists, Lutherans, and Disciples of Christ were wary of the faith healers, snake handlers, and freelance prophets in the Pentecostal movement. They spoke in strange tongues. They danced in church. They fell to the floor when touched by the power of the Holy Spirit. Many Americans laughed at the "holy rollers" and saw this new wave of religious fervor as little more than a carnival sideshow.

Equally scandalous to the churchmen of the day were women at the pulpit. Aimee Semple McPherson, a Pentecostal pioneer and founder of the International Church of the Four Square Gospel, was the best known of the flock and a role model for Virginia's ministry. She and Hjalmer left the Disciples of Christ for the Christian and Missionary Alliance, a less restrictive network of evangelical preachers, and took their show on the road.

Their ministry, the Berg Evangelistic Dramatic Company, arrived in Miami in March of 1925. They started with a tent and a year later opened a 4,500-seat auditorium, the Gospel Tabernacle. Newspaper advertisements for their revivals featured pictures of Virginia and Hjalmer. She was billed as "The Miracle Woman" and "A Modern Prophetess." Her husband was listed as "Campaign Director" and "Song Leader." Attendees were promised a "soul-stirring, heart-warming revival of New Testament Religion."

Not everyone loved the Miracle Woman. On the night of July 24, 1926, someone threw a piece of coral through the window of the Miami church and struck Virginia just as she was about to begin her nightly service. According to the police, the unidentified assailant was a man upset that two young girls had joined Mrs. Berg's church. It was a strange incident—foreshadowing the opposition David Berg would encounter decades later from parents upset that their children had joined his sect. Just days before the attack, Virginia received threatening letters warning her to get out of town or face a fate more serious than "another well known evangelist of the same faith experienced."[4] That was an obvious reference to Aimee Semple McPherson, who presided over the 5,300-seat Angelus Temple on the other side of the country, in southern California. McPherson disappeared in May 1926. She later resurfaced, claiming to have been kidnapped. But according to numerous media reports at the time, McPherson had used the kidnapping story to cover up the fact that she'd really been "shacked up" in a romantic "love nest."

Little David was six years old when his mother's troupe landed in Miami. Some of his earliest memories are not of revival meetings but of his mother constantly scolding him for playing with himself. Virginia went to great lengths to break her son's bad habit, including one terrifying time when Mama Berg walked into her son's room and "caught me playing with it again." Here is Berg's own account of what happened:

> I suppose she thought she was going to make me so ashamed that I wouldn't do it anymore. So she brought in the whole family ... my governess whom I didn't even like anyhow, and my brother and sister, scolding me before all! She brought a washbasin, a little bowl and a knife and she told me she was going to cut it off! Oh, I was terrified! I was absolutely petrified! I almost never forgave my mother for that, threatening to cut it off and embarrassing me in front of the family. But that didn't stop me. It felt too good to quit! I just kept it up in secret, my terrible secret sin.[5]

Berg tells another childhood story about a Mexican babysitter named Maria "who used to suck me to sleep for my nap every afternoon."

> I had orgasms and I really enjoyed it. I always got nice and relaxed and went to sleep right after. So I got started liking sex at an early age. But my mother was not very progressive. She

finally decided she wanted to see what made me want to take a nap every afternoon.

So she snuck in and took a peak and she found Maria sucking me! She slapped the poor little Mexican girl out of the house! Because Mom had been taught, like all other little "good" kids are taught, that it's *naughty*! I don't know what was naughty about it? I enjoyed it! It worked great!

Look at me, I don't think it did me any harm. Of course if you'd ask any of my enemies they'd say, "Aha, see! That's what made him such a sex maniac!"[6]

Meanwhile, Virginia Brandt Berg's ministry had hit the big time. But not for long. It all came crashing down the following year when her church was destroyed by a hurricane that tore through Miami in September 1926. Virginia raised money to rebuild but then had a fight with one of her financial backers. She regrouped and moved into downtown Miami to start the Church of the Open Door in a two-story building across the street from City Hall. She could still pack the place, but the glory days were over.

Little David graduated from Buena Vista Grammar School and went on to Robert E. Lee Junior High and Miami High School. He would later recall how "the rough kids at school" made much of his youth "an agony and a torture."[7]

At age sixteen, Berg got his driver's license and replaced his father as Virginia's chauffeur and right-hand man. Despite their disagreements as to the joys of childhood sex, David and Virginia Berg were close—extremely close.

I was a grown teenager about nineteen, or perhaps twenty, and she was a middle-aged woman of around fifty-five at the time. We were very busily engaged in the Lord's service together, traveling alone together because my father had said he was too old and too tired and had quit the evangelistic road to settle down to a business of his own in California.

She and I were holding this meeting for a small Alliance church in northern California.... One cold night we were sleeping together in the big double bed that [the local pastor] had rented for us, and which rather shocked us when we saw the room! But we hardly dared complain knowing how poor he was and what a small pastorate he had and that he probably couldn't afford separate rooms.

One cold night we woke up in the middle of the night with no heat and quite cold. Apparently, I must have been stirring and my mother must have been cold and realized that I was cold too, so suddenly in an almost impulsive movement she threw her arms around me and snuggled me real tight. My back was to her at the time—I was lying on my right side and she on her right side—so that as she embraced me and pulled me close against her bosom, she tucked her knees up under my knees and wrapped her body around mine!...

My first reaction was absolute terrified shock to think that my mother would get so close to me and wrap her arms around me and her very body around mine in such an almost sexual embrace. It certainly was a loving embrace and affectionate and perhaps she meant nothing by it whatsoever ... but I think for the first time in my life I had sexual feelings about my mother!

And in those days when very young I was quite virile and potent. I can remember having her snuggle and feeling her warm soft body against mine, her bosoms against my back. She had on a nightgown, a very thin nightgown. She was still a beautiful woman at fifty-five, charming and although a little on the plump side, quite pretty and very attractive [and there she was] with her bosoms against my back and her arms wrapped around me and almost her legs wrapped around me. I suddenly got quite an electric sexual jolt that I had never expected before, and I was almost immediately erect!...

Perhaps if I had not been so conservative and extremely narrow minded in my theology and religion at that time and so absolutely frightened of my mother's seeming abandon at the moment I might have [been] a little bit more responsive. Perhaps [I could have] satisfied both of us and our mutual tremendous sexual needs. It could have developed into a beautiful sexual relationship.[8]

By then, David had been driving his mother back and forth across the country for several years. "I had been more faithful to her than her own husband," he confided. "We had a very beautiful, marvelous wonderful mutual spiritual and filial relationship which was beyond what any actual fleshly sex could have ever been."

Since his father had resigned his pastorate in Ukiah back in the summer of 1917, Hjalmer and his wife had been spending less and less time together. Virginia was clearly the star attraction of the Berg Evangelistic Dramatic Company.

Life on the road was hard on David. He never graduated from high school in Miami, but later managed to get his diploma at age nineteen at Monterey Union High School on the central California coast, where his older brother worked as a teacher.

Other young men Berg's age were valiantly marching off to World War II. David was in his twenties and spent the war years helping his mother with her revival meetings—just as he'd always done. Writing in his diary on March 28, 1941, Berg confessed that he "awoke with a deep desire to strike out on my own, at least to 'prove myself.'

"Took stock of my abilities—with not very encouraging results on the side of job experience and health. Fair intelligence and singing voice. Can speak if compelled to. Knowledge of spiritual things. Inclined to feel inferior because of poor physique. Never had a job, was always different from the other boys."[9]

Writing in his diary later that year, Berg reveals how a government agent told him that the best way to stay out of the war was to get ordained and "enter a plea of mother's dependency on my help." Five days later, on September 25, 1941, Berg writes that he was "ordained today by Dr. Jay C. Kellogg, President of the British-American Ministerial Federation. I'm now a full-fledged minister!"

During the war Berg obtained conscientious objector status with the Army Corps of Engineers and a disability discharge because of a heart ailment.

Two years later, he met his wife, Jane Miller, the secretary and youth director at an Alliance congregation in southern California, the Little Church of Sherman Oaks. He was there helping his mother stage revival meetings. They eloped and married in Glendale, California, on July 22, 1944, and took off to Palm Springs. Deborah, their first child, was born September 10, 1945, followed by their first son, Aaron, on June 21, 1947.

Berg was ready to head out on his own. But he was still working as his mother's song leader in 1948 when the Berg Evangelistic Dramatic Company rolled into Richmond, California, for yet another round of revival meetings. "I knew them both quite well," said the Reverend Charlie Dale, the pastor of the Richmond Alliance Church from 1945 to 1952. "Virginia held lots of meetings in our church. She was a good preacher and an intelligent woman. David was uneducated—never really went to college or seminary—and always seemed closely tied to his mother.[10]

"David was ordained [into the Alliance churches] in 1947 or 1948," the old preacher recalled. "I remember that because I gave him a suit of clothes for his ordination—a zoot suit."

Berg started his first and only position as an Alliance pastor when he was assigned to a struggling church in Valley Farms, Arizona.

Valley Farms was born out of the Great Depression, one of thirty-seven communities created by the Resettlement Administration, a federal agency established in 1935. One of the most controversial experiments of the New Deal, the idea behind this part of President Franklin D. Roosevelt's recovery plan was to relocate struggling families to cooperative farms and "garden cities."

By the spring of 1940, the federal government had spent $817,000 to build sixty simple homes and a grocery store/community center in the sun-baked fields outside Florence, Arizona. Government photographs designed to show off the program's collective accomplishments depict children picking flowers outside a freshly whitewashed adobe home, neatly stacked bales of hay in a new barn, and dairy cattle poking their heads through a new fence. Another image, "Leaving the Grocery Store at Casa Grande Farms," depicts three women and a young girl wearing their Sunday best as they emerge through the front door of the new community center.

Berg arrived eight years later with Jane and the first of their two young children. The Depression was over, as well as World War II and the collective experiment at Valley Farms. Berg was almost thirty years old and finally able to step out of his mother's shadow and into his own pulpit.

Sometime between Christmas and New Year's Day, Berg sent out his first fundraising letter—to his mother's network of supporters.

This was intended to be our Christmas greeting to you, but we have been so busy moving, getting settled, and taking up work here that we have been delayed in getting it off to you. We hope you have had a very blessed Christmas season! Our own hearts are simply welling over with praises to Him this season for all the manifold blessings with which He has showered us, especially the glorious opportunity which He has given us here in Valley Farms. We are preparing to build a church in this churchless community, just such pioneering missionary work that we have been longing to do, feeling keenly the Lord's command to go out into the highways and byways and compel them to go in....

How grateful we are for our training in the evangelistic field for this type of work, especially the lessons learned in living the life of faith and for Mother's inspiring example and teaching along this line! She is now in Santa Barbara with Dad preparing for another evangelistic tour.[11]

At the Colorado Springs headquarters of the Christian and Missionary Alliance, it's hard to find any records or any person able to shed light on what happened following Berg's appointment to lead the flock at Valley Farms. But something happened at Valley Farms. There was a sex scandal or a political controversy or something. David Berg got kicked out of town and was never the same again.

His appointment to the church was reported in the February 5, 1949, edition of the denomination's official publication, *Alliance*

Weekly, which lists his name among six "New Workers" sent out to missionary assignments around the country. His name reappears in the magazine two years later, in the May 5, 1951, edition under the "Transfers" section of the church news column. There are twenty-seven transfers reported in the column. Only two pastors, including Berg, are listed as "Unassigned."

The Christian and Missionary Alliance was founded by the Reverend Albert Benjamin Simpson in 1887. Simpson was a Presbyterian minister swept up in the faith healing, holiness, and apocalyptic Christian revivals of the late nineteenth and early twentieth centuries. By the year 2005 the Alliance would claim nearly 2,000 churches attended by 420,000 people in the United States. Internationally, the denomination reports another 18,000 churches and three million members in eighty-four countries.

No one at the Christian and Missionary Alliance could shed light on this early chapter in the life of David Berg. Officials at the denomination's Colorado Springs headquarters said any documents would have been kept at its South Pacific District office in Riverside, California. Don Brust, the district superintendent there, said he could find no records explaining whatever happened to David Berg or his flock.

Harold Mangham, who preceded Brust as district superintendent, remembers the congregation, but not Berg. "Yes, we had a church in that community," Mangham said. "It was an interesting place. Roosevelt set it up. It was kind of like a kibbutz that you might find in Israel." Mangham said he made several visits to Valley Farms and remembers that the congregation was still struggling when he left his post in 1987.

Two young women who were assigned to Valley Farms in 1947 preceded Berg as the first missionaries sent out by the Alliance. One of them was Betty Findley. "We were just missionary girls back then, but we had a large youth group and held six meetings a week at the community center," Betty recalled. "We used to call the place 'Little Russia.' People didn't have their own things—they were all together. They farmed together, and I guess they shared the profits."

Findley stayed at the Valley Farms cooperative until she left to marry and has just a vague memory of the man who would succeed her. "He came after I left, but I remember seeing him at some of our revivals. I didn't really hear anything against him, but I'd like to know why he left, too."[12]

Charlie Dale recalled a story about how David dug a big hole for a swimming pool on the church property, then used the clay to make adobe brick for a little chapel. Deborah Berg remembers her father collecting bricks from nearby ruins to build his church. Berg stated his intentions to build a church at Valley Farms in his Christmas fund-raising letter of 1948. Services were being held in the home of the "women missionaries who preceded us here," he wrote, until "a modest chapel can be erected on the adjoining lot.

"The entire property is being purchased at a very reasonable figure on long-term payments," Berg wrote. "We expect to begin building the first little church in Valley Farms next month, the Lord willing. Far removed from the nearest towns with churches, this village is sorely in need of such a Gospel Lighthouse, especially for the sake of the young people and children."[13]

Valley Farms is a ninety-minute drive from Tucson via the Pinal Pioneer Parkway, a road that winds through desert landscape dotted with sagebrush and saguaro, the stately cactus and proud symbol of the Arizona highway. Most of the sixty homes built by the Resettlement Administration stand today in various states of disrepair. Some have been abandoned. Others have been expanded in an architectural style inspired by generations of poverty and an absence of building codes.

Berg's adobe church was still there. Along its sides the original adobe peeked through cracked pink plaster. Several of the windows were boarded up. There was an old dishwasher, toilet, and other trashed appliances piled near double doors that once led into the sanctuary. A cross of white bricks adorning the building's beige facade confirmed its history as a house of worship, but the Christian beacon was mostly hidden behind an overgrown shrub. There was no evidence of a swimming pool in the backyard, just a weedy lot facing a golden field of freshly cut hay.

No one answered the door, but a neighbor working on a truck provided some information. "It hasn't been used as a church for years," he said. "There were some Mexicans living in there, but I think the place is abandoned."

Ruby Webb was the only Valley Farms resident left from the time Berg was there. Ruby lives in a trailer down the street from the abandoned church. Her place faces a dusty parking area and the only sign of the town's collective past—a brick monument with an old plow and faded letters. "Welcome to Valley Farms—Established 1934."

Ruby moved here in 1941, but had been alone since her husband, Floyd, died in 2002. She said the old collective spirit of Valley Farms died a long time before her husband. According to the local gossip, the church that David Berg built was a drug house in its most recent incarnation. "You used to know everybody in town," Ruby sighed. "Now you have to lock your doors."

She remembered Berg as one of several preachers who came to town over the years and tried to turn the church into a viable congregation. "I don't know why he left," she said. "But I'm eighty-six, and I don't remember lots of things."

Whatever happened at Valley Farms was serious enough to cause Berg's flock to expel him from their fellowship. According to his daughter, Deborah, Berg left amid rumors of a sex scandal at Valley Farms. Around the time of his dismissal, Berg sent his mother a tape recording in which he "categorically denied the charge of sexual misconduct."[14] Berg would say later that he left Valley Farms in a dispute with racist church members over whether he should allow "dirty, barefooted Indians to the church service on Sunday."

Deborah Berg, who was five years old when her family left Valley Farms, would soon have firsthand experience of her father's sexual misconduct. At age seven, she says her father began "attempts at incest" that would continue for five years. "From that time on, I was terrified of being left alone with him. At age twelve I was more consciously aware of the 'strangeness of his actions,' but I still had no understanding of what he was attempting. I determinedly resisted, threatening to jump out of the window if he touched me. He tried to explain he wanted me to fulfill special needs that my mother didn't completely meet. Unlike twelve-year-olds today, I was totally naïve about sex, and it wasn't until I was married that I realized what his intentions had been."[15]

In her account of her childhood, Deborah says her younger sister, Faithy, had an incestuous relationship with their father. "Unlike me," Deborah writes, "she did not resist him."[16] Faithy later defended her father's endorsement of adults masturbating children to help them relax. "It reminded me of how [dad] used to put me to sleep when I was a little girl, three or four. Wow! Daddy did it best! Back rubbin' that is, and front rubbin' too!... Daddy just made me feel good all over.... I don't think it perverted me, none at all, but it sure converted me to his call! So I believe our parents should try it and help our kids to get the natural habit.... Oh, I could write a book, but this is just a look into my childhood sex."[17]

In the end, it doesn't really matter if Berg was expelled from Valley Farms for sexual misconduct or because he could no longer stomach the racist hypocrites in his ignorant flock. Either way, Berg would never again minister to the mundane spiritual needs of an actual congregation. He had convinced himself that he was a prophet, not a pastor

"It seems the Lord is showing me that belonging to anything other than the Lord Himself is too binding, too hindering, too man-made," he wrote in a May 31, 1951, letter to his mother, the same month he was removed from Valley Farms. "It obligates you to follow the dictates of man rather than God. When you follow God instead of man they kick you out anyhow, so you might as well not stay in or get in.... Evidently, I was never cut out to be a kowtowing, hypocritical, beating-around-the-bush, please-everybody pastor."[18]

Following his abrupt departure from Valley Farms, Berg enrolled at a Phoenix college and took courses in philosophy, psychology, and political science. He also signed up for a personal witnessing course at the American Soul Clinic, a missionary training school founded in 1944 by evangelist Fred Jordan. Berg would spend the next fifteen years working for Jordan, helping Jordan promote his missionary training camp and a radio and television ministry called the "Church in the Home." Now he was in Jordan's shadow, rather than his mother's.

In 1966, Berg had a falling out with Jordan and took his kids on the road as the "Berg Family Singers." They were a flop.

At the time, Virginia Berg was retired and living in a Huntington Beach cottage. She had begun to see lots of restless, seemingly lost, teenagers hanging around this town on the southern California coast. They were about the same age as her grandchildren, but they had long hair and wore wild clothing. They smoked marijuana and took other mind-altering drugs. Huntington Beach was turning into southern California's version of the infamous Haight-Ashbury neighborhood up the coast in San Francisco.

Virginia knew lost souls when she saw them. The old revivalist started passing out peanut butter sandwiches to the hippies and the beach bums in Huntington Beach. Then she'd tell them about Jesus. Meanwhile, her son was approaching his fiftieth birthday and had nowhere else to go. Maybe God would give poor David one more chance.

Mama Berg called her son home.

3

Jesus Freaks

SAN FRANCISCO, CALIFORNIA
May 1967 – Corner of Haight and Ashbury streets

GOD WAS SPEAKING to Kent Philpott through his car radio. Actually, it was the voice of Scott MacKenzie singing his new song "San Francisco (Be Sure to Wear Flowers in Your Hair)." But the Almighty was speaking through the music and had a clear message for this young Baptist preacher. "God called me to the hippies," he says. "Right there and then."

Faithy Berg (right) ministers to the hippies in the early seventies.

Kent had just crossed the Golden Gate Bridge and was heading north out of the city on Highway 101. The song came on as his car was approaching the Seminary Avenue off-ramp in central Marin County. Kent was in his second year of studies at Golden Gate Baptist Theological Seminary, selling shoes at J.C. Penny's, and serving as the part-time pastor of a tiny Baptist church way out in Byron, a farming community about fifty miles east of San Francisco. There were no hippies in Byron. It wasn't happening in Byron. It was happening in the Haight, and that's where God wanted Philpott to go.

All across the nation
Such a strange vibration
People in motion.

Philpott wasn't sure where the Haight was, but the next day he headed back into the city to find out. He'd been raised in southern California, joined the military, and converted to Christianity through the work of a Baptist preacher at Travis Air Force Base northeast of San Francisco. Now, at age twenty-five, Kent was on his own mission from God.

"San Francisco," MacKenzie's sentimental ode to peace and love, was an instant worldwide hit when it was released in the spring of 1967. Now everyone knew about the strange vibrations emanating from the intersection of Haight and Ashbury streets.

There was a cultural revolution erupting in this blue-collar neighborhood of dilapidated Victorians and struggling shops. Rents were cheaper than over in North Beach, where the edgy artists, Beat poets, and assorted hangers-on were losing their monopoly on hip. In Berkeley, on the other side of San Francisco Bay, the revolution was political and had a harder edge. It was mellow in the Haight. Golden Gate Park was just a few blocks away. What would come to be known as "the San Francisco sound" was taking shape in the form of rock bands like the Jefferson Airplane and the Grateful Dead. And there was this little chemical called LSD.

Philpott got the call from God just weeks before the official opening of the Summer of Love. By then, the advance guard of the hippie movement—led by Ken Kesey and his Merry Pranksters—had already put on the Trips Festival, a drug-fueled celebration held in January 1966 at the Longshoremen's Hall near Fisherman's Wharf. A year later, there was the Gathering of the Tribes for a Human Be-In in Golden Gate Park. Beat poet Allen Ginsberg chanted "We are one!" Timothy Leary, the former Harvard professor and psychedelic evangelist, made his first public appearance in San Francisco. Hare Krishna devotees danced in ecstasy. Thousands of revelers poured onto the Polo Field, and the bands played on.

That was just a warm-up for the summer of 1967, when the scene got very crowded and very crazy. Suddenly, it seemed like all the loose screws were rolling into San Francisco from across the nation and around the world. There was talk of peace and love, but there was also hunger, homelessness, rape, and lots of people strung out on drugs. For a freshly ordained street preacher, it was an evangelical gold mine.

On his first day in the Haight, Philpott thought it wise to see what was happening—if anything—at an evangelical church close to ground zero. So he found his way to Hamilton Square Baptist Church and was looking in the window when a young man tapped him on the shoulder. "Would you like to meet someone who *really* knows God?" the man asked.

Kent took the bait and began a lifelong friendship with David Hoyt.

Hoyt had also grown up in southern California, but had a much rougher time of it than his newfound friend. He'd bounced around foster homes and juvenile halls and wound up in Lompoc Federal Penitentiary on a drug conviction. In prison, Hoyt passed the time reading about Buddhism, Hinduism, and other Eastern philosophies.

Hoyt moved to San Francisco following his parole in September 1966. By the spring of 1967 he had become a disciple of Swami Prabhupada, the founder of the International Society for Krishna Consciousness, also known as the Hare Krishnas. *That* was whom David Hoyt wanted Kent Philpott to meet. Krishna was the god he was talking about. But that didn't stop the Baptist preacher and the Krishna devotee from developing a close friendship. They got together often, Kent with his well-worn Bible and David holding his copy of the Bhagavad

Gita. "He'd try to convert me to Hinduism," Philpott recalled, "while I taught him scripture."[1]

When Hoyt moved into the Hare Krishna temple in San Francisco, he and Philpott continued their Bible study in the basement and drew in a few other students at the temple. "When the Swami heard about me, I had to explain what I was doing," Philpott recalled. "He agreed to let me continue if I came to *their* worship—the *kirtan*—and stayed for an hour and a half of chanting. They'd go on and on dancing and chanting until they worked themselves into a frenzy. It was like being out on Hippie Hill on acid listening to the Grateful Dead, but it was a worship service. After the *kirtan*, David and I would go in the basement and study the Bible."

Jesus would prevail over Krishna, but it took a dream and a fire to seal Hoyt's conversion. Asleep one night in the temple basement, David dreamt that he was missing out on the Rapture—that all the true Christians all around him were rising up into heaven while his feet stayed on the ground. Then he woke up to find his personal altar ablaze. "I always thought he just left a candle burning," Philpott mused. "But David attributed it to God."

Hoyt moved into Philpott's room at the Baptist seminary in Marin County and stayed through the Summer of Love. "We started an intense on-the-street ministry that summer," Kent recalled. "We'd just walk up to people and tell them about Jesus. That was the whole thing. We didn't even have any literature, but we sure went to town. We were there all the time."

They didn't know it at the time, but Kent and David were helping birth the Jesus movement, a wave of counterculture conversion that would alter the face of American Christianity. Some called them "Jesus people." Others preferred the term "Jesus freaks." By the end of the year, another group of Marin County converts had opened up a coffeehouse in the Haight called the Living Room and soon took their mission down to southern California, opening two more Christian communes. Theologically, they were conservative evangelicals, but sociologically, they kept many of the trappings and the values of the emerging sixties counterculture.

Across the bay in Berkeley, the Jesus movement took form as the Christian World Liberation Front. Jack Sparks, a Pennsylvania State University professor who had been involved with the evangelical Campus Crusade for Christ, started the group and an underground Christian newspaper called *Right On*, which blended the love of Jesus with the radical rap of the New Left. Here's a sample from a Christian World Liberation Front tract entitled "The Second Letter to the Christians."

Dig it! God has really laid a heavy love on us! He calls us His children and we are! The world system doesn't recognize that we're His children because it doesn't know Him. Right on, brothers and sisters, we are God's children even though we're a long way from being what He's going to make us. Don't get hooked on the ego-tripping world system. Anybody who loves that system doesn't really love God.... That world system is going to be gone some day and along with it, all desire for what it has to offer; but anyone who follows God's plan for his life will live forever. Dig it! This whole plastic bag is exactly what Jesus liberated us from.[2]

Two of the fastest-growing evangelical churches of the seventies and eighties—Calvary Chapel and Vineyard Fellowship—were fueled by the Jesus movement of the late sixties. Chuck Smith, who started Calvary Chapel in late 1965, was not an early fan of the hippies. "These long-haired, bearded dirty kids going around the streets repulsed me," he later wrote. "They stood for everything I stood against. We were miles apart in our thinking, philosophies, everything."[3]

To many Americans, the Jesus freaks were a contradiction in terms. The counterculture was supposed to be about sex, drugs, and rock and roll. Evangelicals were supposed to be about piety and sexual purity. But evangelical Christians—especially before the rise of the religious right and its alliance with the Republican Party in the late seventies—*were* countercultural. In the late sixties and early seventies, a growing cadre of avant-garde evangelicals found a receptive audience among the hippies, whose rejection of materialism and search for spiritual experience provided common ground. This was especially true in Pentecostal churches and charismatic Christian circles, where a lively style of worship and openness to religious ecstasy rang true for spiritual seekers of other stripes. Both the hippies and the evangelicals envisioned a world beyond the confines of ordinary time and space. Both practiced spiritual healing and were open to the wisdom of living prophets. In the end, it wasn't a great leap from the Age of Aquarius to the Second Coming of Christ.

Chuck Smith began to change his mind about the hippies when his daughter started dating one. His name was John. A few years back, before his Christian conversion, the young man had dropped acid and reveled in all that sin and sexuality up in San Francisco.

"One night I opened the door and there was John with a long-haired, bearded kid with bells on this feet and flowers in his hair," Smith recalled. "An honest-to-goodness hippie!"

"Chuck," John said. "I want you to meet Lonnie Frisbee."

Lonnie grew up in Orange County, left home as a teenager, and wound up in San Francisco for the Summer of Love. One of the first converts of the Jesus movement, Frisbee helped set up the Living Room in the Haight in late 1967, but headed home the following year. Lonnie still had the fire of a fresh convert when he showed up on Chuck Smith's doorstep.

"I put out my hand and welcomed him into the house," Smith said. "As he began to share, I wasn't prepared for the love that came forth from this kid. His love of Jesus Christ was infectious. The anointing of the Spirit was upon his life."[4]

Smith helped Lonnie rent a two-bedroom house on Nineteenth Street in Costa Mesa and open the House of Miracles, one of the first crash pads for Jesus freaks. Meanwhile, on the other side of Los Angeles, David Hoyt had rented an old sanitarium in Lancaster and founded The Way Inn, another early Christian commune. Frisbee had nearly two dozen converts the first week. He built bunk beds in the garage at the House of Miracles. One kid slept in the bathtub. It was the spring of 1968, and the Jesus movement was taking off.

But Frisbee wasn't the only young evangelist harvesting hippies in Orange County. He and other leaders in the fledgling Jesus movement had begun hearing stories about a zealous band of young Christian evangelists in nearby Huntington Beach calling themselves "Teens for Christ." Frisbee, who was only nineteen years old at the time, asked two street preachers with a little more savvy—Kent Philpott and David Hoyt—to help check them out.

Berg and his family had just arrived in Huntington Beach after their flop as the Berg Family Singers. They arrived at Virginia's cottage in early 1968 with a few followers they'd picked up along the way. Two brothers had joined the troop at the New York World's Fair. David Berg married one of them off to Faithy in February 1967 when his youngest daughter turned sixteen years of age. Another teenage devotee married Berg's son, Aaron, in November. Berg's oldest daughter, Deborah, had already married a man who met the Bergs at a Florida Bible college.[5]

Lonnie Frisbee, Kent Philpott, and David Hoyt arrived late in the day for their meeting with the Teens for Christ. "Berg and his sons were sitting there with some other guys. What I remember most is that they were dressed in black suits. That was very astonishing to us. They looked like establishment-type people.

"It was not like a conversation between brothers in Christ. It was more like, 'Who are you?' Sort of a suspicious tone," Philpott said. "After the meeting, we recommended that Lonnie stay away from them."

Hoyt has a similar memory of the bad vibes in Huntington Beach. "It seemed a little strange to me," he said. "There was a strange spirit there."[6]

Lonnie Frisbee listened to his Christian brothers' wise counsel and stayed away from the Bergs. A few years later, David Hoyt would fail to take his own advice. It was a decision he'd regret for the rest of his life.

Gospel of Rebellion

*David and Jane Berg sit in front of three of their children (l-r)
Aaron, Faithy, and Hosea in this 1964 photo. (Their oldest daughter,
Deborah, is not pictured.)*

HUNTINGTON BEACH, CALIFORNIA
March 1968 – The Light Club

IT WAS JUST a small item in *Alliance Witness*, the official publication
of the Christian and Missionary Alliance.

Information has been received concerning the homecoming of
Mrs. Virginia Brandt Berg, in Huntington Beach, Calif., on
March 15. Her death in her eighty-second year concluded more

than fifty years of evangelism, gospel broadcasting and writing.... She is survived by a daughter, Virginia, and two sons, Dr. Hjalmer Berg and Rev. David Berg, director of Teens for Christ in Huntington Beach.[1]

Mama Berg was dead, but mom was right. There was a sea of lost souls ready to be saved along the California coast.

Things had not been going well for David Berg since his 1966 falling out with Fred Jordan, his old boss from the American Soul Clinic. Berg had traveled around the country in his mobile home with Jane and the kids, singing hymns and preaching about how all the churches were corrupt and the Endtime was at hand.

Berg started using the name "Teens for Christ" in 1966, pushing his two sons, Aaron, nineteen, and Hosea, seventeen, into the limelight. "Here's some good news about teens for a change. They like to witness instead of Watusi, preach rather than protest, and win rather than sin," Berg wrote. "Would you like to have them at your church? Contact or write them *today*. Tomorrow may be too late!"[2]

Early photos of the troupe confirm Kent Philpott's memories. They show Aaron and Hosea in dark suits, white shirts, and ties. Berg had yet to realize that suits and ties were on the way out and the counterculture was on the way in. By the end of 1967 he and his family were broke and on the way to live at Virginia Berg's house in Huntington Beach.

What would one day become The Family got its start when Berg's kids got a job singing one night a week at the Light Club, a youth ministry in Huntington Beach started by Teen Challenge, an arm of the Assemblies of God, one of the nation's largest Pentecostal denominations. Before long, they had taken over the ministry.

His mother's death in March 1968 set David Berg free. He started sounding like a prophet, not an assistant pastor stuck in his mother's shadow. Berg had finally found a following with his radical denunciation of "the system"—the established churches, the government, the business world, and all those clueless parents. It was us-versus-them. He was the Endtime Prophet. They were the established churches. They were the government. They were the corporations. They were all those parents who just did not get it. Berg was still growing up, still rebelling against mother. Notice how a fifty-one-year-old Berg uses the words "our parents" in a sermon delivered to "the kids" on March 8, 1970:

> The parents want them to follow in their footsteps in a selfish dog-eat-dog economy in which they not only murder one another, but they conduct massive slaughters of whole nations....
>
> The young people are sick and fed up with what really amounts to a pagan, cruel, whore-mongering, false Christianity. They're trying to return to the peace-loving religions of old, including ancient Christianity, and the parents will have none of it....
>
> We are the true lovers of peace and love and truth and beauty and God and freedom: whereas you, our parents ... are on the brink of destroying and polluting all of us and our world if we do not rise up against you in the name of God and try to stop you.[3]

Early newspaper accounts on the Light Club began to worry local parents and church leaders. One night a reporter observed a sandal-clad David Berg performing "betrothal ceremonies," including one between a twenty-one-year-old man and a sixteen-year-old girl. Faithy Berg explained the ceremony to the reporter. "It's as good as getting married," said Faithy, who was just seventeen years old and already betrothed. "You make the vows and everything. I guess it's like an engagement, but stronger."[4]

Locals started calling the club "the hippie church." It was at 116 Main Street, just a few steps from Huntington Pier. There were colored lights, Bible verses written on the walls, patches of used carpet, folding chairs, and a half-dozen large telephone cable spools for tables. There was an elevated stage that served as a combination altar/bandstand.

Potential converts walked in off the beach, passing under a white peace dove emblazoned over the door. The Light Club opened nightly at 8 P.M. and kept going until past midnight, fueled by free coffee. Aaron and Faithy would strum guitars and sing pop songs interspersed with spiritual phrases.

Before long, the proselytizing would begin one-on-one. "How are you? Do you know Christ?" It could get intense, especially for those who just came for the free sandwiches. "They are always pushing this religion on us; they never leave us alone," one visitor complained. "When you go in every night, it gets on your nerves."[5]

Berg's early followers took his message to the beaches, parks, and college campuses of southern California. They demonstrated at local churches and accused them of heresy. In late 1968, six of the Endtime Prophet's Christian revolutionaries were arrested and charged with trespassing when they refused to stop handing out religious tracts at a Huntington Beach college. Berg responded by sending eighteen robed members of his teenage shock troops back to the college to picket. Berg stayed in his car during the picketing and watched from afar.

"We had sit-ins, march-ins, protests and everything the kids loved," Berg would later brag. "Everything that was radical. It was just going great! Terrific! And I loved it! I was master-minding the whole thing from behind the scenes with Jesus!"[6]

At first, most people saw Berg's flock as just another part of the Jesus movement—hippies and political radicals who saw Jesus of Nazareth as the symbol of true revolution. "It was happening all across LA and California," said Shula Berg, an early convert who would later have a child by Berg's oldest son, Aaron. "God's spirit was coming upon people. God was trying to reach the hippies and do a whole new thing with the church. The church had no clue what to do."[7]

David Berg's children brought many early devotees into the fold— especially Aaron, who wrote many of the songs that would inspire the first wave of converts. He would also foreshadow the madness that would soon envelop The Family. "Aaron was the big show in Huntington Beach. Here was this guy, writing songs, playing guitar. He'd start singing and his hair, blond and curly, would stand on end. He looked like Einstein," Shula recalled. "Aaron was like an encounter with God. Revivals are started by spiritual anointing, a power encounter with the presence of god. Aaron had that spirit."

In his own account of the early days, David Berg credits his younger son, Hosea, for gaining control of the Huntington Beach club. "He was begging me to come down and teach the hippies the Bible—'Like you taught us, Dad!' But I said, 'Well, I'll have to come down and see first.'

So I was trying to get to know the hippies and see what they were like, hanging around all their haunts. I grew a little beard and I put on some old ragged sneakers, a ragged pair of pants, an old ragged black jacket, my beret and dark glasses and I probably looked like a pusher or something! The police used to really give me the eye when I passed by. But that seemed to be the style, to dress as ragged and as bummy as possible. Only they wore a lot of freaky clothes too, and I got to where I was finally wearing a Japanese kimono, a little more fitting to my style.

So I came into the club one night, sort of staggering in like some old bum. I wanted to see what it was like, because I'd never been there and [Hosea] wanted me to come down and teach. I thought, "Well, I ought to scout out the land a little bit first." So I staggered in the door and saw a spot over in the corner that was vacant—you had to step over bodies and everything to get to it—I threw myself down in the corner. And this nice little blond boy beside me, I remember him yet, he said, "Hi Dad, what's your bag?" I didn't even know what a bag was then.[8]

After a few undercover visits, Berg decided to reveal himself. He waited one night until the Light Club was packed with seventy-five singing, clapping converts.

[Hosea's wife] was singing so I waited till she came to the end of her song and she was just leaving the stage. I knew [Hosea] was probably waiting to introduce me. So I flung the door open and I leaped in and I thundered at the top of my voice—and I can yell pretty loud—"Revolution for Jesus!" And then they roared: "For Jesus!" I said, "Come on, you can do better than that! When I say, "Revolution!" you answer me back, "For Jesus!" So that got to be our battle cry and the way I introduced myself every night from then on.... I really had the age barrier to break, because they didn't trust anybody over thirty. I had to really prove I was one of them.

David Berg took off his tie, let his hair and beard grow, and began to preach "the gospel of rebellion." Some of his early sermons sound like they were written by a teenage rebel, not a man in his early fifties. They were as much a rebellion against all those stupid parents out there than they were a prophetic witness against social injustice.

People never cut their hair until the past hundred years. Men had beards.... Sandals and bare feet were popular throughout the ages. What are the parents complaining about? They're complaining that their children are returning to the customs of their forefathers. It's the parents who are the rebels. The kids want to return to the pattern of the cooperative, socialistic, communal living of the tribalism of their forefathers. That's the most ancient and longest lasting of any economic system—the economic system of tribalism—ancient socialism.[9]

Berg's tribe was growing, and he was about to find another way to break the age barrier. In January 1969, he met and began seducing Karen Elva Zerby, the twenty-two-year-old daughter of a conservative Tucson preacher. Karen was a few years older than many of the teenage converts, but she didn't look like it. "When she lets her hair fall down, she looks like she's about fourteen," Berg recalled years later. "When I used to take her out places with her hair down they looked at me like I was really robbing the cradle!"[10]

Like David Berg, and his mother, Virginia, Karen Zerby was a preacher's kid. She was born in Camden, New Jersey, on July 31, 1946. Her dad was a Methodist minister who served in the Wesleyan and Pilgrim Holiness churches. Her parents moved to Tucson in 1964 when Karen was eighteen.

Her younger sister, Rosemary, said their father was stern, but loving. "We did get paddled and it did hurt. But it was always fair. We knew we deserved it. He talked to us about it. But it was never anywhere but on the bottom. He didn't whip us. He wasn't beating us.

He was a great father. My father is one of the best men I have ever met."[11]

Karen enrolled at the University of Arizona after her family moved to Tucson, but she dropped out after a year to work as a legal secretary and help her struggling parents pay their bills. "Karen was their first child. She had always been good to them," Rosemary recalled. "They loved her. They loved all of us, but she was the first. She had always been there for them. My younger sister and I were the goofballs. Karen wasn't. She had always been the best of the three of us."

Karen agreed. "I was taught by my parents and church that it was displeasing to the Lord to smoke, drink, dance, wear make-up, jewelry or have short hair, attend movies or even watch TV. We didn't have a TV until I was sixteen, and we listened to radio seldom," she said. "To me, obeying my parents was obeying the Lord ... unlike my sister, two years younger, who was very rebellious."[12]

Karen was very idealistic and very religious. Rosemary remembers her walking back and forth under the trees in their large backyard every morning, reading her Bible. She took her Bible to her job at the law firm. This was the late sixties, a time when few young people did that kind of thing. "Karen had never held hands with a man until she met The Family," Rosemary said. "She would maybe bring someone from the church and we'd sit and eat. She went out with other couples, but she hadn't even held hands with a guy. She felt it was not the right thing to do."

According to Rosemary, Karen's dream was to minister to all the teenagers she saw hanging out on the street in Tucson. She had gone from church to church to find someone willing to sponsor her in that ministry, but no one seemed interested. Then, one day in January 1969, she met the Teens for Christ at an evangelical convention in Phoenix. Two of Berg's children, Faithy and Hosea, were singing at the assembly and telling local preachers how to reach counterculture converts. After the meeting, Karen ran into Faithy Berg in the ladies room.

"Hi," Karen said. "I'm really interested, I really appreciated your talk!"

"Thanks," Faithy replied. ""Where are you from?"

"Tucson."

"Oh, we're going to be in Tucson in a week, why don't you come?"[13]

They talked for a few minutes. Faithy handed Karen a card with the address for the upcoming Tucson meeting. They were only going to be there one night, but here was Karen's big chance for her dream vocation. She went to the meeting and ran off to southern California with her new friends the next day.

On the day she left, Karen showed up at her family's Tucson home with—of all people—Jane Berg, the woman she would soon replace as David Berg's primary wife. "I vividly remember watching my mom and dad cry," Rosemary said. "Karen came in along with Jane, who was talking to my mom and dad to distract them when Karen went in and got her things. She just walked out and said she was going off with them."[14]

Karen Zerby and Jane Berg jumped into a van and sped off—driving straight to Huntington Beach. They were just a couple miles away from the Zerby's home in Tucson when Jane turned to Karen and asked, "Honey, what job have you been doing?"

"Well, I've been a secretary," Karen replied, "but I'm glad I'm done with that now."

"Oh, we need secretaries," Jane said. "Maybe you could help out!"

Karen began having second thoughts about running away with the Jesus people.

"I was already so sad I was leaving home," she recalled years later. "I'd never been away for very long from my parents, and I thought, 'How can I bear this? It's bad enough leaving home and my parents, then having to go back to that boring job again.'"

They arrived at the Light Club after midnight. "The kids were still in the club," Karen recalled. "I walked in and there was a group of people there singing. The thing that really impressed me was Aaron standing there with his guitar. The light was shining on him and his beautiful blonde hair and it looked like he had a halo around his head."[15]

Karen started typing letters and other secretarial work in the Huntington Beach garage Berg had inherited from his mother. Virginia

Berg had been dead now for almost a year, and her fifty-year-old son was finally coming into his own. One day, David wandered out into the garage to see Karen.

"It was winter," Berg recalled. "I was afraid she was cold, so I went out there to make sure she had heat. She said she was cold, so I think I put her sweater around her or something."

"I wish you'd pray for my back," Karen said. "I'm having back-aches lately."

"Well, where is it? Is it here? Higher? Lower? Is that it? I'll give you a little massage."

After a few minutes of back rubbing, Berg had made his diagnosis. "Your backache sounds to me like maybe it's your kidneys. Of course, a lot of women get backaches from congestion back here because of sexual tension, they don't have any sexual release, and you're not married."

At that point, Berg says, Karen confessed that she had an attraction toward Jethro, the husband of Deborah Berg, the prophet's eldest daughter. "He's married and has got five children," Karen wept. "I couldn't steal another woman's husband!"

"Well, that's true," Berg replied. "You certainly couldn't have him."

Berg and Zerby related this account of that winter day in Huntington Beach nearly a decade after the event in a 1978 letter entitled "Our Love Story!"[16]

"Of course," Berg recalled in the letter, "I hadn't boned up enough on our doctrine of having an additional wife in those days, but I got around to it real fast after I got hooked on [Karen]. So I didn't know enough then to tell her, 'Well, you wouldn't have to steal him, maybe you could just be added!'"

By the time Karen Zerby walked into the Light Club, Berg was plotting his next move. Concerned parents, police, and school administrators were worried about the beatnik prophet and his diehard followers. Then, suddenly, in the spring of 1969, he and his flock disappeared from the streets of southern California.

They resurfaced when a convoy of cars and campers were spotted in the parking lot of the Sears Roebuck department store in Tucson.

Berg consummated the affair with Zerby in April. They made love in "The Ark," the twenty-six-foot-long 1962 Dodge camper that slept twelve and served as Berg's mobile headquarters in the early years.

"Mostly we were just doing what we used to call 'necking,' just kissing, cuddling, fondling and petting. She was a virgin, so it took me a little while to get her opened up. But, finally, one night we got it together!"

Jane Berg was suspicious of her husband's young secretary. "Once or twice dear little mother came home early and came bursting in the door," David Berg said. "All we had was a little curtain across the aisle to hide the beds. Suddenly we heard mother coming and Maria [Karen Zerby] would scramble out of my bed as fast as she could and go back up in the top bunk and pretend to be asleep.

"We used to park a whole convoy there [in the Sears parking lot] on the weekend when there was nobody there," Berg explained. "It was a good place to park, vacant and lots of room. I think Mother began to suspect something was going on for sure. I hadn't quite sold her yet on the doctrine of polygamy. I was even having a hard time selling [Karen] on the doctrine of polygamy. I don't think I got her sold on that until we got to Texas. But she was at least enjoying participating [having sex with Berg] even if she didn't understand the doctrine."

Berg had been caught, but he was unrepentant. No one, especially his aging wife, could question the Endtime Prophet. His time had come. Young people were finally following him.

Berg saw something in Karen Zerby. She certainly wasn't one of the prettiest females in the flock. She was skinny, bucktoothed, and extraordinarily plain. She was the same generation as Berg's own children, but more of a blank slate. She hadn't seen the shadow side of the Endtime Prophet during all those tough years on the road—his alcoholism, his tirades, his infidelity to his wife, his incestuous impulses. Karen was searching for the truth, and Berg convinced her that he had the truth and could pass it onto her

In recalling her childhood, Zerby said, "Obeying my parents was obeying the Lord." Karen's sister thinks she transferred that loyalty from her preacher father to the Endtime Prophet. "He could definitely mold her," Rosemary said. "If she had faith in him she would give him everything. I heard that later a lot of it was guilt. She felt guilty for things she had done with him and he used that against her."

Tucson was just a stop along the way. Berg put out the word for his flock to meet up with him in Canada. What would later be seen as the founding convention of The Family was held in the summer of 1969 at a campground in the Laurentian Mountains of Quebec. David Berg was the new Moses, and the hippies were his Chosen People. God's prophecy was pouring through him, and his people were finally listening.

> I saw unto thee this night, my children of the hippie army, bow low before Me, for I will give unto thee that which I have long desired to bestow upon My Children. I have said that in the Last Days, I would pour out My Spirit, yet the world has seen but a little sprinkling of the mighty showers. During this year to come right before you I shall pour out My Spirit in mighty waves upon you as you witness to the lost children whom the churches have created by their own whoredom.
>
> Thou shalt see it flow as rivers in the streets, parks and highways. Lo, servants, My hippie children ... I have seen thy tears in the night hours during all thy childhood. I have seen the burdens of thy heart. I have seen thee in all thy struggles against the Evil One, and in thy heartaches, and when the Evil One hath sought to take thy life, and did seek to destroy many of thee through drugs. I waited for the congregations of the churches to minister unto thee. But they hardened their hearts and forsook thee![17]

Berg then called the leaders of the fledgling movement to a meeting in Vienna, Virginia, where his prophecies included a spiritual justification for his sexual affair with Zerby, whom the Endtime Prophet christened "Maria." That prophecy, later published as "Old Love, New Love," declared Jane Berg, his wife of more than twenty years, to be the "Old Church." Zerby was the "New Church."

At that moment, the course of The Family was set. Berg was the Endtime Prophet and Karen Zerby was his queen. They would lead the hippie army through the Great Tribulation and into the new millennium. There was no time to waste. The end of the old order was near. Jesus was coming again. It was time to spread the news.

"Be prepared! Join us now! Tomorrow may be too late!" one early tract screamed. "Come see us TODAY or write NOW for the location of our nearest colony and more information on how to survive in the days ahead!"[18]

Nothing motivates the troops like the end of the world, and Berg would often use his apocalyptic prophecies to inspire his followers to new fields of battle and higher levels of commitment. California was going to be destroyed by earthquakes, so they all fled to Europe. Then Europe and North America were to burn in a nuclear holocaust, so the troops headed down to Africa, South America, and Southeast Asia.

Dates were set. The Great Tribulation would begin in the eighties and last for seven years. Ricky and his mother—Davidito and Maria—would lead the Endtime army. Jesus would return and The Family would be raptured to heaven in 1993. "We were always having to get ready spiritually for the Endtime," recalled one longtime member of Berg's inner circle. "It keeps you in this hyper state of mind—kind of like the war on terror. The bad guys are everywhere, but you can't really see them. It changes the way you think. Why worry about consequences when the whole world is about to end? Why take the time to work out your relationship with your wife? Why take on long-term projects? People were not thinking about things like growing old or sending the kids to college."[19]

It may have all been very exciting, but there was little new in Berg's doomsday scenario. Religious prophets have been warning about the end of world since the world began. In the Judeo-Christian tradition, apocalyptic prophecies begin with the Hebrew Bible and the Book of Daniel, which was written several centuries before the first coming of Jesus and meant to comfort Jewish Zealots living under the oppressive rule of a Syrian monarch. Sometime around AD 70, the Book of Revelation, the last chapter of the New Testament, was written to inspire the persecuted followers of Jesus.

In the modern era, an Englishman named John Nelson Darby pioneered the still popular theory of "dispensationalism" or "pretribulation premillennialism." Darby, writing in the middle of the nineteenth century, envisioned a "Secret Rapture" to snatch true believers up to heaven and concluded that the Book of Revelation was written to describe the last seven years of Earth's history. The basic idea is that the Antichrist is at work in the world, making things worse and worse. Even the churches are corrupt. But before the Antichrist is revealed in the flesh, Jesus will appear and rapture true believers up to heaven with him. They escape the seven years of intense earthly tribulation and disaster. Then there is the final battle of Armageddon, with Christ fighting the Antichrist. Christ wins and Satan is bound and kept away for one thousand perfect years when the lions lie with the lambs. Finally, there comes the Last Judgment. People go to heaven or hell. Human history ends.

This scenario of the end of the world—one favored by many of today's televangelists—has only become the mainstream evangelical scenario over the last fifty years. This vision really caught on in the seventies when author Hal Lindsey published the *Late Great Planet Earth*, the best-selling book of that decade. Lindsey used Bible prophecy to explain how Israel recaptured Jerusalem in 1967. Russia was the home of the Antichrist of that era, so Lindsey predicted a Soviet invasion and Middle Eastern war in the eighties as his Battle of Armageddon.

Lindsey's work foreshadowed the more recent success of Jerry Jenkins and Tim LaHaye, the evangelical authors whose series of *Left Behind* books have sold more than sixty million copies, plus millions more in home video. In their Endtime scenario, the Antichrist uses the United Nations to establish a one-world government, currency, and religion. Baghdad—the old Babylon—is the new world capital.

That's not much different than the gospel according to Berg, where the emissaries of Satan "crept into our institutions in the form of university professors and high school teachers, and into our churches as moralistic pastors.

"The Antichrist agents had thoroughly infiltrated our government agencies and our militaristic establishments so that every move was known by their central intelligence agency in the headquarters of the Antichrist government."

It was not a new message, but it rang true to many in the political left and hippie counterculture of the late sixties and early seventies. Berg disciples spread the ancient warning with renewed fervor. They donned red sackcloth and wore large wooden yokes around their necks. They smeared ashes on their foreheads, carrying Bibles in one hand and large staves in the other, pounding them on the ground in a mournful rhythm. They appeared at churches and government buildings around the nation, generating media interest wherever they went. They warned of impending doom raining down upon a decadent nation. It was quite a sight. John the Baptist had come back to Earth and taken over the dirty bodies of a bunch of crazed hippies.

Meanwhile, Berg was mending fences with his old boss, Fred Jordan, who allowed the hippie army to occupy the televangelist's abandoned ranch at Thurber, an old coal-mining settlement and one of the finest ghost towns in west Texas. Another garrison of Berg's troops went to Jordan's skid row mission in downtown Los Angeles, while others settled in Florida with Jane Berg, who had accepted her demotion and along with her children continued to bring new disciples into the fold.

Faithy Berg was put in charge of the Los Angeles mission, while Aaron and Deborah Berg joined their father at the Texas Soul Clinic. The Berg family had lived on the 400-acre ranch back in the fifties, following Berg's ouster from Valley Farms, but the place had fallen into serious disrepair. Berg arrived with a small army of disciples eager to rebuild the ranch into a basic training camp for his revolutionary recruits. Buses full of dropouts, runaways, and other counterculture flotsam poured into the camp.

Jordan gave The Family positive media exposure on his TV program "Church in the Home." Former hippies and druggies testified before the cameras about how Jesus had saved them from a life of sin. Some even had their long hair shorn on television. By 1971, the mainstream media had discovered the Jesus freaks. *Newsweek* found them on the Sunset Strip in Hollywood. "They roam about in shaggy pairs, praising the Lord and pressing for converts at the drop of a psychedelic Bible tract." NBC's *First Tuesday* newsmagazine gave positive coverage in a nationally televised broadcast that profiled three Jesus people groups, including The Family.

Another group featured in that broadcast was based in Atlanta and run by David Hoyt, the former Hare Krishna devotee who'd found Jesus in San Francisco on the eve of the Summer of Love. After founding a network of Jesus communes in California, Hoyt moved to Atlanta to establish a beachhead in the South. It had been three years since he, Kent Philpott, and Lonnie Frisbee stumbled across the beginnings of The Family in Huntington Beach. It seemed like a century ago.

Berg's following grew rapidly in the early seventies, from a few hundred to several thousand. Accurate membership figures in new religious movements are hard to establish, but The Family would claim to have more than eight thousand members by 1978. By the time NBC found the Jesus movement, David Hoyt had become overwhelmed by his own success.

"We were housing about eighty people in Atlanta, many of them just recovering from being street people," Hoyt explained in an interview decades later. "We were strapped financially. I was only twenty-five at the time and very young to be in charge of this whole thing."[20]

Hoyt saw salvation in The Family. Perhaps they had the organizational skills he lacked. He went off on a secret mission to check out the Texas Soul Clinic. "It was a very dumb mission," he said. "I went incognito, posing as a seeker who'd just heard about their movement." In a few days, Hoyt revealed who he really was, and the courtship began. "They were very excited about working with us. They said, 'We have an excellent band. Let us come and visit you guys.'"

Jeremy Spencer, a guitarist with the rock band Fleetwood Mac, had recently joined the sect after disappearing one night in 1971 while on tour at the Hollywood Bowl. Hoyt agreed to let the band come to Atlanta, but when The Family arrived, they came with more than just the band. "They bused people in and flew in people from all over the county," Hoyt recalled. "From that moment onward it was just major confusion. They had a plan to take over our ministry. That was the hidden agenda. It was a nightmare. I felt terrible for years afterward. I just went along thinking they had the best of motives. They emptied out most of our ministry."

Hoyt and Philpott recalled these events three decades later. Kent Philpott had wound up pastor of Miller Avenue Baptist Church in Mill

Valley, a small congregation in a prosperous Marin County suburb not far from the Baptist seminary where he and Hoyt lived during the Summer of Love. "I don't think David Hoyt has ever recovered from the trauma he went through in Atlanta," Philpott said. "Berg and his children had a spiritual power that was beyond what we could deal with. I believe it was a demonic spirit."[21]

Philpott pulled out an old file stuffed with Family tracts, or "Mo Letters," that he had collected during the seventies and spread them over the desk in his cluttered office. Some of them were yellowed and frayed around the edges. Many of the leaflets are illustrated with covers that make them seem more like underground comics than Bible tracts. There's one with a warning about the chaos coming in the wake of the comet Kohoutek in March of 1973. Another asks, "Are You a Dropout?" with an illustration copying the Zap Comics style of cartoonist R. Crumb. By the mid-seventies, Berg stopped hiding his sexual obsessions, and the cover art started looking more like cartoons from *Playboy* magazine than *Christianity Today.* "Come on Ma! Burn Your Bra!" one tract extorts, while another entitled "Mountin' Maid," reprints Berg's poetic homage to the female breast. One particularly revealing tract, "Revolutionary Sex," has a cover drawing of a hippie couple masturbating in a field of flowers. Two young children, a boy and girl, stand nearby, tenderly touching each other in an act of imitation.

It was quite a leap from the earliest of Berg's letters, written in 1970 and published two years later. They would hardly raise an eyebrow. One early compilation is illustrated with a pastoral scene of sheep in a mountain valley. In the neck of the shepherd's crook is the title, "Letters from a Shepherd." This collection, unlike the later letters to his followers, has Berg's real name on the cover and begins with a poem written by his mother. Looking back at this early tract more than three decades later, there are two lines of Virginia Berg's poem that jump out like an early warning signal:

> *The lectures you deliver may be very wide and true;*
> *But I'd rather get my lessons by observing what you do.*[22]

That's advice David Hoyt wishes he had followed. In those early years, when he joined forces with The Family, Berg had yet to reveal his sexual obsessions. In fact, Hoyt never even saw Berg during his indoctrination into the sect. Hosea, the prophet's younger son, was his main contact. Nevertheless, Hoyt clearly saw the abuse of power and the blind obedience inspired by the Endtime Prophet.

"The lesson for me is to be very, very careful not to give your loyalty to any new teaching, new prophet, special revelation. My loyalty is to God and Jesus Christ and the Holy Spirit and to no pastor, teacher, or evangelist. I don't care how big a following they have. No pastor or leader or man is infallible. You have to keep your eyes focused on what is pure and eternal. Don't listen to the voices of prophets and prophecies. I've got that warning burned on my soul."

Hoyt brought four communes and scores of disciples into The Family. He also helped convince another Jesus movement leader in Seattle to bring members of her flock under Berg's control. But at the same time, The Family's zealous recruitment tactics were making as many enemies as they were converts. Berg had warned his followers that they would face persecution, and like many of his predictions, this one proved to be a self-fulfilling prophecy.

On the Fourth of July in 1971, Ted Patrick took his family to watch the fireworks at Belmont Park in San Diego. At the time, Patrick was California Governor Ronald Reagan's Special Representative for Community Relations in San Diego and Imperial Counties. During the evening Patrick lost track of his fourteen-year-old son and one of his nephews. They had not returned to the beachfront hotel room Patrick had rented. Just after midnight, as the worried father was about to call police, the two boys appeared back at the hotel looking "vacant, glazed and drifting." They met some people with Bibles and guitars, they said, and there was just *something* about them that made it hard to leave. They wanted the boys to go with them, and promised that they'd never have to work, be sick, or go to school again. They wouldn't even have to go to church because all of those things, along with their parents, were "of the Devil." The encounter prompted Patrick to investigate. He let himself be recruited into The

Family, and after several days determined that this dangerous cult was programming innocent recruits into its deceptive fold.[23]

If young people could be programmed, he reasoned, they could also be *de*programmed. Patrick found other southern California parents whose children had disappeared or gone through sudden personality changes after meeting these intense Christian missionaries. They joined forces to help launch the anticult movement of the seventies. Parents began kidnapping their "brainwashed" children for intense "exit counseling." The media-fueled cult wars began and The Family was right there in the opening battle. Berg's prophecies were being realized. The persecution had begun.

Patrick and the other parents didn't know it, but they were playing right into David Berg's hands. "Which of the prophets," the Endtime Prophet asked, "have not your fathers persecuted?"

Persecution is not bad, but good for you! It purges, purifies.... It tests your devotion and loyalty to Him and His, and keeps you closely dependent on Him, crying out for help! It purifies you and makes you mean business! It sees whether you've got what it takes, if you really love Him and His all the way! It purges the ranks of those that don't mean business and who are not devoted, loyal and true, and who will not be faithful unto the end, but who, like Judas, will cop out under pressure and turn on you and betray you rather than suffer and die for you! It really shows you who's who in your own ranks, and who is going to be dependable when even greater pressure comes![24]

Family Circus

ERATH COUNTY, TEXAS
March 1970 – Texas Soul Clinic Ranch

LIKE MOST OF THE BABES on the Jesus bus, Shula didn't have many
other options. Surrounding her on the ride from Los Angeles to west
Texas were street people strung out on dope and kids running away
from home. Others were just lonely or looking for something with
meaning.

In the parlance of The Family, they were all "babes," meaning
babies in Christ.

Honk if you love Jesus!

Shula was a babe. She was also pregnant and looking for a husband.

She had been raised in the Baptist church in Anaheim, back when it advertised itself as the fastest-growing city in America. Then her family moved up to Beaumont, a small town on the eastern edge of the southern California sprawl. After high school she moved into Los Angeles, where she was in a bad car accident. "I was lost," she said. "I had sex with this guy I hardly knew and ended up pregnant."[1]

Shula went to see her older brother. He'd just gotten out of the Navy and had run into a bunch of Jesus freaks on the streets of Palm Springs. "They've got all kinds of wonderful guys in there," he told her. "If you join up with them, God will give you a husband."

The next thing Shula knew she was on a bus full of Jesus people heading for Texas. She needed love, and The Family had plenty of it. They were singing, laughing, praising Jesus. They were headed for the Texas Soul Clinic, the ranch where Fred Jordan had taught David Berg how to win souls for Jesus back in the fifties. Shula rolled into the Texas ranch in March 1970 but was not prepared for what hit her. "I got off the bus, and there was David Berg right there," she recalled. "I remember looking at him and thinking, 'This guy is crazier than a fruitcake. I'm getting back on the bus.' He was speaking in tongues and laying on hands, and people would burst into tears. It's a powerful thing to watch, especially as an outsider. Here he was praying for all these people, and I'm thinking, 'He might as well pray for me. I need it.'

"It was the most intense spiritual experience I'd felt since I was saved as a seven-year-old at a Baptist church camp. Who knows? Maybe I was imparted with his evil spirit. All I know was I fell in love with Berg right on the spot."[2]

By now, The Family was on a roll. Berg had left Huntington Beach for Arizona in 1969 with about fifty followers. "We began sending teams eastward by different routes to cover the major cities of the United States with our witness," recalled Berg's son, Hosea. "We were seeking to reach young people who were the same as ourselves, looking for something to do with their lives and to give their lives to."[3]

After the big gathering in the Laurentian Mountains in Quebec, the hippie army had fanned back down into the United States. At one encampment in New Jersey, a local newspaper reporter came to check out the motley collection of tents, VW buses, trailers, and other vehicles.

"Who are you?" he asked. "What are you doing here?"

"We told them we weren't part of any group or church, we were just children of God," Hosea said. "So they ran headlines in the newspapers about the 'Children of God.'"

Berg decided that name was as good as any, and it stuck for a while. There were more than 100 members of the tribe traveling in about three dozen vehicles when they regrouped in February 1970 at the Texas Soul Clinic.

Those who joined The Family were encouraged to renounce all worldly possessions—to turn over all they owned for the collective good. Cars, stereos, television sets—not to mention bank accounts—were turned over to the group. In the early years, many Family colonies looked more like pawn shops or used car lots, as all the loot piled up for resale. While the proceeds were used to support colonies popping up around the states and overseas, they also provided Family leaders the resources they needed to scout out future encampments and find a network of safe houses for Berg and his growing staff.

Meanwhile, back at the Texas ranch, Shula was still reeling from her encounter with David Berg when she got her first glimpse of the prophet's oldest son. "Aaron pulled out a guitar and started singing: *I'd rather hear from heaven than a thousand times from earth. For heaven knows what's happening, and the men on earth do not.* I got a supernatural feeling that told me, 'You're going to marry him.'"

There were a couple of problems. Shula was pregnant with another man's child, and Aaron was already married to a girl named Sara.

In 1967, Sara Glasswell had been given her mother's permission to travel the country with the Teens for Christ. She would later tell investigators working with the New York Attorney General that she was forced to have sexual intercourse with Aaron in the presence of David Berg. She told them she was then compelled to obtain her mother's permission to marry Aaron. After the birth of her first child, Sara Berg said her new father-in-law told her it was his turn to father her child, asking the teenage girl, "Why can't you have my son?"[4]

Sara said David Berg tried to seduce her several times before he married her to his son. "Of course, I jumped up and ran and things like this," she said. "He never pushed it very far because I guess he was afraid I'd squeal. But once or twice he did make the attempt."[5]

David Berg seems to confirm his early sexual interest in Sara in his own diary. In an entry dated August 10, 1967, when the Teens for Christ were camped at the Texas ranch, Berg writes "kissed Sara in washhouse. She's so sweet and good to me."

Berg officiated at the wedding of Aaron and Sara in November, just weeks before they arrived in Huntington Beach. "After I had married [Aaron] there were several times when [David Berg] tried to get me. He'd ask me to go to bed with him," Sara said. "He said if I'd have his son's children, why couldn't I have his. He told me that nobody would know the difference if it was his or [Aaron's]."[6]

Over the next three years, Sara Berg gave birth to a son and a daughter. She later told New York state investigators that she "continued living with the group almost as a virtual prisoner."

It wasn't until 1970, just a few weeks after Shula arrived at the Texas ranch, that Sara said she was able to escape with her baby daughter. At the time, Shula says, she had no idea that David Berg's advances had forced Sara to flee the Texas Soul Clinic. All she knew, she says, was that Aaron was despondent over the departure of his first wife and baby daughter.

"Aaron was heartbroken. He was crying and weeping," Shula said. "One day I was in the kitchen chopping vegetables. Aaron said, 'You're thinking of leaving, aren't you? You're thinking of leaving because you need a husband. I'll marry you.' Aaron took me up to his trailer and started reading the Song of Solomon to me. I knew this guy was really desperate. So we had sex. Then all hell broke lose."[7]

Two of Berg's other children were outraged that Aaron wanted to take another wife. "Hosea accused me of seducing Aaron," Shula said. "Deborah went crazy."

They hoped their father would end the relationship, but David Berg had other ideas. "Berg came along and said our marriage was of the Lord," Shula recalled. "He said, 'They are two people who needed each other, and they will give comfort to each other.' He shut Deborah up, and he shut up Hosea."

Shula was betrothed to Aaron and about to get her own intimate look inside the Berg family circus.

She gave birth to her first child, a baby girl, later that year. She had joined up with the Bergs so that her unborn child would have a father. But that father was not Aaron, nor would Shula be the mother who would raise her. The little girl was just six months old when David Berg sent Aaron and Shula up to Canada to bring more converts into his hippie army.

How could she explain what she had done? She had given her daughter over to a disciple named Susan in order to be with Aaron. "At the time," she confessed, "I didn't think I was leaving my daughter. I thought I was putting God first. It was a communal attitude. Your kids were everybody's kids. When I came back, Susan and her husband were totally in love with my daughter. Aaron didn't want her. I allowed myself to be influenced by people who didn't really care about me. Deborah was saying, 'Do you want to be with Aaron, or do you want to be with your baby?'"

In 1971, Berg and Zerby went on a secret mission to Israel. The Endtime Prophet had visions of relocating his flock to a kibbutz in the Jewish state. He expected "Hosannas" from the Jews, but wound up getting deported. Few of his disciples at the Texas Soul Clinic knew about it, but Berg and Zerby had returned to the Lone Star State and were hiding out in a Dallas hotel room. Berg would summon his children and other top leaders to the hotel for meetings. One time, Shula was invited to come along with Aaron.

"Berg was blasting the hell out of Deborah and her husband for something. He knew I had issues with Deborah, and I think he invited me in order to impress me."

Business was adjourned. Berg was in the mood for one of his "sharing" parties. By now, the prophet had pulled out a bottle of wine and removed his clothes. He was walking around the hotel room stark naked, proclaiming his favorite proverb.

"To the pure," Berg said, "all things are pure!"

Before long, the sharing was in full swing. "Everybody was having sex," Shula recalled. "It wasn't like an exhibition. It was under the covers. There was one bedroom with two double beds. There was a mattress on the floor in the living room. Hosea and his wife were off in one corner. I shared with someone other than Aaron. Later on, Berg came up to me in the middle of the night and started kissing me and playing around and said, 'Oh, I could make you my fifth wife.' That's all that happened. The next morning, Berg didn't remember a thing. He'd had a couple glasses of wine and didn't remember what he said the night before, and I certainly wasn't about to remind him."

Nevertheless, the young convert had seen what really went on inside the Berg family. She had been initiated into sharing years before the rank-and-file members of The Family could even guess that teaching was coming down the line.

"In some ways, I guess I thought it *was* possible to love everybody," Shula recalled. "Now I see that stuff doesn't really work. I was twenty, but my maturity level was maybe seventeen or eighteen. Maybe I was trying to break away from my Puritan heritage. I had never been a hippie, so I guess I was trying to be one. I was just totally taken in."

Shula's next child, Merry Berg, was conceived while she and Aaron were off proselytizing across eastern Canada. This time Aaron *was* the father. Mothers often know the moment their children are created, and Shula believes Merry was conceived in the back of a van heading through the Canadian countryside. Aaron's mother, Jane, was riding shotgun and her new mate, Stephen, was behind the wheel. By now, Jane had accepted Karen Zerby's rightful "place above all the maidens."

"We [Shula, Aaron, Jane, and Stephen] called ourselves the Fearsome Foursome. It was in some ways the happiest time in my life," Shula said. "We won people to Jesus every day. People were dropping out of society and joining us. Aaron would write three or four songs in a day. He had a powerful anointing on him."

Aaron and his pregnant wife returned to Texas just as the Soul Clinic was breaking up. David Berg had gotten into another battle with his old boss and landlord, Fred Jordan. But there were other reasons to leave. Angry parents and law enforcement authorities were coming after the Endtime Prophet. Berg took off to England with Zerby, and amidst the chaos, Merry Berg was born in Mingus, Texas, on June 5, 1972. Within a month, Shula was flying off to London with a newborn baby on her lap.

Shula's experience was different than that of most recruits. Her involvement with Aaron gave her an early glimpse of what The Family would soon become. Many of those who joined the sect in 1971 didn't know David Berg existed when they were first brought into the fold. All they knew at first was that they were joining a band of Christian revolutionaries who were preparing for the Endtime. They had to be hooked before they were fed the teachings of David Berg through his "Mo Letters."[8]

Consider the story of Jim LaMattery, who joined The Family before he ever heard of David Berg. Family missionaries approached him in a park in San Diego in the summer of 1971. Jim was sitting under a tree. He'd just smoked a joint.

"Want to hear a song?" one of the missionaries asked.

"Um, sure man, I guess so," he replied.

Jim loved music and also played guitar. But he'd never heard this song.

How long you have been waiting,
For somebody to love you?
How long you been waiting,
For somebody to care?

This guy could really sing. Jim asked him if he was in a band.

"Yeah," he answered, swinging his guitar onto his back and sticking his hands into the pockets of his bell-bottom pants. "So what are *you* doing here?"

"Just hangin'," Jim said.

The stranger smiled and turned his head over toward a crimson van that was pulling up to the curb. There was a young girl riding shotgun. Jim gladly accepted his new friend's invitation to come and have dinner with them. They both piled into the van with the girl and her friend, another attractive hippie chick. Strands of colored glass beads separated the driver and front passenger seats from the rest of the van.

All the other seats had been torn out. Intense conversation ensued as the van rolled down the streets of San Diego. They were talking about a revolution of love.

"Love means getting together," said the girl behind the wheel.

"Yeah, and sharing everything," added the one riding shotgun, flashing a smile at the star-struck teenager.[9]

LaMattery went for dinner and wound up staying six years. At first, when he was living at The Family mission in downtown Los Angeles, he didn't even know David Berg existed, or that there was another large group of disciples in Texas. Berg's youngest daughter, Faithy, and her husband were running the colony in Los Angeles.

Jim LaMattery soon took his guitar into the streets to sing about the revolution of love. It was about Jesus, but not the same Jesus he'd learned about growing up in the Catholic Church. This was radical, revolutionary. Jesus as Che Guevara, the Cuban revolutionary, not like that good shepherd from Sunday school. It was radical, but there was also a feeling of safety in the sect. It seemed like the war in Vietnam would never end. The prospect of the draft hung over LaMattery and his generation like a mushroom cloud, and The Family was a ready-made bomb shelter. Just before his encounter with The Family, LaMattery had started a summer job picking apricots on a farm outside San Diego. Here was an alternative—a radical, communal alternative to getting sucked into the military or some dead-end job. They were going to change the world, and they had God on their side.

"They made rebellion look great," he recalled years later. "It was a radical stance against the government. They called it the 'gospel of rebellion.' They used the shell of religion to control people. That put a holy stamp on the whole thing. It wasn't just a playground or some kind of experimental living. You had some very devoted people."

Among those LaMattery brought into the fold was Donna, a nineteen-year-old convert and his future wife. When the word came down to leave the country—that the United States of America was about to face the wrath of God—Jim and Donna didn't think twice. They took off to a new Family outpost in Denmark, on the site of a vacated Danish army base that had been taken over by a band of European hippies.

David Berg's unorthodox ideas about sexual freedom had not yet filtered down to rank-and-file members of The Family. "It was so fundamentalist. It's hilarious to look back on it now," Jim recalled. "It was no drugs, no sex. You were strictly there for God, to be a revolutionary for Jesus."

Shula, who had just flown into England with Aaron and their baby, was getting a very different view of life in The Family. She was about to have one more close encounter with her horny father-in-law.

"We had gone to live in Berg's house in London," Shula recalled. "I was trying to cook for him and keep this house up while I had Merry, a new baby. It was like a month after having her. I was still healing. One night Aaron sent me into Berg's room. He and Maria were watching something on TV about the Royal Family. They were really into the Royal Family. He offered me a glass of wine and started kissing me. We didn't have sex. He told me he had just been with Becky and Rachel [two of Berg's other wives] and was worn out. I think he was just a drunk and couldn't get it up. Well, the next night he comes up to me and starts kissing me again and wanting to have sex. I told him, 'You know, I'm really tired. Can we do it another time?' It was the truth on my part. Obviously, he took it personally. When I told Aaron that I'd turned Berg down and said I was tired, he couldn't believe it. Aaron said, 'What! You didn't have sex with the prophet!' Maybe Aaron was trying to get back in his father's good graces by letting him have sex with me. Berg would play games with his kids—promote one and demote another."[10]

Aaron was already losing his father's trust. Having his wife turn Berg down certainly didn't help his cause. But there were deeper problems. Aaron had long suffered from bouts of depression, and he was once again sinking into that mix of anger and melancholy. He and Shula were sent off to Sweden, where they briefly crossed paths with Jim and Donna LaMattery.

"Aaron was flown into Sweden," LaMattery said. "He was in a world of confusion when he got there, and I was told to babysit him. I knew he had been shifted to me for babysitting duty, but no one told me why. They just said to watch out for him. We had a lake there, and we would go out. He was a great guitar player, but a really miserable guy. Aaron was always a little strange. We would go out to eat and he was always in left field. Back in California, he would go on these crazy expeditions, singing through the streets of LA. But he seemed really depressed and despondent in Sweden."

Shula could see her husband was going down into the spiritual spiral of depression. "Aaron knew that his dad did not want us back in England," she said. "Merry was about nine months old. Aaron was really depressed."

After Sweden, Shula, Aaron, and Merry moved into a Family colony in Paris, where the eldest son of the Endtime Prophet continued his descent. One night she saw him writing a long letter to his father. "He was really depressed. I looked over his shoulder to see what he was doing and he was writing about how Jane [Aaron's mother] would leave him in the house [as a baby], and he'd scream for hours. He put the letter in an envelope, and wrote on it, 'Goodbye dad. You're the best dad a son ever had.' Then he gave it to me to mail. It was a suicide note."

Jane Berg, the Endtime Prophet's long-suffering but ever-loyal wife, was dispatched from London to Paris to deal with her suicidal son. Before she arrived, Aaron's behavior worsened. "One night he wanted to have sex," Shula recalled. "I just said, 'No. I'm tired,' and he pushed me out of bed and onto the floor. It was totally out of character for the way he treated me. It was evil. He was possessed. I called Jane and she told me to lock him in a room and pray for him until she could come and deliver that spirit out of him."

Jane arrived the next day and told Shula she was taking Aaron with her to Switzerland. It was the last time Shula would see her husband.

According to a statement later released by The Family, Aaron Berg died in a climbing accident. He was last seen alive in Geneva on April 3, 1973, when he headed into the Alps "to pray and be alone with the Lord." His body was found nineteen days later at the bottom of a cliff—on Easter Sunday.

Berg claimed his son's death fulfilled one of the "Laurentide Prophecies" issued back in Quebec in 1969 at the founding gathering of The Family. "I saw a vision of Aaron dying on a mountain, and the Lord said, 'Thy Aaron shall be taken from thee and depart on the mount!' And he did! God's word never fails!"

"His music helped start the Jesus Revolution, and he was one of its hardest-working witnesses," Berg said. "But his mind was much stronger than his frail body ... so God has now enabled him to cross forbidden borders, escape his enemies and help us as never before!"[11]

Shula knew it was no accident. She knew from the beginning that Aaron committed suicide, and David Berg had blood on his hands. Years of paternal abuse and cruel manipulation, she says, caused her husband to take his own life. Her theory as to what destroyed her husband would be confirmed fifteen years later in another one of Berg's prophecies. Then, in the eighties, the focus of the prophet's wrath would be his granddaughter, Merry, the child of Shula and Aaron Berg.

Merry Berg did not have a stable upbringing after her father's death. Shula took another husband in the inner circle, a loyal devotee named Ralph Keeler Irwin, but the marriage never really took. Merry was shuttled between Ralph, Shula, and her grandmother, Jane Berg, and her new mate, Stephen.

In the aftermath of Aaron's suicide, Jane Berg sent Shula and Merry to Spain with two trusted members of the inner circle. "Jane invited me back to Paris six months after Aaron died," Shula said. "I was really out of it. The full impact of what had happened to Aaron had just hit me. Berg wanted Jane to take care of me. They said, 'Pick any of these guys you want to marry.' Jane called Ralph and I in and did this prophesizing thing over us. She talked me into having sex with him. I didn't get involved with anyone else at the time. If I was going to get pregnant, I wanted to know who it was. And I got pregnant."

Don Irwin was born into The Family in 1974. Shula, Ralph, Merry, and little Don were together off and on over the next few years. They were a family—of sorts—but this was the seventies, and this was The Family. It was a chaotic time. There was a battle raging for control of the sect in several continents around the world. There was also a big proselytizing push at the time in—of all places—Libya and Tunisia. Then, amidst all the chaos all around the world, another child was born.

6

My Little Fish

TENERIFE, CANARY ISLANDS
January 1975 – Emergencia Maternidad

RICKY WAS BORN just after noon on Saturday, January 25, 1975, on Santa Cruz de Tenerife, in the Canary Islands, the Spanish archipelago that dots the North African coast between Morocco and the Western Sahara. His biological mother, Karen Zerby, and his spiritual father, David Berg, hopped in a taxi that morning and rushed down to a little clinic near Plaza Charco. They'd stopped at the more upscale Bellevue Clinic, but no one was around to help with the delivery. "There was

The "flirty fishing" team in Tenerife. Front row (l-r) are Sue Kauten, Queen Rachel, David Berg, and Karen Zerby.

no room in the inn, so we had to go down to the stable," Berg would later explain. "Hallelujah!"[1]

They came to the Canary Islands to conduct an experiment. Ricky was the experiment. On the second day of his life, Ricky was taken from the clinic to his new family's home, where a series of nannies would help raise the Prophet Prince.

He had dark curly hair, long black eyelashes, and a birth weight of 7.7 pounds. Berg was sure that had prophetic significance, as he had a long fascination with the mystical properties of the number seven. Berg was forty-nine years old (seven squared) when the world finally began to realize—in 1968—that he was the long-awaited Endtime Prophet. At the time of Ricky's portentous birth, David Berg weighed 77 kilos. Not only that, the prophet calculated that the Prophet Prince was born in the seventh hour of the seventh day. (That numerology works if one considers that the day starts at 6 A.M. and Saturday is the final day of the biblical week.) To make the timing of his birth even more auspicious, the child was born in 1975 on the 25th day of the month. Two plus five equals seven. And it doesn't stop there. The bill for the overnight stay at the *Emergencia Maternidad* was 7,000 pesetas.

David Berg christened the baby "Davidito," or Little David. According to the Endtime Prophet, Ricky and his mother, Karen "Maria" Zerby, were destined to be the two witnesses credited with ushering the apocalypse in the eleventh chapter of the Book of Revelation.

> And I will give my two witnesses authority to prophesy for one thousand two hundred and sixty days, wearing sackcloth.... When they have finished their testimony, the beast that comes up from the bottomless pit will make war on them and conquer them and kill them.... Their dead bodies will lie in the street.... For three and a half days members of the peoples and tribes and languages and nations will gaze at their dead bodies and refuse to let them be placed in a tomb.... But after three and a half days, the breath of life from God entered them, and they stood on their feet, and those who saw them were terrified. Then they heard a loud voice from heaven saying to them,

"Come up here!" And they went up to heaven in a cloud while their enemies watched them.[2]

Sara Kelley, a devotee who would emerge as Ricky's most influential nanny, arrived on the island with her husband, Alfred, on March 19, 1975. She was given a copy of a child care book entitled *How to Raise a Brighter Child* and told to keep detailed records of the newborn's activities and handling. "Someday," Berg told her, "you will be writing his story to share with the whole world."[3]

Sara's tale would be called *The Story of Davidito*.

How do you begin the story of the King and Queen's little brown prince? We've always considered him a King too, not just a prince, because ever since the very early beginning at birth, he was special. I guess that's the most important thing to emphasize from the start, that he is special, exceptional, and Dad [Berg] has always said to me, "Now remember, honey, he's different. I've known a lot of children and had plenty of my own, but he sure is special, an exceptional child. So don't expect every baby to be like him. It must be something spiritual."[4]

Ricky had four nannies and teachers in the early years of his life—including Sara Kelley and Sue Kauten, who would go on to serve as his mother's longtime personal secretary. Sara would have the greatest impact on Ricky's life. She would chronicle the highly sexualized environment in which he was raised. But decades later, on the other side of the world, Sue Kauten would pay the ultimate price for the child-rearing experiment on the isle of Tenerife.

It all started as a kind of lark. Sara and Sue were among the first Family staff summoned to Tenerife, a sun-drenched Canary Island known for its tropical parks, beaches, quaint fishing port, and lively nightlife along Veronica's strip—a street lined with nightclubs full of globe-trotting party animals.

Tenerife was the third stop on Berg and Zerby's exile from the United States. The first stop was their failed mission to Israel, where the Endtime Prophet had to scrap his vision for a Family kibbutz. After a brief return to the United States, they flew off to London, where they set up shop in an apartment in Bromley. They started "witnessing" in nightclubs and discotheques.

It was prime mission territory for Berg, a prophet who definitely liked his drink. Berg soon found that potential converts were more interested in dancing with his young wife than listening to what he had to say about the end of the world. It was here, amid the mirror balls of London's swinging social scene, that the Lord gave Berg his most infamous revelation.

Berg was to become God's pimp. Karen and the rest of his female disciples would be heaven's harlots. They would bring men to Jesus—and The Family—by selfless acts of sexual sacrifice. Berg gave his erotic evangelists detailed instructions, right down to what they should whisper into the ears of potential converts on the dance floor of discipleship:

> Even when you're dancing, you meet them at the club and you put your arms around them and you snuggle up to them and you love them up and kiss them, you feel their bodies against you and you feel them getting hard and all you have to say is, "You mean to tell me you don't believe in God?"
>
> "Listen, feel me, I am the love of God, I am *God's* love for *you*! I am God's *love* because He *created* me for you. He created me a woman and a woman's love and a woman's breasts, my pussy and everything for your pleasure. Doesn't that prove that God loves you? Why can't you understand that that *proves* that God loves you."[5]

"Flirty fishing" originated in London, but it wasn't until 1976 that Berg sent out a flood of letters to trusted members with explicit illustrations and provocative titles like "God's Love Slave" and "The FF Explosion." Even before the letters went out, the flirty fishing crew was creating quite a stir on Tenerife. All these American women were hitting the clubs in low-cut dresses, flirting with men, and talking about Jesus.

At the time, hardly anyone in The Family knew the whereabouts of their prophet. New members of the team would be flown into Barcelona, met by a trusted insider, and taken aboard a tramp steamer. "You drop off the face of the earth and wind up on this island in the middle of the Atlantic. It was an adventure," recalled one member of the Tenerife team. "We were all young, in our early twenties. It was an idyllic place. You were living on this tropical island with this big volcano. It was a relatively simple existence, but it was exciting. None of the bad stuff had really kicked in yet. You have a sense that you are chosen to be there. It makes everybody there feel important and special, but it also creates a high level of paranoia."[6]

Mostly, it was just a lot of fun. "It's not like you were in some conservative backwater. Most of the tourists were northern Europeans who were pretty tolerant of our weirdness. We just came across as other people on holiday. That was our front. There were all these gorgeous girls, and there was David Berg test-driving FFing (pronounced 'eff-eff-ing') before unleashing it on the entire Family. It was all pretty amazing."

To others, flirty fishing didn't seem all that strange. Miriam Williams was only seventeen when she met some of Berg's disciples in Greenwich Village in 1971. She soon went off with them to a commune in upstate New York. "It was a campground with about 300 people," she said. "People were living together, sharing everything. It was a mixture of Christianity and communism. It appealed to me."

Later, as a Family missionary in Europe, Miriam found herself sharing more than her material possessions. "At first, it was just flirting, but if necessary, you'd have sex with men to get them to join," said Williams. "Most of us weren't that shocked by it. It wasn't that much different than the whole hippie, free love thing. We were already having sex with people in the group."[7]

It didn't take long for the European press to smell a story on Tenerife. Ricky had just celebrated his second birthday when a pair of Swedish journalists came to the island in February 1977. "Our Tenerife Family had their first magazine interview by two Swedish reporters, to whom Dad gave a beautiful witness, and they took lots and lots of pictures of everyone, especially Mommy [Zerby], Daddy [Berg] and Dito [David-ito/Ricky]," Sara wrote. "We were very busy meeting reporters and new people and even stopped on the street by complete strangers."

Swedish journalists were the first to publish an infamous photo of the Tenerife flirty fishing crew. The picture, later published in *Time* magazine in August 1977, and countless times thereafter, shows the Endtime Prophet surrounded by twelve of his holy hookers, all of them with big smiles and visible cleavage. Bearded and beaming beneath his receding hairline, Berg sits in the front row with Sue Kauten and Queen Rachel (an early Family leader) on his right and Zerby on his left.

Flirty fishing was now in full swing. Berg's sect rented several homes, including an old villa with a special FFing room. "Some of the girls would come in there. Some would go to the guy's place if you could trust them. There was a rule you weren't supposed to sleep with anyone on the first date," one member of the crew recalled. "Berg ran a tight ship. Everybody had to write reports. 'Whom did you see? What did you talk about?' Berg called himself the fisherman. He was a spiritual pimp. He ran this line of girls. He'd say, 'Ok, we're going to focus on this guy.' Either he had money or was considered to be spiritually hungry. Berg would read the reports, then get some revelation."

In *The Story of Davidito*, Sara recalls how she first learned that "FFing" had something to do with Ricky's not-so-immaculate conception. "The Lord has reminded me many times how Davidito was conceived by the ultimate in love, total sacrifice and total giving," she wrote in her diary, "and that the Lord is using him to teach us about love."[8]

About six weeks after Sara came to the island, Berg and Zerby had been gone the whole day and well into the night. Ricky spent much of the day out on the porch, bouncing up and down in his new "Johnny-Jump-Up." Mom and Dad came home around 11:30 P.M. with a shy, young Canarian named Carlos, the biological father of the Prophet Prince and a waiter in one of the hotels where Zerby and Berg stayed when they first came to Tenerife.

Berg sat in his chair next to the fireplace of their home, sipping a glass of wine and gazing at Carlos with a strange look of affection. Then he moved over and sat beside the young man before taking Karen and the handsome waiter into Ricky's dimly lit bedroom. They all looked down at the baby asleep on his stomach.

"What dark hair he has and so brown," Carlos said.

"Why not?" Berg replied. "He was born in Spain. He's Spanish."

"So Carlos was the one the Lord had used to give us Davidito!" said Zerby, who had never been sure. "Do you really think so? Do you really think it's Carlos? Why him?"

"Honey, he loved you from the first. He loved you the most, he fell so hard for you," said Berg, raising his wineglass for another toast. "He still loves you, and the Lord wants to bless him."

Berg sensed that Karen—not to mention Carlos—was a little uncomfortable with this strange introduction to their son. Berg later spent half the night berating Zerby for not showing enough love toward the biological father of the Prophet Prince during his visit. The next day, they invited the Spanish waiter back to the house after work. Berg told Zerby to put on one of her long, sexy dresses and try, this time, to be more loving toward Carlos. Sara helped prepare the love chamber with candles. It was the first time the new nanny had seen flirty fishing in action. "It was such a beautiful sample and she showed so much love and obedience to the Lord's words," Sara wrote in her diary. "They made love on the floor!"[9]

Ricky was still an infant when Berg began plotting his next move. One week after Sara chronicled Zerby's exploits in the love chamber, the couple was off with the baby Ricky to Libya. In the month's preceding Ricky's birth, Berg's disciples around the world had been distributing a tract praising the dictator, entitled "Khadafi's Third World." Why this intense interest? Perhaps Berg respected Khadafi's cocky willingness to stand up against American power, or he was drawn to the Muslim leader after Berg's rejection by the Israeli government. Maybe he was looking for another hideout from the news media, government investigators, and dismayed parents. And, like other apocalyptic prophets of the mid-seventies, Berg saw shades of the Antichrist in the fiery colonel. Maybe he was someone The Family could use—at least until the Great Tribulation.

Khadafi didn't take the bait, and the royal family moved on. There was a trip with mommy and daddy to a villa on the Italian coast and a train ride to Barcelona in August 1975. They were back on Tenerife in September to move into a larger house to accommodate the ever-growing staff needed to serve the royal family. The new house had a red-tiled roof, swimming pool, and large walled garden with palm trees. It was located on the edge of a village where Carlos was raised, El Barrio del Durazno, in the lush green valley of Orotava.

Perhaps Berg thought that being closer to the family of his son's biological father would ease tension over the unusual family arrangement. It did not. Carlos and his family were distancing themselves from the inner circle. The handsome waiter even started talking about marrying his childhood sweetheart. "Dad became so indignant he threatened to blast them all away at our next family fiesta for not loving their new family member, Davidito," wrote Sara, who like other disciples now referred to Berg as "Dad." "Because of their final decision to reject Davidito, the Lord said later in Prophecy that the family would be cursed."[10]

Sara recounted all this in her *Story of Davidito*, published by The Family in 1982. It's a strange book, full of advice on such everyday matters as child nutrition, teaching toddlers to read, and clothing suggestions for small children. Berg's personal experience is often used as the model. "Dad [Berg] never liked putting on tight turtlenecks because of having to wear them as a child," Sara advised. "His mother probably forced them over his head, and they always gave him an uncomfortable feeling of claustrophobia."[11]

But it was not the helpful hints on dressing children that would make *The Story of Davidito* the most controversial publication in the history of The Family. The most explosive and embarrassing sections of the book were the pages devoted to the young prophet's sexual education. It began early, when he was an infant in Tenerife. Sara writes:

> He gets quite excited when I wash his bottom and his penie gets real big and hard. I kiss it all over till he gets so excited he bursts into laughter and spreads his legs open for more. I wonder what it's going to be like when he begins to talk and asks for more? When playing on the floor he'll oftentimes spread his legs open for me to kiss his penis (what we call his "penie"). He got to where he liked it so much he'd pull people by the hand down

onto the floor and would spread his legs apart for "the treatment." So we had to explain to him that there are a lot more important things in life than just sex, and a time and a place for everything![12]

What is most extraordinary about *The Story of Davidito* is the innocence with which sexual acts between adults and children are described and photographed. Sara writes about sex play with toddlers on one page, then nonchalantly jumps into a discussion of how Ricky's stamp collection is "a tremendous teaching aid in geography."

Children learn by imitation, and for the children in The Family, that was the way to teach toddlers sex education. Kids were encouraged to watch their parents make love and then try it themselves. After a while, however, even Sara began rethinking that parenting tip. "Davidito is jealous when Alfred [Sara's husband] and I begin loving up and tries to pull us apart, so the best thing for now is that we just not make love in front of him. Davidito loves to watch Dave and Sally [two other staff members] go at it, though. He begins to pant and bounce along with them, then sits down in exhaustion with a big sigh when it's all over, just like he's been through it too! Praise the Lord!"[13]

Ricky got a sex partner closer to his age when Sara gave birth to her own child, Davida Maria Kelley. She was fourteen months younger than the Prophet Prince, but within a year of her birth was engaged with simulated sex acts with her older playmate. Ricky would watch couples make love by the pool and imitate the action with Davida, whose name is pronounced "Da-VEE-dah." The same kind of sex play went on at night when the children would sleep in the same bed with their adult caregivers. Sara writes of how Ricky was at first jealous of her baby daughter, but jokes about how "he finally found something he thinks the baby is good for." When Sara first told Berg and Zerby how Ricky would climb on the bed, crawl up on Davida, and start humping away, they didn't believe her. "They both love it, really," she told them. "Dad and Maria [Zerby] came to see for themselves, and sure enough, Davidito once again climbed on top of Davida and began banging away with a big smile!"[14]

Berg's theories about childhood sexuality were being put into practice. He was finally getting back at his mother for publicly chastising him for playing with himself.

"Children should be taught that their sexual parts are just as good as the rest of their body and that sexual activities, feelings and pleasure are no more evil than eating or other physical functions or exercise," Berg wrote. "The prohibitive and condemnatory attitudes toward sex of our overly religious so-called 'Christian' Western culture has produced generations of over-sexed children with an abnormal desire for sex and an absolutely manic craze for everything sexual due to their early sexual frustrations. Only in the present hippie generation have young people finally returned to a more normal attitude toward sex."[15]

In *The Story of Davidito*, Sara did not merely describe the sex play between the eighteen-month-old Prophet Prince and his five-month-old consort. The most explicit chapter of her book, "My Little Fish," includes nude photos of Ricky and his mother striking sensual poses in bed—along with snapshots of Ricky "banging away" on top of Davida.

At the time, Berg was certainly not the only advocate for allowing sexual play among children and teenagers. Berg was writing in 1973—when attitudes toward human sexuality and sex education were changing. One example was a book entitled *Show Me!: A Picture Book on Sex for Children and Parents*, published in 1974 by St. Martin's Press. It was widely available in bookstores until the late seventies, when new laws were passed prohibiting the display of photographs of sexual acts involving children under sixteen years of age. *Show Me!* was much more explicit in its presentation than *The Story of Davidito*.

On the other hand, St. Martin's Press had already pulled *Show Me!* from the stores by 1982, the year The Family published *The Story of Davidito*. Even back in 1973, when Berg wrote his treatise "Revolutionary Sex," he insisted that his followers conceal their hands-on experiments in childhood sexual education. Children in The Family were taught never to reveal their sexual play to outsiders.

"It must be made very clear to your children that such sexual freedom must never be indulged in or practiced openly in the presence of visitors, strangers or uninitiated relatives and friends who have not been properly re-educated in the revolutionary sexual freedom of natural living! In other words, you will not be able to indulge in such God-given freedoms in the presence of the average Systemite or even new disciples or their children or those who have not yet been properly educated in the liberty-loving ways of God's revolutionary naturist."[16]

Actually, it didn't take long for the Systemites in Tenerife to go after the Endtime Prophet for his freewheeling sexual teachings. Sensational press coverage of The Family had forced Berg and his followers to flee the United States. Now the European press, especially the German magazine *Stern*, was onto the story. Reporters staked out the villa that an Italian count had turned over to the cult. "In this estate, surrounded by olive trees and terraced vineyards, the sect has its operational headquarters, which is top secret—known only to a handful of people," *Stern* reported.[17]

Journalists also caught up with Berg in Tenerife, where the prophet was spotted having a fine time. "The man with the white beard in his late 50s was spotted every night with a dozen beautiful women in the upscale bar 'Los Caprichos' in Puerto de la Cruz and bought drinks for hundreds of Marks every night. Germans and tourists from other countries flirted with the women, who were ordered to sleep with anyone who looked like they had money."

One Berg devotee, a twenty-one-year-old nurse from the Italian resort town of Rimini, explained that flirty fishing was not conducted for the money or with lust in her heart. "What I do here has nothing to do with group sex," she wrote in a letter to her parents. "I don't sleep with just anyone, only with those that search for Jesus. What could be better than to give my life and my body to Jesus."[18]

It was soon time to get out of Tenerife. In February 1977, a local judge summoned Berg to court. Catholic Church leaders had complained about the sect, prompting a closer look at the visas of these unorthodox American missionaries. At first, Berg held his ground. In early March, the entire Tenerife Family held a prayer vigil outside the courthouse in Orotava to support their spiritual leader. Ricky's picture—his hands folded in prayer while Berg was in court—was published in the local paper.

Fearing deportation, Berg and Zerby fled the island, leaving Ricky behind with Sara. They followed on a flight to the Portuguese island of Madeira, where the Unit was reunited. It was the beginning of their "gypsy travels."

Sue Kauten soon joined the family at their hotel on Madeira. Sara now had her own child and initially found herself torn between her spiritual responsibilities for Ricky and her motherly concern for Davida. Sue's arrival helped The Family get back to Job One—the sexual education of the Prophet Prince.

One night, right after his nap, Ricky, now aged two, joined Sara and Alfred in their bed. "We were all three loving up when Dito looked at me with those big dreamy Canarian black eyes and said, 'Sara, I yub you!' He pulled me down to kiss him, then pushed my head down to kiss some more!"[19]

There was another move in May. Sara, Alfred, and Ricky fled to Lisbon to prepare a new home. But reporters working for *Stern* had caught up with them, and they wouldn't stay long.

All five of the inner circle were forced to flee from Portugal in the middle of the night. "Diabolical German news reporters of the vicious anti-Christ [sic] Jewish *Stern* magazine were right on Dad's trail and hounding us at our very front door," Sara wrote.

They would move five times in the next six weeks. Members of the Unit were moving around at a pace even faster than David Berg knew as a child growing up with his itinerant evangelist mother. There was a sudden move to Switzerland, where Ricky learned how to ride a bike; then to the island of Malta, where they lived in a small apartment on the bay; and after the police started an investigation there, onto Sicily and then back to Switzerland. There were immigration officials, local police, or the news media asking too many questions, and The Family was always on the run. In August, at a casino in Lisbon, they were "besieged by antagonistic German reporters by surprise! The whole house was in an emergency security state the next day. Not only were we concerned about the safety of the King and Queen, but also our Little Prince!"[20]

The reporters' arrival at their home in Lisbon that day was Ricky's first real lesson in security training.

"Who's at the door?" he asked.

"They are people who want to come in, but we don't want to let them in," Sara replied.

"What people?"

"They're mean people who don't love Jesus and don't love us because we *do* love Jesus."

"Are they sitting outside in the parked car?"

"Yes, they are."

Then, according to Sara, Ricky said, "They're mean people and they don't love Jesus, but we're not afraid because we have *Jesus*, and Daddy's not afraid because *he* has Jesus!"

At 4:30 A.M. the next morning, Berg and Zerby slipped out a back door into the night. Then a taxi quietly backed into the driveway of their home to pick up Sara and Ricky and take them to a small downtown hotel.

They moved again in early September—this time to Madrid and then on to a safe house out in the Spanish countryside. But no amount of moving would get in the way of the sexual education of the Prophet Prince. Sometimes, before he went to sleep, Ricky would jabber to his stuffed animals, giving them voices.

"You go fuck Pat, and you go fuck the big girl in the kitchen!"

"Oh, you don't want to? Oh, OK, I'll fuck Pat!"[21]

One day, not long before his third birthday, the Prophet Prince was thumbing through a copy of *Playboy* magazine. He came to the foldout, turned to Alfred, and said:

"Oh, she's pretty. What's her name?"

"Sheila," Alfred answered.

Ricky asked if he could put her picture on the wall by his bed, just like Daddy, so he could kiss her nipples and pet the Playmate on the foldout. Alfred replied:

"I think Sara's prettier than her, don't you?

"No," Ricky answered

Later that night, the Prophet Prince wanted to take nude photos of Sara in bed. Alfred got a chair for Davidito to stand on and showed him how to work the camera. "He was so excited he could hardly stand it," Sara recalled.

Sara's sex play with Davidito varied from night to night. "He'll sometimes just jump on top of me real quick, hunch away and then jump off again and say, 'Do you like that, Sara?' But his usual, more gentle and preferred approach is, 'Let's go wash penie,' and then I know what he really wants.

"Daddy told me he wants Davidito to have all the love he ever needed and wanted and didn't get," Sara wrote. "And thank the Lord we can enjoy sharing real 'loving up' together. It all comes about so sweet and naturally that it makes me wonder what all we must've missed in our own childhood. It's wonderful to be able to pour into the children all your 'dreams-come-true.'"[22]

Ricky celebrated his sixth birthday, and Davida turned five during the Unit's eight-month stay at an old farmhouse in Puyricard, a hamlet in the south of France. Berg would spend most of his time in a trailer behind the house with Zerby, a tape recorder, and a bottle of wine. "Basically, every word he said was recorded," one staffer recalled. "If you were walking around in the yard with him, you have to take a tape recorder. And God help you if you screwed up and didn't turn it on."[23]

Berg would come down to the farmhouse on most nights for the evening meal. "Dinner could go on for hours," recalled one regular guest. "Berg was a religious drunk. You listened to him. It was stream of consciousness. It would be about something he'd been reading. If someone had been bad in the group, you'd hear a rant about that. If he was in a good mood he'd start singing a song or want to hang around and play with the kids."[24]

That's an adult recollection. Davida has her own memories of what it was like when David Berg decided to play with the kids. More than two decades later, as an adult living in New York, Davida offered her own firsthand memories of what it was like living as a child with the Endtime Prophet, a man she called "Grandpa."

According to Davida, Berg sexually fondled her on many occasions and performed oral sex on her when she was a child. "Growing up in the Unit, there was absolutely nothing wrong with adults having sexual interaction with children. The whole thing was encouraged," Davida said. "As Grandpa put it, 'God created us to enjoy it at a young age so I don't see why age should have anything to do with it.'

Grandpa was the mouthpiece of God. Everything he did was done in the name of Jesus and, therefore, it couldn't be wrong."[25]

Grandpa loved to watch Davida dance. One day at the farmhouse in France her performance was staged against a backdrop of palm trees and a bucolic blue lagoon. Davida stood before the stage set and struck a sexy pose. She was five years old. She was topless and had a gauzy sarong tied about her waist. She had one arm on her hip and the other seductively raised behind her head.

For Grandpa, it was a Kodak moment. No one knew it at the time, but this photo would later illustrate the final page of *The Story of Davidito*—right above a caption describing Sara's daughter as "Dancing Davida, the Hawaiian Hula Honey."

"Our children have learned that this dancing is not only for fun, but it's for Jesus," Sara wrote. "Isn't it wonderful how the Lord made so many events in our life for Him so exciting and just so much fun! Hallelujah."[26]

Davida's dance may have been exciting, but it was not for just the Lord. It was for Grandpa Berg, a man who loved to watch videotapes of young girls performing sexy dances. They were taped and sent to him from Family colonies all around the world. But the dance of Davida was the most exciting. She wasn't just on the TV screen. She was right there in the flesh, ready to be sent to the Endtime Prophet's bed whenever Grandpa was in the mood.

Dozens of these family photos illustrate *The Story of Davidito*, but there's something especially eerie about this family scrapbook. The heads of all the family members are covered over with drawings of their hair and facial features. They are half photograph, half cartoon. And they are always smiling.

Their faces were altered for security reasons. No one was to recognize the members of the inner circle—not even Family members who were sent *The Story of Davidito* as their child care manual. But the concealment of Ricky's and Davida's identities went much deeper. They were to have no personal identity. Ricky was Davidito—prophecy embodied. Davida was a child sexuality liberated. They were not raised to be normal children. They were born to be exemplars of the great child care revolution of David Berg.

No one knows better than Davida what Ricky went through as a child. She lived with him and the Unit until she was eleven years old and he was twelve. Growing up, Davida had no concept of "sexual abuse." Going off with Grandpa or another man was "love up" time. As she remembers it, members of her Family would get together in a gathering that could begin as a meeting or celebration and end up as a disco and an orgy. "We were all naked and getting molested when we were four or five years old. Everybody was having sex, and the kids would get involved."[27]

Davida's earliest memories in the Unit involve moving and moving and then moving again. Her childhood was spent on the run. She and Ricky traveled across Europe, to South Africa, and finally to the Far East. They were always moving, yet never really leaving the cocoon that was the Unit. "We never had other interactions with kids. We'd see them on the streets or at the zoo," she said. "It was us, Grandpa [Berg], Maria [Zerby], my mom and dad and immediate staff—security, cooks, secretaries, writers, and editors."

It would be a few more years before the teachings of the Endtime Prophet would be made flesh. Merry Berg, the child born to Shula and Aaron Berg, would be brought back to the Unit. Merry was a few years older than Ricky and Davida. She was the first to sexually come of age. Her presence was needed to make the teachings flesh.

While Davida called David Berg "Grandpa," she was not actually related to him by blood. Merry, on the other hand, was the daughter of Aaron and the biological granddaughter of David Berg. But there was no need to worry about incest. This was the gospel of revolutionary sex. What was good in the heart of the prophet was right in the eyes of the Lord.

"To the pure," as Berg liked to say, "all things are pure!"

7

Teen Terror

Children of God in the south of France in the seventies. Standing front and center are Merry Berg and Don Irwin.

ANTIPOLO, PHILIPPINES
February 1987 – Sunflower Street

RICKY, THE SPIRITUAL son of David Berg, was twelve.

Merry Berg, the Endtime Prophet's biological granddaughter, was fourteen.

In the gospel according to Grandpa, it was time for them to make a baby, to continue his dynasty, to make the teachings flesh.

David Berg had not seen his granddaughter since 1972, when Shula and Aaron and the infant Merry left the Endtime Prophet's hideout in London. Berg had christened Merry with the biblical name "Mene Mene," from an Old Testament story about how the Prophet Daniel interpreted strange writings on a wall that foretold the destruction of Belshazzar and his kingdom.[1]

As would often be the case, Berg was half-right. Merry Berg *would* play a key role in the destruction of a kingdom. It would not be the kingdom of Belshazzar, but the kingdom of Berg. In the process, Merry would nearly destroy herself and help inspire Ricky to embark on a murderous rampage of revenge.

Hundreds of kids were born into The Family during the seventies, but none of them were made to live out the Endtime Prophet's teachings like Ricky, Davida, Merry, and Zerby's daughter, Christina

Teresa Zerby. Christina, called "Techi" in The Family, was born in the south of France on March 19, 1979. Her biological father was Michael Sweeney, a one-time Berg insider who would soon be ousted in a power struggle among the prophet's top lieutenants.[2]

During the eighties, the Unit remained on the run. They were in France until June 1981, when Berg predicted a nuclear holocaust would soon devastate Europe and North America. They moved to Cape Town, South Africa, to escape the coming horror.

Membership in The Family—always hard to determine with any certainty—peaked by the early eighties. Several thousand members left in 1978 and 1979 as Berg's teachings got more bizarre and leadership struggles broke out in various parts of the world. In 1978, before the wave of defections, The Family claimed 8,000 members. Only about ten percent of them were living in the United States, but babies kept being born in colonies around the world. The number of children born into The Family peaked in 1983 when the sect reported 746 births in a single year. Nearly half of the reported membership was children.[3]

Berg and his staff—now called "World Services"—moved from South Africa to the Philippines in 1982. They stayed at the Admiral Hotel in Manila and then moved into a house in Greenhills, San Juan, a wealthy Manila subdivision. They rented some cottages at the Tropicana Hotel Resort in southern Manila for a few months. They then found a more permanent headquarters at a hilltop hideout in Antipolo, in an exclusive development overlooking the sprawling capital city.

Merry was summoned to join Grandpa in the Philippines in late 1983. There were now four children in the Unit. Ricky was eight, Davida was six, and Techi was four when eleven-year-old Merry arrived. Here's how Ricky, referring to Merry as "Mene," remembered that time in the Philippines:

After she arrived, things started changing for us. . . . It raised the standard considerably for us, and made it harder to keep up.

Maria [Zerby] and Sara [Davida's mother] were obsessed with their image and the reflection we cast on it. We not only had to be "good kids," but we had to be the best! After all, we were "Grandpa and Maria's kids." We were supposed to be super-kids, commissioned with taking over The Family when Berg died, and leading God's Endtime Army through the Great Tribulation!

If we were going to be able to do that, then why on earth shouldn't they expect Techi to keep up with someone like Mene who was only seven or eight years older than she was, and certainly hadn't had "as good training"?

We still were kids, and we wanted to play with our toys and just have fun, instead of worrying about watching all our actions and making a good impression on our teachers.

Mene didn't seem to be interested in playing games and playing with toys. She didn't seem to view school and "Word Time" as something to endure, as we did. She was always held up as the example for us to follow, and we started resenting her for being smarter, more liked, and the center of attention, mainly from Berg.[4]

Merry's life of sexual molestation and abuse started when she was seven years old and sent to the sect's "Music with Meaning" camp in Greece. Music with Meaning was a Family radio program translated into seven languages and broadcast on radio stations in dozens of countries between 1976 and 1984, making it one of The Family's most successful operations. Girls sent to the camp were supposed to be recording Christian songs and learning that part of The Family's music ministry. But their duties also included starring in those erotic dance videos David Berg loved so much.

Shula agreed to let Merry attend the program with two of her friends. "They wanted to be there and sing. I felt like that was what Aaron would have wanted—to have his daughter used with music," Shula said. "It was supposed to be temporary."

Merry's sexual abuse intensified when she was sent from Greece to the Philippines to be with Grandpa. She would later testify before a British court that she was repeatedly fondled and abused by her grandfather during her four years in the Philippines.

In a 1995 judgement in a British custody case involving another child in The Family, Lord Justice Alan Ward wrote that Merry was called to Berg's quarters and sexually molested "on a number of occasions."

"He was invariably impotent," Ward wrote. "They did not have sexual intercourse, though he once tried to penetrate her, so there is no evidence of incest strictly defined. He did rupture her hymen with his finger. They had oral sex that was oral sex by him on her."[5]

Merry told the British court that Berg even staged a mock marriage ceremony, gave Merry a silver ring, and proclaimed, "I, David, now wed thee." Unable to consummate the incestuous marriage, Berg turned to Ricky, his spiritual son.

"Berg was looking in some warped way to carry on his line through Ricky and Merry," explained Merry's brother, Don Irwin. "He seized on this idea that Ricky should start having dates with Merry."[6]

This forced sexual relationship between Merry, aged fourteen, and Ricky, aged twelve, was acknowledged in one of the most incriminating documents ever produced by The Family. Years before Ward began his lengthy proceedings in the British custody case, Family leaders issued a letter entitled "The Last State? The Dangers of Demonism!"

"[Merry] *was* having regular dates with [Ricky] and we suggested she should put off [her] interests in other boys and sex, except [Ricky], until she was stronger in the Lord," the letter states. It goes on to say that Merry "resolved in her own mind that if she couldn't have the sex and men that *she* wanted and choose, that she'd get it from the Devil himself!"[7]

Merry testified that she was subjected to violent exorcisms to beat the devil out of her. "Many times they would beat me," she said. "They took my head and beat it against the wall and bruised me. I was helpless and knew nothing else. It all felt like torture and once I fainted, throwing up. They said I was throwing up demons."

"Dangers of Demonism" was meant to be a warning to other rebellious teens in the movement. The letter contains the transcript of a recorded conversation between Berg and Merry during one of the violent exorcisms designed to rid her of the Devil's influence.

Merry enters Berg's room in the Philippines and greets Grandpa with a hug and a kiss.

"Praise the Lord, Honey. How are you? Bless and help her, Lord, as we talk to her about her problems. In Jesus' name. Thank you, Lord!"

Suddenly, Berg begins yelling, "Hallelujah! Hallelujah! Hallelujah!" and starts to speak in tongues as he grabs the girl and violently shakes her to emphasize every command.

"Get out of her, Devil! Get out of her in Jesus' name! Get out of her! In the name of Jesus, get out of her! Hallelujah! In Jesus' name! I rebuke you, Satan! Look at me! Get out of there!"

Berg slaps her in the face.

"Do you hear me?" Berg yells, slapping her again.

"Yes sir!" Merry replies.

"Do you understand what I am talking about?"

"Yes sir!"

"That's what you're going to get if this thing comes back again!" Berg screams, pushing her back into a chair. "How can you, my own granddaughter, supposed to be one of my saved children? How could you invite Satan in and put curses on others, send little devils to other people? I don't ever want to hear about that again!"

Another slap.

"Is that clear?"

"Yes sir!"

Berg goes on to repeatedly berate and threaten his granddaughter. He tells her that her mother, Shula, was insane, as was her father. "If it hadn't been for the Lord, he would have jumped off the cliff a long time before that," Berg said.

"I have a rod here. Will you please bring it to me," Berg says. "You see this? Pass it to her, let her feel it. I want you to feel this, how heavy it is."

Berg is right in his granddaughter's face.

"That is a rod! I am going to take this rod to you and I am going to beat you with it the next time any of this stuff comes up. Do you want me to help you know what you're going to get? Come here, I'll let you feel it just one time. Bend over."

Bergs spanks her with the rod.

"Did you feel that? Well next time your buttocks are going to be bare and you're going to really feel it! You're dangerous. You're going to go stark raving mad and do something terrible if you keep playing around with those devils."

Justice Ward's 121-page ruling was neither a victory nor a defeat for The Family. The judge said he believed that The Family changed its practices regarding the sexual abuse of minors by the early 1990s. He allowed The Family member involved in the case to retain custody of the child in question. Nevertheless, the public release of testimony by Merry Berg and other second-generation victims painted a damning portrait of life in The Family in the eighties.

Merry Berg told the judge she had "begun to realize grandfather was a hypocrite who made rules for people which were not necessarily for him. He would write one thing one day and the opposite the next because God was changing. He was very contradictory. He was a chronic alcoholic.... I now look back at his writings as the ravings of a drunk madman."

Justice Ward sided with Merry, concluding:

Who could blame the girl for lacking respect for a man so revered by others when she knew from her personal knowledge that he was foul mouthed, drank too much and sexually abused her? For this she was brutally punished. Her crime was to have yielded to Satan. That led to a time of two months when she had five major exorcisms performed over her.[8]

Merry still failed to give Berg the respect he thought he deserved, so she was sent to a "Victor Camp" in Macao, the most notorious of several Family detention camps set up in the late eighties.

According to The Family publication cited in the Justice Ward's decision, Macao was supposedly "a voluntary program established to help a small handful of teens who needed more individualized guidance and encouragement to overcome long standing serious personal problems."

While in this program, the teens received exceptionally close shepherding in a small personal family atmosphere, with lots of love and prayer, individualized personal training, hours and hours of personal counseling, specialized Word classes that were often spoon-fed to the teens, and a consistent daily schedule of typical boarding school-style discipline, administered with patience, prayer, reasoning and understanding.

Justice Ward took extensive testimony on the situation in Macao and concluded that The Family's description of life at the camp was "a travesty of the truth." He found that "children were subjected to a regime of physical and psychological brutality." Merry Berg told the judge about another girl at the reform school who was slapped and became so upset that she could not talk properly but was stuttering incoherently. "The reaction of the shepherds was to say that she was possessed of deaf and dumb spirits and so they held an exorcism, talking in tongues over her," Ward writes.[9]

Another teenager sent to Macao told the judge that "most of the children there were shipped in from other countries because they had deep psychological problems as a result of being in The Family. In my opinion, I would call them 'mental.' Three of them were completely irrational and were hallucinating. Some of them thought that they were seeing demons.... Most walked around dazed. I and a few others were the only ones who were not 'mental.'"[10]

Among the abusive practices Ward condemns were putting teens on silence restriction, isolation, and hard labor. "The Macao experience is a shameful example of putting into practice the belief that the end justifies the means," the judge concludes. "The means was a form of physical and mental atrocity mercilessly dished out to young, often already emotionally damaged children. There seems little acknowledgement from the leadership of the abusive nature of that regime. In my judgement, the leadership must stand condemned."[11]

Not surprisingly, Merry Berg's experience in Macao did not resolve her emotional problems. After her release, she was sent to the United States to live with her grandmother, Jane Berg, and then with Deborah, the Endtime Prophet's eldest daughter and Merry's aunt. By the early 1990s, when Merry entered her twenties, she had found enough stability to testify in the British court case and give several media interviews about her abusive upbringing.

Her public denunciation of the cult prompted Berg and Zerby to unleash a vicious campaign to vilify her among The Family flock. "Why would anyone in The Family accept the word of this crazy girl, who completely yielded herself to the Devil?" Zerby asked in a 1992 letter. "She was fucking the Devil and throwing violent curses on everyone around her, describing these in vivid, gruesome detail!"[12]

James Penn, a top-level Family operative who defected in 1999, confesses that he was given "the shameful task" of devising a strategy to undermine Merry Berg's decision to tell the truth about her abuse. He explains that Berg, Zerby, and Peter Amsterdam—now one of the top two leaders of The Family—were afraid of Merry "not because she was crazy, nor because she was lying, but because she was telling the sordid, shameful truth about the abuse she had personally suffered at their hands."

"[Merry] was their worst nightmare come true. Her testimony, fully corroborated in Family publications, validated the accusations of child abuse, and directly implicated the leader. The usual suspects, weak and immature Family leaders or members, were nowhere to be found. [Merry's] testimony struck at the man-god, the head and heart of the movement, and threatened to destroy him."[13]

Merry Berg was a great threat to The Family leadership, but she was just one of many second-generation kids hitting their teenage years and causing big problems for The Family. Most adult members joined the sect in their late teens or early twenties, but they were willing converts. Those who couldn't stomach the unquestioning obedience Berg demanded in the early days had already left the cult or had been kicked out. But here was a new generation of disciples who never had a choice as to whether or not they wanted to be children in The Family. And for the first time in their lives they were starting to realize that difference.

Teenagers can be a handful, and The Family was running out of hands. "Teen Combos" were set up to centralize the oversight, education, and indoctrination of teenagers. Troublesome kids were sent to Victor Camps for re-indoctrination.

Many of these kids' parents had joined the movement to get off drugs or away from their own dysfunctional families. They had no idea how to be parents themselves. So where did they turn for advice? They turned to Sara Kelley, the mother of Davida and Ricky's primary nanny and sexual playmate. Sara became the Dr. Spock of The Family. Her *Story of Davidito* became its child care bible.

"My mother was sent to be a leader in other communities—to teach them about how to be like Grandpa and reprogram everybody," Davida said. "That's when I started meeting kids who never saw Grandpa and only read books about us. We were the closest thing to Grandpa they would ever get to. They all knew who I was. I was very famous."[14]

Children in The Family learned to read with a series of "Life with Grandpa" comic books—sanitized stories of what it was like to grow up around the Endtime Prophet. Davida started telling her new friends some real slices of life with Grandpa. "I mentioned something about sex, or being intimate with Grandpa, and my mother immediately freaked out and hushed me up and said, 'Don't talk about love-up time. Do not mention that. You do not discuss having sexual conduct with Grandpa, and if you happen to slip up and you say something, the first thing you are going to do is go back to the Unit.' I'm thinking, 'Why, is there something wrong with it? You mean people out here don't fuck their kids? They are not required to have sex with adults?'"

Davida was sent to a Victor Camp in Japan, and later to another camp in Brazil. "It was a way to reprogram our little heads," she said. "That is where you would go if you are really bad or rebellious and not wholehearted or have an attitude or dare to be different. If you have independent tendencies, that is condemned. In Japan I got public spankings. I took a banana out of the refrigerator without asking permission. It was a walk-in refrigerator full of bananas and fruit and vegetables. I happened to grab a banana. They made an example. This is what happens to bad, bad naughty girls. They made me drop my pants in front of fifty kids."

Davida said Grandpa never had sexual intercourse with her. According to the Endtime Prophet's own code of sexual morality, girls did not reach the age of maturity until they were twelve years old. Davida and her mother left the Unit when she was eleven, but that didn't stop Berg from using Davida for his own sexual pleasure while she was still with the Unit. One of his favorite acts, she said, was to perform oral sex on her. "It was very oral," she said, "and very hands on."[15]

Davida and the Unit were in Manila when the Prophet Prince celebrated his twelfth birthday. Ricky was now old enough to have sexual intercourse with teenage girls and adult women. And, according to Davida, one of those adult women was Karen Zerby, his own mother. "I saw his mother having sexual intercourse with him while I was getting molested by Grandpa in the same bed," Davida said. "That was disturbing. I'd never seen her [Zerby] have sexual contact with the children."[16]

(Karen Zerby declined to be interviewed for this book, but Family spokeswoman Claire Borowik, called the incest allegation "an absolute lie.")

It was in the Philippines that Davida first realized there might be something wrong with sex play with adults. "I went into my mom's closet and found this book about sexually abused kids. It was a book for kids to read. It said something like, 'This is wrong. Adults do this because they were abused themselves.' I was like, 'Oh my god! You mean adults are not supposed to have sexual contact with kids. I said, 'Look, mom. This book says its wrong for adults to have sex with kids and that if it happens you should say something.' My mom said, 'Where did you find that?' I remember feeling sick to my stomach. I always knew there was something wrong with being dragged out of our beds at three in the morning and being forced to drink wine and willingly have sexual interaction with Grandpa."

Political turmoil in the Philippines forced Berg, Zerby, and the rest of the Unit to find a new base of operations in late 1987. After a brief stay in Tokyo, they moved onto the grounds of the 21st Century International School, known to Family members as Heavenly City School. The complex of buildings in Chiba prefecture would be the headquarters for various projects, including the taping of Family audio/visual products and the re-education of second-generation teens. At times, the population swelled to more than three hundred residents. Berg was at the school less than a year, but long enough for him to write a series of letters on education and Japan, including "The School Vision!" and "It's Japan's Hour!"

Students at The Family's showplace school were used to getting strange instructions from the resident shepherds, but some of the Japanese marching orders were particularly puzzling. "They told us if we saw someone walking around and didn't know who they were, we were not supposed to look at them," recalled Daniel Roselle, a former student. "Not long after that I was cleaning windows and saw this guy with a beard walking a dog. We knew he was Berg, and we knew we weren't supposed to look."[17]

Heavenly City was also part of the Davidito experiment. Ricky, who had just turned thirteen, was put in the regular Family population, and he was to be carefully observed. Word soon got around the student body that the famous Davidito was in their midst—the boy they had read about for years in "Life with Grandpa" and other children's literature.

"One day we saw a boy about twelve or thirteen walking around in baggy jeans," Daniel recalled. "Ricky has a distinctive look. Everyone was saying, 'Is that Davidito?' We called him 'Petey' then but we knew who he was. It was 'Don't ask, don't tell.' He was shy and quiet. He just wanted to be accepted. We'd been told he was this model child, but he just wanted to fit in."[18]

Celeste Jones, who had been one of Merry Berg's friends at the Music for Meaning camp in Greece, was at Heavenly City School when Ricky arrived. They were both thirteen years old at the time. "He seemed really sweet, but so shy and timid. He had no confidence in himself. He wasn't very talkative. He didn't have social skills."[19]

Celeste remembers Ricky as a kind of handyman, coming around fixing things, and almost always accompanied by an adult shepherd. "We all knew who he was, but we couldn't talk to him. They told us not to. He'd just look at us with this long face."

Finally, Ricky's shepherds eased up and allowed him to mingle with the rest of the kids. The Prophet Prince had a taste of freedom, but it didn't last long.

"There were a few guys there who had been in 'the System' for a time," Roselle recalled. "They'd be doing things like break dancing. We thought they were cool, but the leaders saw them as 'worldly.' Ricky and I were on the periphery of the cool guys, but then they started cracking down on them, making them clear brush on this hill.

It was the kind of physical labor punishment that later became standard at the Victor Camps."

Ricky was just starting to hang around with the cool guys when word got back to David Berg. He ordered Ricky back to the Unit and threatened to send him to a Victor Camp. As with Merry Berg in the Philippines, the threats against Ricky were published in a 1988 letter—this one entitled "Our Teens—The Devil's Target!"

"Do you want to be put in detention with some of the bad apples, some sort of detention reformatory colony and have to be locked up in your room at night because you're such a bad example?" Berg asked Ricky. "If you keep on that trail, boy, I'd rather disown you! Do you hear me?"

"Yes," Ricky replied, meekly.

"Let me tell you, brother, if you ever got into that cesspool of the System and had to go to a System school and see what the Devil's children are really like, it's like Hell on Earth. You'd come running back to Mama and Daddy with your tail between you legs, saying, 'God help me! I don't ever want to be with people like that again. It's like living in Hell!' All those stories he [one of the 'cool guys' who had lived outside The Family] is telling you about how wonderful it is, what excitement and blah blah ... I'm talking to you! How could you have gotten mixed up with a guy like that?"

"Well," Ricky replied. "I guess I just wanted to see what the other side was like."

"Why?" Berg countered. "Brother, let me tell you. I was raised around the other side and I know what it was like. It was Hell on Earth!"[20]

Berg's outrage sparked what became known as "the shakeout" at Heavenly City School. "There was this big meeting with Peter Amsterdam and Sara Davidito [Davidita's mother and Ricky's chief nanny]. They gave us this long lecture about being cool," Roselle recalled. "Mostly it was just about listening to 'System' music. I was one of the kids called up front. I thought, 'Me?' They yelled at us for three hours. I remember Peter Amsterdam telling me to 'get that smirk off your face.' I just started crying. And I never saw Ricky after that."

Japan was a turning point for Roselle. "Something clicked for me when I saw what happened in Japan. Ricky was a normal kid, but they couldn't let him be a normal kid. Here was this guy who was going to be our prophet, and he was more desperate to fit in than I was."

Seeing the Prophet Prince in real life was also a wake-up call for Celeste Jones.

"Ricky and those guys were just being normal boys—telling jokes and being frivolous. There was nothing really bad going on. Then all of a sudden we got herded in and blasted by Peter Amsterdam. We were put on punishment and scrubbing toilets for months."

For Celeste, the crackdown was another example of the unique style of child abuse in The Family. Yes, there was sexual abuse. Some kids were physically beaten. But in a way the worst abuse was the constant changing of rules and expectations. They were always on edge. David Berg would get a new prophecy or get pissed off about something and everything would change.

"One day you were supposed to have sex, and the next day you weren't even supposed to hold hands. It was all on a whim. It was crazy," she said. "There was nothing you could grab onto. Then you were separated constantly from who you knew, from your family and friends."

What happened to Merry Berg was a perfect example.

"They come out with a new letter, and say Merry is possessed by the devil. That letter was shocking. That was not the Merry I knew. It was scary. Then they started looking at us, and you do *not* want to be singled out. It was so driven into us that we represented the future, but we weren't turning out like they thought. So they clamped down really hard."

Merry's brother, Don Irwin, was living in a "Teen Combo" in Thailand. He had the same feelings and the same fear of being sent to a Victor Camp.

"I told them I wanted to go to university, and next thing I knew I was sitting in a room with three people sitting around me telling me there were going to be complications if I kept up this hankering for worldly knowledge. It just freaked me out. I had no choice. I wasn't with my biological parents. The only recourse you had was to submit to them, have the demon cast out of you, or get sent to a Victor Camp."[21]

Berg's letters about Merry's punishment and Ricky's bad behavior did what they were supposed to do—at least for Don Irwin. They terrified him and kept him from acting out at his Teen Combo in Bangkok. "Any type of somewhat lucid, smart person over the age of twelve who knew how to read and reason could see that if they rebelled they were going to drop their ass into Macao."

Irwin starts talking faster. It had been more than fifteen years since he read those letters, but the fear returns to his voice when he starts talking about growing up in The Family.

"There were a couple of girls in Thailand in 1992 or 1993 who rebelled and wouldn't say uncle, and they sent them to Macao," he said. "They were there one day, and the next day they weren't there. You'd see some of the kids come back. When you are fourteen or fifteen you don't understand what post-traumatic stress syndrome is and what trauma is. You don't understand girls who are acting out and flirting and trying to get sexual attention from people because you don't understand what being sexually compulsive is after being sexually abused as a child. They are either sexually compulsive, or asexual, or very maladjusted or very fearful. It was a traumatic thing to see. You didn't understand what you were seeing as a fifteen-year-old. Now, looking back, I see what it is. It was freakish."

Irwin said he and other young people at the Teen Combos and Victor Camps were trapped. They couldn't go home—wherever home was. "If you are not with your parents, who is going to help you to go to the states and go to high school? Nobody is. You are at the mercy of whatever random clown Zerby decided to make the head of that location."

Ricky suffered sexual molestation as a child and teenage boy, but he was more enraged by the sexual abuse he saw Davida and Merry suffer at Grandpa's compound in the Philippines. Years later, Ricky would dream of revenge when he'd think about what happened to Merry in the Philippines.

"We would often see multiple, large black and purple bruises on her [Merry's] body as she was escorted from room to room like a scared, demoralized little prisoner of war," he recalled. "They also tried to keep [Merry] away from us, explaining that she was violent, and had visions of cutting people up with knives. Well, let me tell you, when I think of those sick, fuckin' perverts, thoughts about edged weapons are never far from my mind."[22]

Sue Kauten, a.k.a. "Joy."

8

Joy

SEATTLE, WASHINGTON
May 1993 – King County
District Court

SUE KAUTEN WENT by many names, but "Joy" best describes her. Just try finding a picture not dominated by her gaping smile and dark, compassionate eyes.

"We called her Joy. Such an appropriate name for her. She was a joy to be around," recalled Jeannie Deyo, one of Karen Zerby's two sisters. "She was undoubtedly one of the most unique people I had ever met. She was a ray of sunshine in our lives."[1]

Over the years Sue was also known as "Cedar" and "Trust." Family leaders often changed their names to arouse less suspicion when unrelated devotees crossed borders with other people's children—and to make it harder for reporters, government agents, and angry parents to track them down. On May 10, 1993, Sue signed papers at King County District Court legally changing her name to "Angela Marilyn Smith." But her given name was Susan Joy Kauten.

Sue left her family home in Winchester, Virginia, when she was eighteen years old, right out of Edison High School. There was a young man, a pregnancy, a parental argument, and an abortion. It was the early seventies. Sue moved in with her brother, John Jr., his wife, Tina, and their baby daughter in their apartment in Charlottesville.

John Kauten was nine years older than Sue and often called on to babysit her when they were growing up. Sue loved her big brother, and cried when he left to go into the Navy in 1962. But she always knew she could go to him when she was in trouble. After he came back from the Navy, but before he got married, Sue would come over to his apartment and clean the place for him. "She really cared a lot about people. She liked to please," her brother recalled. "Sometimes she was so nice I almost felt uneasy."[2]

It was the tail end of the sixties, not the decade, but the era, when Sue ran off with The Family. Her brother used words like "hippie" and "flower child" to describe her back then. "A lot of people were running away from something. Trying to find a family," John said. "I think Sue was just looking for somebody who really cared."

Sue struck out on her own and moved to Vienna, Virginia—the same town where David Berg revealed the founding prophecies of The Family. There, she fell in with a group of early devotees and was soon on her way to Texas for missionary training. Sue moved in with a band of "babes" packed into a big house in Houston.

Anneke Schieberl, a devotee who left the fold in 1978, remembers Sue from the beginning. "We were in basic training together," Schieberl said. "You could tell she was going to do whatever it took to be in this group. She was always smiling and cheering. She was always telling me to 'get the victory, sister!' She just bought into the whole thing wholeheartedly."[3]

Schieberl grew up in the Baptist church in Houston, and like Sue, was enraptured by the positive energy of the Jesus movement. "When I first met them they were dancing and singing and living communally. It seemed like everything I had ever wanted," Schieberl recalled. "But in the beginning, it was very puritanical. You had to pray before you were allowed to date."

There was no sex before marriage.

"They called it betrothal," Schieberl said. "I remember this one brother walking up to me one day and saying, 'I've been praying, and God said we should get married.'

"I looked at him and said, 'Well, God didn't tell me anything.'"

Schieberl said the sexual mores in The Family changed gradually—one revelation at a time. "We were like frogs in water that gets hotter and hotter until you don't realize you're being boiled alive. First there was this beautiful, romantic story about Maria [Zerby] meeting this man in London and showing him Jesus' love. He turned out to be the first fish of flirty fishing, and before long everyone was supposed to be doing it."

Schieberl also met her husband, Ron, in the early years. He was a convert from California who would become one of the top European leaders in the sect. But they were never sold on flirty fishing.

"At first, we would get around it by going out to piano bars in Italy, then come back and lie and say, 'Oh yeah, we picked up this guy.' I kept thinking that this was just a phase Berg was going through, but it just kept getting bigger and bigger and out of control."

Sue Kauten first appears in the written record of The Family when she and her partner at the time, Monty, came from South America in 1976 to serve on Berg and Zerby's staff on Tenerife. Sue had been working for Deborah, Berg's oldest daughter, until Deborah had a falling out with her father and began working on her tell-all memoir of Berg's sexual excesses and theological errors. Perhaps Sue knew too much to be left unattended. Berg heard that she was a good typist, secretary, and "had a lot of other talents!"

Sue's "other talents" were of a sexual nature. Zerby, Sara Kelley, and Sue were the first "flirty fishing" team for The Family. Here's how Berg remembers her from the good old days in the Canary Islands:

"God bless dear Sue. She had the talents and she's still using them, thank God! She's got a lot of talent—some ways you don't know about! Or maybe you do! God bless her! She's a good FFer too. I'll tell you, this is the FF team I started off with, Maria [Zerby], Sara and Sue. They're top-notchers. They really know what they're doing! I started off with that little team in Tenerife. I think they can probably remember the first night we went out. Hallelujah! So if you want to know anything about FFing, you can ask them."[4]

Monty was another story. He never got used to sharing his lover with Berg and all those potential converts Sue would approach at the clubs in Tenerife. "Monty could do a lot of things," Berg would later recall in one of his letters, "but his worst fault was he was almost insanely jealous of Sue, jealous of me, jealous of her fish. He just made her life almost Hell on Earth by nagging her all the time about her other loves and being disrespectful and almost insolent toward me—disobedient."

Monty got tossed, and Sue settled in as Karen Zerby's executive assistant. "Her biggest job turned out to be Maria," Berg would later say. "I think she fell in love with Maria before she fell in love with me! She made herself so useful—indispensable. Maria just figures she can't go on without her! Because she's always there, always willing, works night and day, knows no hours, brings Maria something to eat any time of day or night, is willing to go down and cook it herself, fix it if it isn't fixed, or fuck me, or go to town and shop or whatever is needed. She's willing to do anything, any hour of the day or night."[5]

"Dear Sue," Berg said. "She's so super conscientious and over conscientious and careful and always afraid she's makin' a mistake or something and always trying to be so attentive and so careful and tryin' to do her job overly well, always wondering or worrying if she's not doing it right or something. She's got such an inferiority complex about that. She's so faithful and so diligent and so careful with every detail and takes such good care of us and the work and everything."

"It's good she is," Zerby added.

"Of course it is," Berg replied. "But I mean sometimes she almost overdoes it."[6]

Davida was just a few months old when Sue and Monty arrived in the Canary Islands to join the inner circle. Davida doesn't remember Sue's arrival, but she does recall her later on as one of the pillars of the Unit. "She was one of the nannies, but she wasn't as hands-on with Ricky as my mom. She was foremost a secretary. We saw her every day, but she wasn't an integral part of my upbringing like my mom. She would babysit Ricky, but she was just one of many adult women who molested him."

During the seventies, eighties, and well into the nineties, Sue Kauten followed Berg, Zerby, and the rest of the Unit across Europe to South

Africa and from there to the Philippines and beyond. It took patience and devotion to put up with the royal family, and Sue persevered.

"When you were on their staff, the whole idea was to be yielding and hope they wouldn't go after you," explained one staffer who worked with Sue. "Berg could be very charming, but he had these mood swings. But that was God manifesting before us. You didn't want to get in the way of God's spirit, and God was working through whatever Berg was doing. We'd just go with that. You weren't paid to be an individual with your own opinions. When someone said 'Jump,' you asked, 'How high?' You had to be yielding, beaten down. Sue was a perfect example. Mindless. She would just do what she was asked. Sure, she liked to help people, and they took advantage of that. She'd do anything, and she wouldn't think twice."[7]

That kind of loyalty and service would keep Sue at the center of the inner circle for more than two decades. Davida's mother, Sara, was Ricky's primary nanny and sexual playmate, but Sue was an important part of the team. In the "Prophecy for Davidito" letter, where Ricky and his mother are identified as the "two witnesses" who will usher in the Endtime, Sue is listed as one of the four teachers of the Prophet Prince.[8]

When Berg was sick, Sue was among those who nursed the Endtime Prophet back to health, tucking Ricky into bed with Berg, laying on hands, and serving Berg "fortified health or wine drinks." She would also care for Ricky when he was sick, playing with him and his toy cars. Sue was also a key player in the morning conferences with top staff, when Berg would get updates about what was going on at Family colonies around the world.[9]

As Sue settled into her new post in Tenerife, The Family was expanding across Europe. There were colonies in England, Holland, Scandinavia, Germany, and Switzerland. They had a major presence in Italy, including an estate in Zoagli, near Genoa. That coastal palace was courtesy of Victor Emanuele Canevaro, the Duke of Zoagli, an Italian count brought into the fold by Barbara Kaliher, an early Family leader and one of Berg's mistress wives. Kaliher, a stunning brunette once crowned "Queen Rachel," married Canevaro in the spring of 1973. She was at

Zerby's side helping deliver the Prophet Prince at the Tenerife clinic, but left The Family during the leadership battles of 1979.

Sue Kauten kept in Berg's good graces.

By 1979, Sue was living on the French Riviera with Berg, Zerby, Ricky, Davida, Sara Kelley, and other key staff. In March, Zerby gave birth to her only other child, Christina Teresa Zerby, a.k.a. "Techi." After Techi's birth, Sue and the Unit moved to a house in Cagnes Sur Mer.

In *The Story of Davidito*, Sara writes about how four-year-old Ricky "was having lots of fun too with all the girls in the house, including dear Sue who's been our close friend and sister for so many years. Once at the dinner table Sue was stumbling over saying a big word, 'phenomenom ... phenommalnon ...' when Davidito casually looked up from his plate and said clearly, 'phenomenal.'"[10]

Ricky had his own memories of Sue during his childhood years in Europe and the Philippines. He remembers her as one of several young women who would be put on the Endtime Prophet's sexual "sharing schedule." Berg would take his daily swim before one of the girls would be summoned to have sex with him in the pool. "Some of the girls had exceptionally loud orgasms, especially Sara. In fact, they were so loud that someone hearing them for the first time would no-doubt believe that she was faking it. But because we were all used to hearing them at that insane volume for many years, the thought never crossed my mind," Ricky wrote. "I think Joy [Sue] holds the record for the most times to have an orgasm at one time with Berg. I think it was in the upper twenties."[11]

There was a pool with an underwater shelf at the deep end—complete with a picture window looking into a basement office—at one of the homes in the Philippines. People would stand on the shelf with the heads sticking out of the water and their bodies visible through the basement window.

"Often I'd walk in, and people would be fucking on the pool shelf," Ricky recalled. "A crowd would be gathered around in the office, watching them. There were certain favorites, like some occasional lezzie-action between Sue and Amy, or certain other couples who could put on a good show."

Sue accompanied the Unit when they left Asia and moved to the West Coast of Canada in November 1988. They lived in a rented house in Vancouver, British Columbia, before moving to a small farm in the suburban city of Surrey.

Ricky turned eighteen in January 1993, and just as Sue Kauten would do later that year, the boy once known as "Davidito" went to the King County Courthouse on March 15 and legally changed his name to "Richard Peter Smith." He gave a false Seattle address. Ricky spent much of 1993 and early 1994 traveling in Europe and the U.S. and Australia with Berg and Peter Amsterdam, returning to British Columbia in March.

On July 13, 1994, Ricky returned to the King County Courthouse and changed his legal name once again—this time to Richard Peter Rodriguez.

Sue remained part of the inner circle through Berg's death in 1994, but was then eased out of the Unit. She wound up back in the United States. In San Diego, she helped longtime Family leader Grant Montgomery set up The Family Care Foundation, a charitable front group that raised money and channeled it to Family colonies around the world.

Sue's reassignment to the states gave her an opportunity to reconnect with John, her long-lost big brother. When she first came to visit him in Winchester in the late 1990s, it had been more than two decades since John had seen his little sister.

"When she first joined, we didn't know where she was. She'd write a letter or make a phone call. Later on we'd get e-mails," John said. "I would tell her, 'Any organization worth its salt allows a sabbatical to visit your family.' Her argument was, 'We have reasons for keeping our identity and location secret.' As years went by I realized she was influential in the organization. Every chance I got I'd say why don't you come home. There's always a place for you here."[12]

Now that Sue was back in the states, John was finally getting a chance to reconnect with his little sister. They would take bike rides along the old railroad bed that leads into Vienna, Virginia. Sue confided to her brother that there were changes in The Family that she did not like. In the last few years, she was helping out at the Zerby family's nursing home in Tucson. She wanted to do something other than take care of old people for the rest of her life. She started talking about going back to school.

"All she had was a high school education, as far as a piece of paper goes, but she was fluent in all these languages, Spanish, Italian, Russian, Portuguese, Japanese. She couldn't write them all, but she could converse. One time when she was here, we went out to a favorite little Italian restaurant in town. Two guys who knew the owner came in and started talking Italian. Sue said something to them, and they started having a long conversation. She knew a lot of people in Italy and had been to the town they were from."

Sue's visits back home became more frequent. Then, in 2004, she got involved with a man who was not part of The Family. Her new boyfriend, Dave Carpenter, was giving her the courage to cut her ties to the movement she had dedicated her life to for the past twenty-five years. They'd met at Elderhaven, the board and care home in Tucson owned by Zerby's parents and her sister, Jeannie. Sue had been caring for Carpenter's father there and saw the chance to make her first clean break. As late as August 2004, Sue had been working to set up a Family orphanage south of Mexico City. But by the end of the year, she'd moved into Dave's apartment in Palo Alto, California, and gotten a job at Restoration Hardware, an upscale chain of home furnishing stores.

But that relationship, too, had its problems. Sue confided to her big brother over the phone that she was moving out of Dave's place and getting her own apartment. The job at Restoration Hardware, however, was going great. She sounded happy and ready to move on with her life. John was thrilled with the news, and remembers thinking, "Finally. She's come back to us."

Sue and John spent about half an hour on the phone the afternoon of January 8, 2005. Sue told him she was in Tucson tying up some loose ends and planned to fly back to California in the morning and start her new life. She had one last appointment. She told John she was planning to have dinner that night with an old friend. "He has some issues that he wants to talk about," Sue said.

It was the last time John Kauten would ever speak to his sister.

David "Moses" Berg reads to Ricky, the
Prophet Prince.

Expert Witness

SYDNEY, AUSTRALIA
January 1994 – Church
in the Marketplace

DAVID MILLIKAN HAD
spent enough time
studying The Family to
know that the eighteen-
year-old guy waiting
to meet him was the
famous Davidito. Rev.
Millikan was one of the few people on the continent of Australia who
possessed a copy of the long-suppressed *Story of Davidito*, and those
childhood pictures of the Prophet Prince cavorting with his nannies
were finely etched in the minister's memory. You could still see the
Spanish influence of Ricky's biological father, who was now just a
footnote in The Family's twisted saga.

Ricky's spiritual father, David Berg, was still alive, but very ill and
would be dead by the end of the year. Amsterdam was firmly in place
as Zerby's new consort and guiding light into the new millennium or
the end of time, whichever came first. Peter Amsterdam was Ricky's
shepherd on this secret mission to Australia—one of several attempts
to contain government investigations of alleged child abuse at Family
colonies around the world.

Millikan, an ordained minister with the Uniting Church in Australia, was known to be a sympathetic scholar of new religious movements. He had defended The Family after a series of police raids in Australia in 1992 rounded up scores of children and placed them in temporary state custody. Millikan knew all about The Family's history of sexual experimentation, but thought the sect had since changed their child-rearing ways. He saw the police action as an outrageous abuse of state power.

By early 1994, when Ricky arrived in the country, the controversy over the raids was finally quieting down. Millikan was in his church office one morning when the phone rang. It was one of his local contacts with The Family.

"We've got something very exciting for you, but we can't tell you on the phone," the voice said. "Can we come by and see you?"

Two Family leaders in Australia soon appeared at Millikan's office. They insisted that they take him out of his office before they'd give him the news.

"Can you guess?" they asked, breathlessly.

"Amsterdam's here," said Millikan.

They were shocked. "How did you know? People in The Family here don't even know!"

"Just a guess," the minister replied.

"OK. You can't tell *anyone* about this," one of them said. "Not even your wife."

"No way, mate," Millikan countered. "I'll tell my wife whatever I bloody want."[1]

They worked out a deal. Millikan could tell his wife, but no one else. Two days later, Millikan was to show up on the front steps of the Sydney Town Hall at exactly 10:30 A.M. and wait for his contact. The minister got there a bit early and waited through the appointed time. He had a feeling he was being watched. He also felt like he was in some bad spy novel.

Millikan was just starting to get impatient when someone he recognized as a top-level Family operative walked up to him.

"You've been watching me, haven't you," the minister asked.

"We just wanted to make sure you were on your own," the man replied. "Can I buy you a cup of coffee?"

They had coffee and made chitchat. Finally the man said, "Shall we go?"

They walked out to the street to a hail a cab. Millikan noticed that the guy let a couple taxis go by before hailing one to stop.

"Where to, mate?" the driver asked.

"Just head down the road. Straight ahead," the mystery man told the driver.

Millikan almost started to laugh when his contact told him they had to get out of that taxi and hail another one.

"Security," he explained.

They finally pulled up to an apartment complex in the Sydney suburb of Randwick. They entered one of the apartments, and there sat Peter Amsterdam, Ricky, and two women. "They were two very good-looking women with long hair," Millikan recalled. "They were also extremely good typists. Their job was to take down everything that was said on two laptop computers. They took turns typing."

Millikan started talking to Ricky. It didn't take long for Millikan to bring up *The Story of Davidito*. "I told him I was appalled by what I saw in that book," the minister recalled. "I told him it fell into my definition of child abuse, and as far as I was concerned, it was abusive behavior." Ricky handled it with aplomb.

"What happened with me was not people using sex out of lust and desire," Ricky told the minister. "It was Father David trying to create a more open world. We believed it was just an expression of the law of love."

Ricky told the minister he was a "test tube" for Berg's ideas about child sexuality, but all that was just a small part of growing up in the Unit. People have blown it all out of proportion, Ricky said.

"They believe it had a bigger emphasis and played a greater part than it did," Ricky said. "If they think my early life revolved around sex it's going to seem very weird, but I know that wasn't the case, so it was not such a big deal."

Millikan found that Ricky had no trouble talking about his early sexual experiences. He told the clergyman that he had a girlfriend and had other enjoyable relationships with young women. "I really don't think it hurt me in any way," he said. "I never felt uncomfortable with it."[2]

Ricky's interview with Millikan was part of a worldwide Family counteroffensive against a wave of negative media coverage and government actions in the early 1990s. In September 1993, Merry Berg had talked about her childhood sexual abuse on the NBC News program *Now*. That same month another of Berg's granddaughters, Joyanne Treadwell, the eldest daughter of Deborah Davis, said her grandfather molested her when she was five years old. Critics of The Family had released portions of *The Story of Davidito* to show that the son of Karen Zerby had also been abused as a child.

Meanwhile, two Family defectors, Daniel Welsh and Ed Priebe, were causing real problems. Welsh, an early Huntington Beach convert known as "Samson Warner," had left in 1986 and joined another charismatic Christian church. Priebe, known in The Family as "Hart Inkletter and "Eduardo," had been one of the Jesus freaks who joined in the summer of 1971 when several Jesus people groups on the West Coast combined forces with Berg. Priebe left the fold in 1990 and like Welsh joined another charismatic Christian congregation.

Priebe flew back to the Philippines in 1992, where he had worked as a top Family operative. He hoped to gather evidence about how Berg had used his sacred prostitutes and other means to compromise political and military officials in the Philippines. Priebe also hoped to find Amy, a Filipino disciple he knew from The Family.

Pretending to be a high-level Family leader, I got the phone number of the home from a Family friend, and then had Samson Warner phone the home, imitating Berg's voice perfectly and telling the shepherds to pick me up at the airport. So while I blame The Family for officially promoting deception, I've been guilty of the same since leaving them. The shepherds picked me up and drove me to the home where they informed me that there were some hot videos in a storage depot. It turns out these were the last remaining videos proving children had been sexually exploited in The Family, so I asked them to give them to me. To make a long story short, I came out with sixteen trunks of videos and literature and Amy made the decision to leave The Family and marry me.[3]

Within a year, those incriminating videos would find their way onto television back in the United States and around the world. There were police raids and temporary removal of children from Family colonies in Australia, Argentina, France, and Spain. Heightening the public alarm in 1993 was the February 28 to April 19 standoff in Waco, Texas, between federal law enforcement officials and followers of David Koresh, the apocalyptic prophet and leader of the Branch Davidians. That drama began with a shootout between the Branch Davidians and the U.S. Bureau of Alcohol, Tobacco and Firearms that resulted in the death of four federal agents and an unknown number of Branch Davidians. It ended with a federal assault on the Waco compound and a devastating fire. Investigations found the remains of seventy-five men, women, and children in the smoldering ashes.

Like the 1978 mass murder/suicide in Jonestown, the 1993 Waco standoff sparked hysteria on both sides of the cult wars. To some, the lesson was the danger of authoritarian cults brainwashing adults and stealing the minds of their children. Others saw the federal government's invasion as a reckless overreaction and an assault on the Constitution's guarantee of religious freedom for all Americans. For the leaders of The Family, the horror of Waco and the sudden crackdown on its colonies around the world inspired a new approach to dealing with the Systemites.

Ricky became a key part of that public relation's campaign. Millikan's interview in Australia was just one piece of the PR puzzle. Ricky was also interviewed and analyzed by two members of the faculty at Oakland University in Rochester, Michigan—sociology professor Gary Shepherd and psychology professor Lawrence Lilliston. Both had written on new religious movements and were known to be sympathetic to the argument that such groups often face unfair persecution and stereotyping by powerful interests in mainstream society—especially the news media.

Lilliston and Shepherd's "Psychological Assessment of Children in The Family" included an interview and examination of Davidito shortly after his session with Millikan. Ricky had turned nineteen, but was still on tour with Peter Amsterdam. They spent several days at a motel near the Michigan college. Lilliston subjected Ricky to a battery of psychological tests. Shepherd and his wife invited Ricky and Amsterdam to their home to have dinner.

"My impression about Davidito was that he was shy and quiet and reserved," Shepherd said. "But once the ice was broken, he opened up. He was a bright guy, articulate and well informed about the world generally. We talked about his interests as a young adult Family member. I was aware of his designated status as an infant and young boy, and that he had been projected to be a great leader in The Family and had been celebrated in various publications. I was also aware that those leadership projections were not being fulfilled.

"I asked him what he saw himself doing in The Family. He had a lot of interest in music. He was not gifted in the performance of music, but he thought he could identify and arrange new music that would be more appealing to second-generation kids."[4]

Larry Lilliston, who had spent much more time with Ricky, did not respond to requests for an interview. Shepherd said his colleague was suffering from health problems and had "zero interest in revisiting this topic."

Shepherd and Lilliston's assessment of the Prophet Prince was published in a 1994 anthology entitled *Sex, Slander, and Salvation: Investigating The Family/Children of God*. Like Millikan, the two scholars refer to *The Story of Davidito* and "critics [who] suggest that this book is a manual for sexual abuse of young children." Lilliston and Shepherd concede that the book describes Ricky's "early witnessing of sexual behavior and encouragement to explore his own sexuality."

"While these experiences would be characterized as sexually abusive or neglectful by most child abuse experts," they wrote, "there is no report of [Ricky] having been actively molested or abused by adults. Moreover, there is no evidence of long-term negative effects on [Ricky]."[5]

Shepherd and Lilliston's report primarily concerns their 1993 study of thirty-two children in two Family homes in California. Once again, they found that "the charges of widespread, institutionalized child abuse are clearly unfounded. The children we studied are simply too healthy to be products of a system in which abuse occurs at a high level."

They even conclude that "the findings regarding these young people are quite probably reflective of child rearing and educational practice found generally in Family homes." They base this conclusion on the fact that kids moved around a lot from home to home around the world, and from later visits to a Family home in Michigan and two in Washington, D.C.

One critical assessment of this study criticized the two Oakland University professors for not revealing that The Family paid them for their work. It also says they had no data to allow them to generalize about child rearing conditions elsewhere in The Family, especially at the leadership level. Carol Buening, an adjunct faculty member with the Ohio State University College of Social Work, writes:

> Lilliston and Shepherd's methodology and their contractual status with The Family squarely place their work in the realm of program evaluation, and it is a misrepresentation to present it as research.... The evaluation was commissioned by an organization that wanted to demonstrate benign outcomes in its child-rearing practices.... Despite the inherent limitations of program evaluation, Lilliston and Shepherd conclude that because their subjects come from international backgrounds, "the findings regarding these young people are quite probably reflective of child rearing and educational practices found generally in Family homes." The evaluators' methodology does not support publication of such a conclusion. It is bad social science to make a generalization based on the untested assumption that a sample is representative of its population....
>
> There is a significant body of evidence that children in these "World Service" homes—or any home where top leadership was present for any length of time—grew up in sexualized environments where overt forms of sexual abuse did occur.[6]

Millikan's and Shepherd and Lilliston's assessments of Ricky and other children raised in The Family comprise three of thirteen chapters in the *Sex, Slander and Salvation* collection. According to the co-editor of the anthology, J. Gordon Melton, the book was largely the work of academic experts hired by Family lawyers in the British custody case heard by Lord Justice Ward. Melton said the co-editor of the collection, James R. Lewis, received Family funds to publish the book.

Ricky's teenage interviews and psychological assessments by sympathetic scholars were conducted over three very important years in the history of The Family—the period between the 1992 filing of the British custody case and Ward's voluminous ruling in November of 1995. These were the years when the outside world first heard Merry Berg's hellish testimony about what happened to her inside the walls of Berg and Zerby's compound in the Philippines. High-level defectors leaked damning documents and videotapes of erotic performances by young girls for the pleasure of David Berg. News outlets around the world were sent some of the steamiest pages from *The Story of Davidito*. How could the leadership of The Family explain all this away? There was only one way. Ricky himself would have to testify for the defense. Ricky had not been living up to his early billing as the mighty prophet for the coming apocalypse. At least he could be paraded before a few accommodating academics to show the world that it really wasn't so bad to be a child in The Family.

Millikan, Melton, and Lilliston were among the experts presented by The Family's lawyers during more than two months of hearings in England. Millikan and Melton shared a room in London during the court proceedings. "Family lawyers were supposed to pay us to testify in court," Melton said. "We never got paid for our time—or at least I never got paid back for my time. They barely covered my expenses."[7]

Another expert called to The Family's defense was Susan Palmer, who teaches a course on new religious movements at Dawson College in Montreal. Like Shepherd, Palmer had been invited to spend a week at a newly established Family colony in San Diego. It was a large, ranch-style home, shaped like an "L" with a swimming pool in the backyard. Family insiders would call the place a "show home," a special colony established for inspection by religious scholars and the news media.

Palmer happened to be staying at the San Diego home the night of September 8, 1993—the same evening that the NBC television show

Now, hosted by Tom Brokaw and Katie Couric, broadcast a special report on The Family. Recent raids on Family homes in Argentina and allegations of child abuse there had put The Family back in the news. The piece by NBC correspondent Fred Francis included an interview with Merry Berg and a scene where twenty-year-old Merry was first re-united with Shula, her long-lost mother. There was also recent footage shot at the San Diego show house that hosted Palmer that very night.

Everyone in the home gathered to watch the show. When the TV reporter mentioned that Family members in Argentina had been arrested on charges of rape, kidnapping, child abuse, and sodomy, some of the teenagers watching the program started screaming at the screen.

"Sodomy!" one exclaimed. "Eooh! Gross! That just *proves* they don't know anything about us. Grandpa's *always* been against sodomy!"

"If we're a so-called sex cult," asked a gorgeous eighteen-year-old girl sitting next to Palmer, "I don't understand why *I'm* not getting any."

"Yeah!" her peers agreed. "How come there's never any sex coming *our* way."

"Shhh," cautioned the shepherdess. "Let's listen."[8]

After her week with The Family in San Diego, Palmer concluded that the best way to describe the members of this new religious movement was as "Christian Fundamentalists with a heavy millenarian and communal emphasis.

"In another hundred years," she adds, "it appears likely that The Family will enjoy the social status of a small Christian church or denomination—quite as respectable, upwardly mobile and certainly less 'heretical' than Christian Science or the Latter Day Saints."[9]

Palmer was among those who testified in London in the child custody case before Justice Ward. The British judge was not impressed with her presentation, saying he was "less than fully convinced of her objectivity and her ability to see the whole picture." Ward was especially troubled by Palmer's statement that she began her research into the treatment of children in The Family "tending to find new religious movements delightful and amusing."

"They knew I would not be hostile or critical," she told the court. "As a sociologist, I am value-free."

Ward's ruling in the case—brought by a grandmother of a child born into The Family—was issued in November 1995. While the decision allowed the four-year-old boy's mother to remain in The Family, the judge's three-year investigation produced shocking revelations about the treatment of minors in The Family during the seventies and eighties. In the end, however, Ward was convinced that The Family had changed its ways.

> Significant numbers of children, more within The Family than outside it, had masturbation and even sexual intercourse forced upon them by adults. I am, however, equally satisfied that The Family have made determined efforts to stamp out this unacceptable behavior and that they have been largely successful in that endeavor. Whereas the blame for the abuse that has occurred is to be laid at Berg's door, the credit for effecting change most probably can be given to [Zerby]. She and World Services have, however, failed fully to acknowledge The Family's responsibility for this past misconduct....
>
> They must denounce David Berg. They must acknowledge that through his writings he was personally responsible for children in The Family having been subjected to sexually inappropriate behavior; that it is now recognized that it was not just a mistake to have written as he did but wrong to have done so; and that as a result children have been harmed by their experiences.... The Family must be encouraged honestly to face up to this shameful period in their history so that those harmed by it, victims and perpetrators alike, can seek to come to terms with it.[10]

In response to Ward's judgement, Peter Amsterdam issued a statement that fell far short of denouncing David Berg.

> The judgement refers in particular to "The Law of Love" and "The Devil Hates Sex," and we accept that as the author of ideas upon which some members acted to the harm of minors in The Family, he [Berg] must bear responsibility for that harm. Maria, and all of us in World Services leadership, also feel the

burden of responsibility.... Father David's statements in his discourse entitled "The Devil Hates Sex" opened the door for sexual behavior between adults and minors, such sanctioning being the direct cause of later abusive behavior by some Family members at that time.[11]

David Berg did not live to read the Ward judgement or see Amsterdam's statement. But that did not stop Berg from participating in the sect's response to the Ward judgement. In a purported prophesy from the grave, the Endtime Prophet apologized to anyone he hurt in The Family. "I did not intend to hurt, but I see now that I did hurt others at times by my words, by my actions," Berg said in a prophecy channeled through Zerby.[12]

In that same October 1995 communiqué to Family members, Zerby and Amsterdam said that the "Law of Love" sometimes led to "quite a wild time, with a lot of sexual activity." They also conceded that literature was published that "challenged the barriers between adult/minor sexual contact, opening the door to some members crossing over that barrier."

At the same time, Zerby defended the Law of Love and said The Family will never renounce it. "Many of those outside The Family misunderstand the Law of Love. They strongly criticize it, and think it deals only with sex. They don't seem to understand that this principle governs more than just our sex lives; it governs every aspect of our lives.

"We try to show show love and kindness in all we do. Of course, unlike most Christians, we feel that God's Word grants us freedoms in our sexual lives as well.... We do not believe, however, that these freedoms extend to adults having sexual contact with minors."[13]

In the decade since they issued that statement, Berg's writings have been sanitized and his reputation restored by Zerby and Amsterdam. In 2006, a person interested in the history of The Family could go to its Web site and read this about "Our Founder":

David Berg called on his followers to devote their full time to spreading the message of Christ's love and salvation as far and wide as possible, unfettered by convention or tradition, and to teach others to do the same.

David Berg's lively, down-to-earth, and sometimes unconventional approach to heavenly matters makes his writings a unique contribution to Christian literature....

Though the world may know him as David Berg, to The Family he was known as Father David, Moses David, "MO," or as most Family members came to call him affectionately—Dad. He truly was a Father in the Lord to those who knew him, either personally or through his writings.

In November 1994, The Family commemorated his passing from this life into the next. Surely he has now heard his Savior's "Well done!" for his life of Christian service.[14]

10

Elixcia

BUDAPEST, HUNGARY
August 1994 – Family International Offices

ELIXCIA WAS SIXTEEN and working in an office set up to translate Family publications into Russian, Croatian, Hungarian, and other Eastern European languages. The place was perfect for The Family. It was a huge facility originally built to house workers with Hungary's state-owned electrical utility, but leased out to private concerns

Elixcia Munumel and Ricky Rodriguez.

after the fall of Communism. Around sixty members of the sect were housed and employed at the compound, which included a recording studio to dub Family videos into the various languages.

Ricky was just passing through. He was nineteen and heading to Russia from his mother's hideout on the Portuguese coast.

Elixcia was sitting at her computer terminal learning how to type when the famed Davidito walked into the office. He and his shepherds were getting a tour of the facility. Their guides were reeling off statistics about worker productivity in Elixcia's unit when her eyes met his.

"They introduced me and I just turned around and smiled," Elixcia recalled. "I was so shy. He was wearing a pair of red shorts that runners wear, split up the side. Really short ones, with a white seam that went up the side. I remember thinking, those are *really* short shorts. He was wearing a blue tank top, muscle shirt. It was the summer, so it was really hot outside. He didn't say anything. He just smiled and they all walked out."[1]

Elixcia had good reason to be flustered. This was no ordinary visitor. This was Davidito, the little boy she and other Family children had read about for years in their "Life with Grandpa" comic books. Elixcia learned to read by memorizing all those stories about the adventures of Davidito, Davida, and Grandpa as they moved from Tenerife to Portugal to the Far East. She'd read them over and over again. There was the story about Davidito's "miracle ride" on the big yellow duck at the playground in the park. There was the story entitled "Three Little Accidents" about what happens when little children disobey. There was the tale about the time Davida dressed up like a sexy gypsy girl and danced for the Prophet Prince. Suddenly, here was Davidito in the flesh, twenty years old and quite hot!

"We all knew about him. He was like a storybook character," Elixcia said. "All the girls always talked about how they were going to marry Davidito when they grow up. They had their little crushes on him."

Ricky was now—at least legally—an adult. At nineteen, he was starting to openly question his mother's demands that he play the role of the Prophet Prince. In Russia, he'd gotten in a little trouble with Davida, his spiritual sister from the early days in Tenerife and the south of France. They were smoking, drinking, and hanging out with outsiders—refusing to be Karen Zerby's obedient representative.

"There was a lot of pressure on him all the time," Elixcia said. "He didn't do anything that much different than other people, but the Jesus freaks among us, the people that really followed Karen, were disillusioned by him."

Ricky convinced his mother to let him move to Budapest to help with repairs at the compound and to be around when The Family moved into a new Hungarian headquarters elsewhere in the city. Elixcia was running the kitchen when Ricky arrived and moved into a bungalow with some other teenage boys. One afternoon she went up to the cottage to tell the guys lunch was ready. "One of them made a little guy remark about girls. You know, at sixteen everybody is so stupid. I sat at the edge of the bungalow talking to them. It was really weird talking to Ricky like a normal person. For my whole life, he wasn't real. He was something you read about."

A few nights later, Ricky and Elixcia found themselves alone in the big house at the Budapest headquarters. There was a party that night at a hall the shepherds had rented away from the compound. Sect leaders didn't want young people mixing with outsiders at clubs or other venues. "Systemites" were to be avoided—except for proselytizing and fundraising.

Elixcia didn't feel like going to the party, and unbeknownst to her, neither did Ricky. She was walking up the grand stairway, a graceful half-circle rising from the ground floor to the second story of the main building, when she saw him. It was about 9:30 P.M., and everyone else had just left for the evening. Elixcia looked up and Ricky was coming down the stairs. "I was so shy. I remember looking up at him at the top of the stairs then looking down at the ground as I walked up the stairs. My heart was pounding. I didn't know what to say."

"Hi," she said.

"Hi," Ricky replied. "Why didn't you go to the party?"

"I don't know. I just didn't feel like it."

"What are you going to do?"

"I was thinking about getting a movie from the video collection."

"Hey, do you know how to play cards?" the Prophet Prince asked.

"No."

"Well," he said, smiling. "I can teach you."

"Cool."

"Great," he said. "I'll go over to my room to get some music and a deck of cards and meet you back at your room."

Ricky returned and sat down next to Elixcia on the bed. He'd brought some tunes from Russia, rock music that Family members were not supposed to hear. He told her about Russia. He taught her the poker hands—straight, flush, Royal Flush. "We talked forever," Elixcia recalled. "We talked that night about angels. He asked about my mother and father. I told him about growing up in Venezuela. A car accident when I was three. Busting my nose. About being a tom girl."

Elixcia's father was a British hippie and son of a United Kingdom diplomat. He'd inherited his family estate at age eighteen and took off to live the surfer's life in Australia. Later, he traveled to South America to go up the Amazon River. Then, in Venezuela, he met The Family. He had grown up in a strict Christian boarding school and hated the way they worshipped God and the hypocrisy of that scene. He joined the sect in 1976 and soon brought Elixcia's mother into the fold.

Her mom was the first daughter of a wealthy Venezuelan man and his mistress. They later married and had four children together. "My grandfather adored my mother and wanted to give her the best education possible and sent her to one of the top Catholic boarding schools," Elixcia explained. "She became a clothing designer. My grandfather wanted to buy her a factory, her own company, but then she met and fell in love with my father."

Elixcia was born in Caracas on April 4, 1979.

Flirty fishing was in full swing, and Elixcia's mom was sent out to the clubs to be a fisher of men. Dad stayed home to watch the baby and got to know—in the biblical sense—another woman in the house while his wife was out fishing. "My mother came home one day and my father was in this other woman's room doing 'the naughty.' My mother got upset, left the house, and went to my grandmother's house. My father tried to call her. She was mad. She expected him to come and find her, but he never did."

Elixcia was seven or eight months old at the time. Her parents split up and assumed joint custody, but her mother still followed her father around the world. "My father decided he wanted to go to India and my mother followed him. Wherever my father went, my mother followed," Elixcia said. "I still think she's in love with him."

Now, as she told Ricky her story, Elixcia was the one falling in love. She and Ricky stopped playing cards and started showing each other their childhood scars—not the emotional ones, not yet, but the physical scars from the time a red hot lamp fell on Ricky's cheek or the scar from Elixcia's car accident when she was three years old.

"We spent most of the night together," she said. "I was sitting with my legs crossed and he kept putting his hand on my leg, very gently rubbing it. I remember kissing but not doing anything else. I was scared. He tried to play around with me, but I was shy. I was sixteen. We did make out. Around two or three in the morning he left my room. I said something about having to get up early. The next day a whole vanload of people came in the morning because we were moving. I went down to the kitchen to help pack stuff up, and when I went back to my room there was a beautiful red rose sitting on my pillow. Just a single red rose."

Michael "Tiago" Rugely was managing the Budapest print shop when Elixcia met Ricky. He saw her falling for him and urged her to slow down. "When Elixcia likes you, she really likes you. She'd say, 'I love Ricky. I want him so much. I'll even have his baby if not him.' She was fifteen or sixteen and would say things like that. I'd tell her to calm down. Ricky is someone who needs his space. It took years for me to communicate that to Elixcia. I'd say, 'If you hang onto him that tight, you'll lose him.' Ricky was a free spirit, and he had lots of girlfriends. Elixcia was never crazy about that."[2]

Tiago was born in Paris in 1974. His father, known as "Black Peter" in The Family, was one of the earliest members and the first African-American to join Berg's sect in 1969. He married Tiago's mother, a young convert from Los Angeles, who would go on to have thirteen children.

Like all children his age, Tiago grew up reading stories about Davidito. "As a kid growing up, you always wanted to meet him.

You respected him, but in some ways you felt bad for him. His parents were often rebuking him. When the Davidito book came out, you didn't know what to think. Here was this kid posing nude in this highly sexualized environment. You knew something was wrong with this picture, but you weren't sure what to think."

Tiago was nineteen when he met Ricky, and his print shop was in full swing. Packets of information would be sent to potential converts who would reply to an Austrian address listed on recruitment posters plastered across Eastern Europe and the former Soviet Union. "It was like a normal office," Tiago said. "When Ricky first came through, there was always a crowd around him. He came over and said 'Hello,' and I walked around and gave him a tour of the place. He was on his way to Russia."

They soon became friends. "I'm a quiet guy. I used to be shy, somewhat of a loner. Not very flamboyant. Ricky was very much like that too. Eventually we would click. He just wanted to be accepted for who he was. He didn't want to be the guy with all the answers. People would ask him, 'Where did Moses David die?' and things like that. Our friendship was at a different level. He was like a brother.

"One of the first things he told me was he was happy to get away from his mom. He said he was the happiest he'd ever been. He was so happy to get away from her. He didn't miss anybody from his past and was happy about the way his future was looking."

At first, Elixcia and Ricky dated in secret. They would take long walks along the windy roads behind The Family compound on the outskirts of Budapest. Family members were given a weekly allowance of alcohol—three beers and two glasses of wine. Ricky and Elixcia would save theirs up and take it out into the woods, make a little bonfire, and spend as much time alone as they could without arousing suspicion.

Secrets are hard to keep in The Family. Karen Zerby had spies everywhere and soon learned that her son was spending too much time with his latest lover.

"Karen liked people to have sex with as many people as possible," Elixcia said. "That kind of detaches you from one person and makes you more part of the whole group. That way you don't have selective relationships."

Ricky and Elixcia seemed to have other plans.

They moved from Hungary to Zerby's secret compound at a large beach house outside Lisbon. It was now early 1997. Controversy surrounding child sexual abuse in The Family had prompted a new set of rules about sexual relationships for anyone under eighteen. Ricky was over twenty-one and Elixcia would not turn eighteen until April 4, 1997. They were not supposed to have sex until her birthday, even though they *had* been sexually involved since 1994, just a few days after Ricky left that single red rose on Elixcia's pillow.

"Karen knew we were dating in Hungary. Everyone knew. We just supposedly weren't having sex. We would sleep together. I'd crawl into his bed in the boy's dorm. We were always together. We'd eat together. Watch movies together. We were always sitting next to each other in meetings," Elixcia said. "Everyone knew about our relationship in Hungary and knew Ricky was off-limits. Girls still asked to date him. I had to let them date him because it was part of our policy, and we didn't want people to know we were having sex."

As soon as Elixcia turned eighteen, the couple no longer had to pretend their relationship was platonic. Ricky's mother grudgingly allowed them to stay together, but saw her control over her only son was slipping away. "Karen really struggled with us," Elixcia said. "We'd come to meetings and sit in the very back and be cuddling the whole time—almost disrupting things at times."

There wasn't much Zerby could do. Ricky was now an adult. He was twenty-two years old—the same age his mother was when she joined up with The Family back in Tucson in 1969.

David Brandt Berg, 1919–1994.

11

Loving Jesus

VANCOUVER, CANADA
October 1996 – World
Services Publication Unit

NOTHING TESTS A NEW religious movement like the death of its founder.

David Berg died sometime in 1994, at the age of seventy-five, leaving Karen Zerby and Peter Amsterdam firmly in control of Family missionaries around the world. Merry Berg, the shattered granddaughter of the Endtime Prophet, had gone public with the story about her physical, sexual, and emotional abuse in the Philippines in the eighties. Under pressure from the British court and Lord Justice Alan Ward, Zerby and Amsterdam publicly acknowledged that their spiritual leader created an atmosphere in The Family that allowed the sexual abuse of children. They promised they would never let that happened again.

> We do not consider it right or good, we do not think or speak favorably of, nor do we officially [or unofficially] consent to, confirm or sanction sex with minors. As a result of this fact, I reject, disown, abandon and give up by open profession every

single writing of any person in The Family which may appear to approve of it. Without condition or limitation, we command The Family not to indulge in sex with minors.[1]

Family leaders never released an exact date or cause of Berg's death, but the Endtime Prophet was apparently flown from British Columbia to Portugal toward the end of his life. He died at Costa da Caparica, a beach resort near Lisbon. Some believe Berg died of alcoholism, but the prophet himself denied that charge in a message sent from the grave. Speaking through Zerby, the spirit of David Berg admitted he was *once* an alcoholic, but said the disease is not what killed him.

I did not die a premature death from having been an alcoholic. I died because it was my time to come home to be with Jesus. I let go and gave up the ghost because the Lord showed me that Mama [Zerby] was ready to carry on without me, which has certainly been true. Isn't she doing great! I could die—although it's really passing from death to life—because I knew The Family would be able to carry on without me, and you folks are doing great, too.

Alcohol had nothing to do with my death. I died in my sleep and had a wonderful homecoming, and drinking played no part in hastening my death. In fact, I lived years longer than I ever expected.[2]

Whatever the cause, some veteran members of The Family thought Berg's death could set the stage for better times in the movement. There was a new charter designed to give members more rights, freedom, and protection from authoritarian leaders. The Family survived the police raids in Australia, Argentina, and at other colonies around the world.

Many of those raids were an overreaction based on agitation by defectors who used incriminating documents from the seventies and eighties to convince authorities that child abuse was widespread and continuing in the nineties. It was not. The situation *had* changed for younger children in The Family. Nevertheless, scores of children were taken from their homes and put in protective custody. Few, if any, child abuse convictions resulted from those raids. It was easy for Family leaders to condemn the raids as acts of religious persecution—further evidence that the Systemites could not be trusted and the Endtime would soon be upon them.

James Penn, the longtime operative destined to play a key role in the Ricky Rodriguez saga, had almost persuaded himself that something righteous and worthwhile could come out of the movement he had helped shepherd for twenty-five years. "James Penn" is the pen name of a Family devotee known over the years as Gideon Valor, Felipe, Jay, Ray, and Phil. He had joined another Jesus people group in Vancouver in the fall of 1970 and became a member of The Family in the summer of 1971. Penn spent years working in World Services and the Unit on various continents and through various stages of the craziness.

"Looking back, I think that the only way I managed to cope with all of Mo, Maria, and Peter's 'high weirdness' was by subconsciously 'compartmentalizing' my mind. I knew Mo, Maria, and Peter [meaning Berg, Zerby, and Amsterdam] were responsible for the abuse of many children in The Family. Yet I still had some sort of fundamental faith in them and in the good that many Family members were doing. I hoped for a better future. If The Family could just win these persecution-related battles, I reasoned, then as an organization, we could reform and purge the excess. Hopes of a brighter tomorrow kept me going."[3]

Penn's optimism was short-lived. Within a year of the founder's death, Zerby received a series of bizarre prophecies from Jesus and from the spirit of Berg. Other voices of the dead came forth—including those of Genghis Khan, Jerry Garcia, and River Phoenix. Perhaps the highlight of that period was the time that Art Linkletter spoke from the grave to a member of Zerby's staff. That communication was particularly miraculous since it turned out that Art Linkletter was still alive.

As a member of the research division of World Services, Penn was among those called upon to translate the latest "doctrinal weirdness" coming from Zerby and Amsterdam. For him and several other long-time members on the edge of leaving, the "Loving Jesus" revelation of 1995 and the "Marriage of the Generations" campaign the following year showed The Family had not changed all that much. "While The Family disavowed flirty fishing and cracked down on sex between adults and minors, it never renounced the Law of Love—one of the doctrines that most separates The Family from the rest of Christendom. Karen Zerby was obsessed with getting Family members to be sexually active," Penn explains.

"Lots of sex with multiple partners is good. Monogamous relationships are bad. In any discussion on the Law of Love, she will insist that sex is not the primary issue. But when the dust settles, you're expected to have lots of sex! In addition to promoting the Law of Love, [Zerby] was eager to introduce the 'Marriage of the Generations,' which encouraged young Family adults to have sex with Family members of their parents' generation. Maria hoped that this would help break down the barriers between the two generations."

"Marriage of the Generations" was introduced as a pilot project at a 1996 Family leadership summit in Maryland and presented to the larger Family two years later. Zerby and Amsterdam were on a crusade to convince twenty-one-year-old girls to get over any problems they might have with sex with men old enough to be their fathers. Family publications called on members to "more fully live the Law of Love."

Penn was at the tipping point.

"Once again, they were deliberately, systematically creating an oversexualized atmosphere in Family homes.... Even if this time around, no children were directly involved, what is young Susie supposed to think when she can't find mommy because mommy is off servicing some man? You can't hide these things in a home. Children inadvertently see things they shouldn't see."

Then there was "Loving Jesus!" In this revelation, Jesus told Zerby that it would be wonderful if his followers would masturbate while praying to him. Some selections:

"As a bride learns the ways of love and the ways to please her husband, so much My children learn of the ways to please and to love Me.

"We shall have a great feast and we shall have great love, and we shall have a great, great, great big orgy together! This is My call to all the young virgins: Come unto Me. I want to marry you. I want you in the bed of My love....

"So I'm coming. And it's coming! And you'll be coming! And we'll all be loving together...."[4]

Speaking through Zerby, Jesus anticipated that this new revelation would just cause more controversy for The Family.

"The world and the church are going to stand back in awe, and they are going to scoff and say, 'The children haven't changed!' But I say unto you, the children *have* changed, because they are no longer children, they are brides! They are going to be experienced lovers, and they are going to revel in the ecstasies of My love."

After hearing from Jesus, Karen Zerby could only say, "Wow! How sexy!"

"God is anything but conservative! He's *radical* and He doesn't seem to care if people know He's wild and free!" Zerby says at the end of her letter to the flock. "May God bless you and help you to spend good loving time with Him—time in His Word, praising Him, telling him you love Him and letting Him fuck you with His Word!"[5]

David Millikan, the Australian clergyman and Family sympathizer, remembers asking Peter Amsterdam about the Loving Jesus revelation. Millikan thought The Family would clean up its act after Berg died. He was puzzled. "Amsterdam told me The Family was in danger of becoming too conservative. He said the thing that gave them their edge was the sexual openness. If they turn away from that, what do they have to make them unique?"[6]

Zerby and Amsterdam's campaign to impose the Loving Jesus teaching on members of The Family—including teenage members—was a revelation for James Penn. He could no longer live in The Family and live with himself. He left the fold and explained why in a February 2000 manifesto entitled "No Regrets." It was posted on the Internet and became a rallying cry for disillusioned members of the second generation. It had a major influence on Ricky's decision to leave The Family.

Penn describes how he became increasingly upset at Zerby's attempts to indoctrinate the second generation. "For many years, most of us assumed that our children would follow in our footsteps, and we did everything we could to facilitate it. We did not view our children as individuals who would find their own way in life, but rather as disciples of the future.

"As the years passed and the children grew up, some began to leave The Family. At first, most of us were shocked. How could these kids turn their back on God and all the godly training that we had poured into them? Nevertheless, many Family members gradually came to accept that not every child born of Family members was going to remain in The Family. Each child would eventually have to make a personal choice as to what he or she wanted to do with his or her life."

Ricky was about to make his choice.

12

Moving On

DULZURA, CALIFORNIA
March 2000 – Family Care Foundation

RICKY WAS LIVING at The Family Care Foundation headquarters in southern California when he first announced he was leaving The Family. The foundation's offices are at Brookside Farm, a four-acre spread along Marron Valley Road in Dulzura, a small town east of San Diego. The wooded compound consists of several buildings and a collection of

*Ricky
Rodriguez
and Davida
Kelley.*

small trailers and RVs surrounded by a stone wall. There's a swimming pool, a small overgrown vineyard, a large trampoline, and a sign warning, "Caution: Children at Play." Two peacocks and a donkey share the grounds.

James Penn had just issued his "No Regrets" manifesto. Ricky had been hanging around Brookside Farm, living in the basement of the main building, keeping quiet, and working on getting his driver's license, getting ready to make his move.

Other staff members at the foundation spent their days processing donations, reading Family bulletins, and performing religious devotions. "It was kind of like working at a nonprofit, except that you were living in this cultist environment," said former foundation accountant Jonathan Thompson.[1]

Despite Family claims to the contrary, Internal Revenue Service documents filed by The Family Care Foundation show deep ties between the organization and The Family International. Those documents and annual reports from 1997 to 2003 reveal that the foundation raised more than $9.9 million in donations including cash and other gifts for projects around the world—such as assisting orphans, educational programs, and disaster relief.

Penn, who spent more than a decade in the inner circle of The Family, describes the foundation as a public front enabling The Family to attract tax-deductible donations from people who would never endorse the cult's "bizarre beliefs and practices."

"People wouldn't give to a charitable foundation if they knew that its leaders endorsed the sexual abuse of minors and religious prostitution," said Penn, who helped start the foundation before leaving The Family in 1998.[2]

One of the larger donors was the Flora Family Foundation, which gave the San Diego charity $61,500. Stephen Toben, president of the Flora Family Foundation, said his organization was unaware of any connection between the San Diego charity and The Family. Toben's foundation, established by the family of Hewlett Packard cofounder William Hewlett and his wife, Flora, learned about the charity while searching on the Internet for groups working on international development projects.

Another source of income for The Family Care Foundation were donations made through the U.S. government's Combined Federal Campaign, which allows federal employees to deduct money from their paychecks for approved charities. An official with the program, which is run by the U.S. Office of Personnel Management, said the campaign did not keep statistics on how much money it funneled to individual charities. In 2003, the campaign raised $250 million for 15,000 participating charities.

Larry Corley, executive director of The Family Care Foundation, said his organization uses donations to fund many "independent projects around the world."

"It is not a front for The Family. It is not tied to The Family," Corley insisted. "There is no relationship, period."[3]

But former members say The Family runs the vast majority of projects funded by the foundation. On top of that, all six officers listed on Internal Revenue Service documents filed by the foundation in 2004 had ties to The Family.

One of them was Angela Smith, a.k.a. Sue Kauten. In addition to Kauten and Corley, the four other officers listed on the foundation's IRS forms were:

— Grant Montgomery, the program director and highest paid official with The Family Care Foundation. He was the former "Prime Minister" and third-ranking leader of The Family.
— Dr. Chris Mlot, the foundation treasurer and board member. She was a longtime member of the sect and shown on property records as the owner of one of The Family's properties in the San Diego area.
— Cheryl Brown, whose birth name is Kathleen Fowler. She was another longtime member of The Family and the registered domain owner of the sect's Web site, www.thefamily.org.
— Kenneth L. Kelly, the brother of Peter Amsterdam, whose birth name is Steven Douglas Kelly. Kelly co-owns Family property with Mlot, and according to Penn, was closely tied to the sect and has several children with Mlot.

Despite these deep connections, Family spokeswoman Claire Borowik insisted the sect "has no say or vote on the activities of The Family Care Foundation board."[4]

"There is no legal relationship between The Family and The Family Care Foundation," said Borowik, although she conceded that the foundation "has under its umbrella many projects run by Family members."

Thompson, who left The Family shortly after Ricky's departure, said the San Diego–based charity was always careful to conceal any link to The Family.

Nevertheless, Thompson said the foundation does get legitimate donations from outside sources for rank-and-file members doing good work. "They are people who are just part of a messed-up system," Thompson said. "They've helped a lot of people."

David Millikan, the new religion expert in Sydney, was willing to give The Family the benefit of the doubt. "In Australia they are finding it hard to define the nature of what they are doing. They are making a push into charitable works, which is a bit of a departure for them. They were setting up a ministry in prisons, and they were doing a good job. They are faithful people. Then one of the other prison chaplains got wind of who they were, and they got tossed out. They had been looking for something to give them a purpose in society and trying to gain respectability. It was quite devastating for them."[5]

At the same time, The Family Care Foundation has funded some of the more notorious members of The Family.

Two members accused of sexual molestation in child custody cases in England and California in the 1990s went on to start charities funded by The Family Care Foundation. One of those cases is described in court documents filed in San Diego in connection with a 1998 custody case. They tell the story of a girl born into The Family International in 1981 and sexually abused from age five to sixteen.

Her alleged abusers included a stepfather, Phillip Slown, who she says repeatedly molested her in Thailand, where her mother was serving as a missionary for The Family International. According to an investigative report by the San Diego County Department of Social Services, the girl "experienced multiple incidents of sexual abuse with numerous men."

"This group has advocated sexual activity with minors as a pathway to God," the report found. "Her mother continues to interact with this religious group and she encouraged sexual behavior between her daughter and three men as recently as March 1997."[6]

Slown went on to start a charity known as From the Heart to help "at-risk youth." It was based in San Francisco between 1997 and 1999—during which time the organization received more than $70,000 in donations collected by The Family Care Foundation.

"They did a really good job with drug addicts and street kids, but I haven't heard from them in a long time," Corley said. Slown could not be reached for comment, and his San Francisco phone number had been disconnected.

One of those accusing Slown of child molestation is Kristianity LaMattery, born in Laredo, Texas, on April 18, 1976. Kristianity was the child of Jim LaMattery, the convert who had joined The Family in San Diego in the summer of 1971 and later crossed paths in Sweden with Aaron and Shula Berg. But by the time Kristianity was born, Jim had separated from his wife, Donna. By then, some of Berg's offbeat teachings about sex and the Bible had filtered down to disciples in communes around the world. "I kept going on about, 'Hey, that's not what the Bible says.' They didn't like that. But here I am in love with this woman, and I have her child and this was going to be my career in life."[7]

Jim and his family were kicked out of the Scandinavian mission and put on a plane back to Texas. Jim had had enough. He was out. Donna remained a true believer, and their marriage ended.

LaMattery would eventually win a custody battle for Kristianity and his other daughter, but it would be eighteen years before he ever saw them again. He was unaware that his brother—a sibling Jim had recruited into The Family—took Kerinina and Kristianity to Mexico and then Thailand. Their mother would go on to have nine children by seven different men—including one with Jim's brother.

Kristianity LaMattery was eight years old when she got her first lesson in flirty fishing. She and her sister were taken into the shower by their mother and given some detailed instructions on feminine hygiene. Here's how Kristianity recalls their conversation:

"Mommy has to sleep with a lot men, honey, and it's important that she keep clean."

"Why?"

"Because God is asking me to."

"But what if they are all fat and ugly?"

"You just pray to the Lord, dear, and he will give you the strength to do it."[8]

Donna's motherly advice may seem bizarre, but it is important to hear it with the ears of a child who knows no other way of life.

Growing up, Kristianity said, the abuse never seemed like abuse. "If Mommy does it, then it was normal." When Kristi was around age seven or eight, her mother moved the two girls back to Texas. Donna was now mated to two different sect members, including Slown. They were all raising money to go to Thailand.

"We had this fish that would lay me on the back couch and molest and rape me," Kristi recalled. "A lot of the fish weren't people who'd actually join [the sect]. Many fish had things to donate—housing, clothes, and food—and got sex in return."[9]

Eventually, Donna, the two girls, and Slown moved to Chiang Mai, a town in northern Thailand. During the day, Kristi would go out with singing teams to sell Christian books, posters, and tapes.

"We never really did any missionary work. We just sold products and begged," she said. "You were placed on teams depending on how pretty and cute you were. My sales pitch was, 'Hi, my name is Kristi and we're missionaries with a nondenominational organization trying to raise money for a really good cause.'"

At night it was a different story. According to Kristi, Slown would have the girls sleep in bed with him. "He'd lie in bed and masturbate himself," she said. "When we'd shower with him, he'd have us masturbate him."

Amid rising complaints of child sexual abuse in The Family, sect leaders issued new guidelines in 1986 that were supposed to stop the molestation. "They sent visiting shepherds out to talk to the teen girls," said Kristi, who was in Thailand when the shepherds arrived. "They said if I felt something wasn't done to me in love, I could tell them about it. I told them."

The shepherds talked to Slown. "Then they told me he was all better, and that I had to talk to him about it," Kristi said. "He said, 'You feel like I've done things that haven't been in love. But I love you, sweetie. Let's pray.'" The abuse, Kristi says, did not end.

Donna separated from Slown in 1990. Two years later, when Kristi was sixteen, Donna and her children moved to Galva, a small town in Illinois. Donna was no longer a full-time missionary with The Family, and Kristi was finally getting a taste of life in the real world. Her mom let her take a job in the local convenience store, where Kristi met Alan, the store's eighteen-year-old assistant manager. "He really liked me, and I started witnessing to him. He was a fundamentalist Christian, so we got along great. We were all gung-ho for the Bible and the Lord," Kristi said. "My mom's thing was to get him hooked. I started having sex with him, and he freaked because he was a regular fundamentalist Christian."

Alan eventually realized that his new girlfriend had grown up in the notorious cult called The Family. His shocked family urged Kristi to leave the sect. "That was the first time I ever heard anyone talk that way about the group I'd grown up in," she said. "They explained what rape was, and I realized that was what had happened, and why I felt so horrible about it." Alan and Kristi moved to Chicago to live with Alan's sister, who encouraged Kristi to find her biological father.

Kristi found Jim LaMattery in San Diego, where he was working as a real estate agent.

"Somehow, I always knew she would come of age, rebel against her mother, and find me," LaMattery said.

Soon after their 1993 reunion, Jim LaMattery reconnected with his older daughter, Kerenina. Then, in 1997, one of Kristi's younger sisters, sixteen-year-old Miriam, went to San Diego to stay with Kristi.

Miriam was the child born to Donna and Jim's brother, John, which makes her Jim's niece and both sisters and cousins to Kerenina and Kristi. In San Diego, Miriam turned out to be too much for her sister Kristi to handle. The sixteen-year-old wound up living in several teen shelters, one of which brought her to the attention of child welfare workers with the San Diego County Department of Social Services.

After interviewing family members, county social workers concluded that Phillip Slown had sexually abused Miriam from 1986 to 1990. In a March 4, 1998, report, the county also determined that Miriam's mother sexually abused her by "having sex in front of the child" and telling her that she should "show men God's love" by having sex with them. In her interview with child protective services, Donna denied she knew of any sexual abuse of her children. But she admitted that "there was a lot of sexual freedom among the adults" in Family colonies and "some people will make mistakes in large groups."[10]

"Flirty fishing is not against the Bible," Donna told the social worker. "The Bible clearly states to love thy neighbor as thyself."

Donna conceded that her children "did receive harsh discipline from Phil" and that Miriam told her Slown was sexually abusing her. She also told the social worker that she and Slown had some "real fights," including one over him beating another one of his stepdaughters for wetting the bed. Nevertheless, Donna said, "It is hard for me to believe that he [Phil Slown] would sexually abuse the kids."

Another alleged molester funded by The Family Care Foundation was mentioned in the lengthy child custody decision rendered in England in 1995 by Justice Ward. The decision names "Paul P.—Josiah" as a member of the sect's Music with Meaning team in Greece. "He corrupted and abused the young girls who were part of the singing and dancing troupe," Ward writes.

Penn and other former members said Ward is referring to Family member Paul Peloquin, known in the cult as "Josiah." One of his accusers is Celeste Jones, the girl who was with Merry Berg at the Music with Meaning camp. Peloquin was later funded by The Family Care Foundation for a project in Africa called "Focus on Kidz." He could not be reached for comment.

Celeste Jones and Merry Berg were among the young girls filmed performing erotic dances at the Music with Meaning camp in Greece. "When I was five, we were already watching these videos being made of adult women dancing," Celeste said. "Then one of the adult men would say, 'Oh. Why don't you do a dance for me?' Sometimes it was just play. Other times I felt uncomfortable. It depended on the person."[11]

Celeste was most uncomfortable with Paul Peloquin, one of the instructors and cameramen at Music with Meaning. "They'd have these orgies in an army tent at night. People naked and dancing. For me, the abuse didn't so much happen there. All of us would be running around and pinching the adults' bottoms and silly things like that. For me the abuse was in private. It was by Paul Peloquin. He was the main one. It went on until I was about ten to eleven years old."

Corley said he was not aware of the abuse allegations against Slown and Peloquin. But Corley did acknowledge that Ricky was living at the foundation compound in the year 2000. "Ricky was never part of The Family Care Foundation," Corley said. "He passed through briefly."

Yet it was at the foundation's Dulzura headquarters in the summer of 2000 that Ricky first announced that he was leaving The Family. "After I got to the States," Ricky would later write, "I decided to leave The Family and get a job. I didn't even know how to open a bank account or write a check, make up a resume or how to lie about having a high school education. It was very discouraging."[12] He revealed his intentions to Jonathan Thompson, his roommate in Dulzura, about two weeks before he told Grant Montgomery. "I was not planning on leaving at the time. I was playing the role of the reformer," Jonathan said. "We talked about Family policies we didn't agree with—like restrictions on the kind of music we could hear."

Ricky later told Grant he was leaving, and Grant called everyone to a meeting to announce the news. He talked about how hard and disheartening it would be for all the kids who'd grown up reading the "Life with Grandpa" stories.

Ricky had hoped to transfer to a Family colony in Mexico with Elixcia, who had gone to England to live with her father, one of the top Family leaders in Britain. Ricky talked his mother into buying a car so he could drive down to his new assignment in Mexico. She didn't trust him enough to just send the money, so she had Grant Montgomery buy the car and turn it over to Ricky.

Instead of taking the car down to Mexico, Ricky sold it and used the money to fly back to England and meet up with Elixcia. For a few months, Family leaders thought they might be able to keep Ricky in the fold. But before he left San Diego, the Prophet Prince began meeting with some angry second-generation defectors. He was starting to see the toll The Family's teaching had taken on other people his age. In a May 2000 letter to his mother and Peter Amsterdam, Ricky wrote:

> You are unable to see how you have hurt so many people's faith [with] prophecies that are not only ludicrous, but obviously the figment of some misguided person's imagination.... You're poking your finger in God's eye time and time again whenever you badger and condemn His little ones. One of these days God will judge you for it and when that time comes I certainly wouldn't want to be in your shoes....
>
> There's a lot of lost and broken young people still out here in The Family who haven't left yet. They need love; they need acceptance. What they don't need is for someone like you to take them on some kind of guilt trip, making them feel worthless just because they're not "on board" with your pride trip....
>
> I'm not looking for a fight with you, but if you push me, believe me, you'll have a nice one, and using the techniques learned by your example over the years, I guarantee it won't be "fair." Just forget all that crap about me writing some kind of sniveling back-pedaling "explanation" to The Family about how committed I am now/again to your BS, because it's not going to happen.[13]

Ricky and Elixcia had not officially left The Family, but they were clearly on the way out. In September, they flew to Venezuela to stay with Elixcia's mother and work out problems with Elixcia's passport.

"We found out later that the main reason the home [in Venezuela] agreed to let us come there was because they wanted us to take care of their kids," Ricky explained. "After a while I wrote my mom and asked if she could send us $400 a month to help with our home and puppet show ministry. She agreed."

In November, Ricky revealed that he was thinking about announcing for a second time that he was leaving The Family. He told Gabe Martin, a longtime Family insider, that he decided long ago that he would not take any leadership role in the organization. "I knew everything there was to know about jumping through the right hoops and playing the game correctly," Ricky said. "But I had to act different parts and play different roles all my life, and I was just plain tired of it!"[14]

One month later, in December 2000, Ricky gave the first indication that he might take violent revenge against his mother and Peter Amsterdam. He wrote in a letter to James Penn:

I am one of those people who have suppressed my feelings and emotions all my life. I didn't appreciate being treated like a commodity by my mother or having to swallow Peter's bullshit. But I tried to stay on the fence all these years because I just wasn't sure what the truth was, and I wanted to be sure before I went one way or the other.

These feelings of anger have not gone away, in fact they grew stronger even though I tried to push them away and sit on them. Now I'm beginning to get in touch with my emotions and feelings that I have hidden away for so long. To tell you the truth, I'm finding little love there, only hate for my mother and Queen Peter. . . . Some days I have come so close to snapping and going back to their compound—but not for a social visit, and not as a repentant prodigal, but as an avenger.[15]

Over the Christmas 2000 holiday, Ricky found respite housesitting an old friend's place outside Vancouver, not far from where he'd lived during his teenage years. He planned to have Elixcia join him in Seattle, settle down, and start to live a normal life—whatever that was. Ricky had made his final break, and he used the time in Vancouver to write his official resignation letter informing Zerby that he and Elixcia were leaving The Family.

We cannot continue to condone or be party to what we feel is an abusive, manipulative organization that teaches false doctrine. You have deceived people and led them away from the truth in almost every way imaginable, and worst of all, when they are no longer useful to you, they are discarded. You have devoured

God's sheep, ruining people's lives by propagating false doctrines and advocating harmful practices in the name of God, and as far as I can see, show no regret or remorse. I could talk for hours about it all, but what's the use? You'll never change.[16]

Ricky knew that publicly denouncing his mother and Peter Amsterdam would end any financial assistance he had been getting. He learned that The Family had given "severance pay" to some insiders who left the fold. Some might call it "hush money." Ricky decided he deserved the same. He asked for $36,000 so that he and Elixcia could "make the transition out of the cult."

In his private resignation letter to his mother, dated January 16, 2001, Ricky reminded Zerby that he has "not shared the knowledge I have of the many wrongs and abuses I witnessed while growing up.

"I have not tried to make the talk-show circuit or sell my story to the newspapers," he wrote. "I haven't tried to turn The Family or anybody else against you and that does not have to change. I see no reason why we can't work this out in a civil manner, but don't jerk me around, because this is for real."[17]

Ricky and Elixcia started getting a monthly stipend from Zerby. The money stopped coming in 2002. That spring, Ricky broke his public silence, wrote an essay entitled "Gospel of Rebellion," and posted it on the Internet.

Berg used the Bible as a means to get what he wanted, and nothing more. Whenever something in the scriptures would conflict with what he wanted to believe or do, he would either twist it around, or simply reject it as being a personal interpretation of the author, or non-applicable in light of his special "End-Time Prophet" anointing. We were taught to accept his interpretations of verses as truth, and gloss over any scriptures that would cast any doubt on his beliefs.

Because of Berg's very small ego, he would slip easily to the depths of despair whenever he would hear any news report or read any article that had anything negative to say about him. He would get depressed for weeks at a time, and would drink so much at night that Maria [Zerby] thought it was going to kill him. So Maria tried to protect him from any hearing about any "negative" publicity or news at all.

I think Maria realized maybe more than anyone else how little of Berg's beliefs and actions were actually based on the Bible at all, because she was the one who was closest to him. But of course, that didn't stop her one bit from doing anything she could to hold onto that power and control that they had over people.[18]

About two weeks later, Ricky posted a second article entitled "Life with Grandpa" on www.movingon.org, a Web site for second-generation Family defectors. Much of that posting was about what happened to Merry and Davida and other girls in the Philippines.

[Davida] was put on Berg's "sharing schedule," or "scaring schedule" as some people called it.... Even as young as Davida was, she was still put on Berg's "scaring" schedule. She wasn't very happy about it, but because of her mother's prodding, pushing, and threatening, she consented. The fucker was just totally obsessed with sex! Thinking about it now, it's almost unreal!

Berg sometimes used the teen girls he had sex with to keep [Zerby] on her toes and get her to do what he wanted. For example, he would drink himself totally plastered at night, and because [Zerby] wanted to get some sleep and because she knew it was bad for him, she would try to ration the wine and get him to stop and go to sleep. It was a losing battle, but night after night, year after year, she kept on fighting with him about it

At different times during those years, Techi [Ricky's younger sister] and I would sleep in bunk-beds or walk-in closets adjacent to Berg's room with beds built into them. Berg liked having us there, but often he would be so loud that we would all be awake for hours listening to his drunken ranting and off-key singing.[19]

Ricky had finally made the break from The Family—and from his family. Now came the hard part. How would he deal with his rage toward his mother? How would he begin to make it in the real world? Should he become a leader of second-generation defectors? Should he just move on? Should he track his mother down and get revenge?

Leaving home and family can be hard for any young person. All adolescents have some difficulties establishing their own identities, but imagine how hard that would be for someone who never had control of something as basic as his own name.

Someone Ricky trusted gave him some advice. "Get a life. Just live your life, and don't let these people destroy the rest of your life."

Ricky tried. He got work on an Alaskan fishing boat. It was hellish labor, but he made some money. He and Elixcia got a little apartment in Seattle and tried to start a life.

His older friend—the one from his mother's generation—saw that he couldn't really do much more to help Ricky and Elixcia. All three had been in The Family. They had all been damaged. But there would always be a gulf between the adult members and children born into The Family. It was an emotional difference—the difference between guilt and anger.

"We're really not in the same boat," his older friend explained. "We [the original members] joined of our own volition and built the system that oppressed these young people from day one. Our guilt and complicity in that can be overwhelming. What can you do to help these young people? You can't undo the harm."[20]

Ricky had lots of secrets—the alleged incest with his mother, his forced sexual affair with Merry when she was just fourteen years old. His story is unique, but he was by no means the only one struggling to overcome a traumatic childhood in The Family.

Don Irwin, the brother of Merry Berg, said it was particularly hard for those kids who grew up in the Unit. "They have such an intense deck stacked against them. They were essentially kept for the purposes of Berg's perversions and foolishness and crimes. The guy would get drunk, buzz up Sara [Kelley] on the intercom and say, 'Bring Davida over.' And she did. Ricky was right there to witness the terror of his friend being carted off to service this lecher and made to receive corporal punishment if she wasn't enthusiastic or didn't perform well. It was just hopelessness. Utter hopelessness.

"You have to stop thinking of this as a religious group or cult and start looking at it as an organized crime syndicate. Then things begin to make a lot more sense. Berg attempted to implicate as many of his top lieutenants as he could in his crimes, so they could not turn on him and so his behavior would seem normal. It's very difficult for them not to be invested in the defense of their leadership when they themselves have so much blood on their hands."[21]

In Seattle, Elixcia enrolled in nursing school. She was moving on with her life, but Ricky couldn't shake his past. "It was hard for Ricky to be with me," Elixcia said. "We pushed each other. We both had low self-esteem. I was going to medical school, and it was hard for him to see me do so well."

Ricky started up a telephone and e-mail friendship with another second-generation defector, Sara Martin, who lives in San Diego and goes by the name Sarafina. She had been searching for an old friend and posted a notice on movingon.org. Ricky saw it and e-mailed Sarafina. They started e-mailing each other and talking on the phone. "He was telling me how unhappy he was in Seattle," Sarafina recalled. "Elixcia had gone through a lot herself, but was moving in another direction. It was hard for her to be around him. He had a lot of anger toward his mom. He said, 'People looked up to me and thought I had this perfect childhood. But I didn't. I saw things they can't imagine seeing.'"[22]

Ricky was starting to see how his childhood experiences—being raised by Berg and Zerby to be the Prophet Prince and role model for the second generation—was a unique form of child abuse. Most of his peers didn't have parents who would "try to brainwash you with the fact that they were God's anointed prophets and to go against them meant you were going against God," Ricky said in an e-mail to a friend. "It takes a lot more juice to 'move on with your life' when that whole fucked up shit gets mixed in there."

Only the children of the inner circle—Davida, Merry, Techi, and Ricky—had parents who would "write volumes and volumes teaching thousands of other people how to fuck up their own lives and the lives of their kids."[23]

Ricky was also spending a lot of time e-mailing Tiago, his old friend from Hungary and someone who would listen to him talk about his troubles with Elixcia.

"Ricky didn't think he promised a monogamous relationship," Tiago said. "They got married, but partly to help her with her green card. She had a Venezuelan passport. He was helping her get her citizenship."

Others say the couple was madly in love, but just had too much baggage from the past. Ricky ended up getting his own apartment in Seattle. He was spending more time on the phone and Internet with Sarafina. Gabe Martin, the longtime Berg/Zerby operative, was Sarafina's uncle.

Ricky found that telling his story on the Internet didn't seem to help him, and it was having little effect on the operations of The Family. Ricky started talking to Sarafina about suicide. She invited him to come down to San Diego, where a number of key second-generation defectors were living. "I told him I know how hard it is to be alone and have no one but yourself when you think about all of these things," Sarafina said. "We were working on some things, and having fun together. I told him about how we have barbecues on the beach and go jet skiing. He would talk for hours. He really needed help. We were hoping to point him in another direction."[24]

Ricky moved down to San Diego and into Sarafina's small apartment in June 2004. One of her two roommates had moved out, and Ricky took her place. She introduced him to a friend and former roommate, Jennifer Schroeder, who had moved up to the San Francisco Bay Area, but still made lots of visits down to the sunnier climes of southern California. Ricky and Jennifer soon became good friends—and got romantically involved. He started teaching her a bit of karate.

Since leaving The Family, Ricky had studied various forms of martial arts. He loved kung fu movies. "Maybe it was a way of letting out his anger," Jennifer said.

Jennifer had never been in The Family, but heard all the stories from her other friends in San Diego. "I sat through many conversations about the horrific acts that happened to them when they were children," she said. "There is a lot of pain, anger, and grief. Some of them can't handle the real world outside the cult because it is so different. They don't have the social, intellectual skills that we have all learned through schooling and life. Ricky was a great friend and a great guy. He was trying to cope with life. He just wanted someone to love him."[25]

Ricky's descent into depression and rage was not done in private. His friends saw it. In San Diego, and in Seattle before that, he wrote about it on the Internet. Some of Ricky's postings were to vent. Others were designed to set the record straight—or at least to explain why he demanded hush money from his mother. But his most poignant message came at the end of a long posting during the summer of 2002. Ricky longed for a normal family life, but it just wasn't happening. One day before he left Elixcia in Seattle and moved down to San Diego, Ricky took his laptop down to a waterfront park he liked to visit.

It's a picture perfect day; the sky is deep blue; there are white puffy clouds in the sky. I can see Mt. Rainier in the distance, and its majestic beauty is stunning.

There's a young couple nearby, walking with their twins. The twins are dressed the same—no shirts, with cover-alls, and baseball hats.

Seeing kids with normal, loving parents who really seem to care about them is a bitter-sweet experience for me. On one hand it hurts because I'm reminded of the stark contrast between parents who most likely want what's best for their kids, and the kind of parents I had, who were really only concerned about my welfare as far as they could use me for a favorable political commodity.

On the other hand it brings me such joy to see kids like these little twins running around, because I am so thankful that they have a good shot at happiness and success in life. They have a loving, caring family to stand behind them, and don't have to struggle with the horrible memories and abuse that many of us who grew up in The Family do.

It gives me hope that one day Berg and Maria's evil legacy will die with The Family, and it will be only a distant or, better yet, forgotten bad memory.[26]

By the end of the summer of 2004, it was clear that Ricky Rodriguez was one of the second-generation defectors who was *not* moving on. "I haven't visited this site much for a long time," Ricky wrote his final Internet communiqué. "I was under the mistaken impression that having written [about my story] I could leave it all behind, start a new life that had nothing to do with the cult, quit talking to anyone who had anything to do with the cult, and really 'move on' with my life. I know now that will never happen. I can't run away from my past, and no matter how much longer I live, the first 35 years of my life will always haunt me."

Ricky then issued a call to arms. "Something has to be done to stop these child molesters and it would be nice to find some people who think the same way. Every day, these people [who] are alive and free [are] a slap in the face to the thousands of us who have been methodically molested, tortured, raped, and the many who they have as good as murdered by driving them to suicide."[27]

Anneke Schieberl, the Houston convert who went through basic training with Sue Kauten back in 1971, was now living in San Diego with her husband, Ron. They had been out of The Family for more than twenty-five years, and their home had become something of a way station for second-generation defectors trying to break free.

"We'd been helping ex-members since 1978," Schieberl said. "Sometimes it's good, sometimes not. A lot of times it's a mercy job.[28]

"Ricky helped us get this house ready so we could move in," she said. "He'd come over here to talk. He just wanted to hang out. He said there wasn't a moment in his life when he didn't think about the shame of his childhood. The word he used was 'embarrassed.' He was so embarrassed by the things they did to him when he was growing up.

"His rage about The Family was constant, but he was trying not to talk about it publicly," she added. "He said he couldn't cause anymore trouble because of what might happen to Techi."

Ricky was worried about Techi, his younger sister still in The Family. He told friends that one of the main reasons he stopped posting his recollections on the Internet was the threats he received regarding Techi. He feared public denunciations of his mother could make life worse for his little sister. Ricky began pretending to seek some kind of reconciliation with his mother. He put out feelers through his relatives in Tucson. After moving to San Diego, he made several visits to The Family Care Foundation and met some people who had his mother's ear. He hoped that the ruse would allow him to contact Techi and get her out of The Family.

Sarafina introduced Ricky to the leading second-generation defectors from The Family. Many were stuck in the pain and anger of their childhood and spent countless hours on four different Web sites started by former members. They were looking for ways to bring the child molesters of The Family to justice by encouraging the FBI and local law enforcement to file criminal charges, gathering information for possible civil lawsuits, and keeping The Family story alive in the news media. They soon discovered how hard it was to build strong civil or criminal cases against Family leaders. Most of the sexual abuse happened outside the United States in the seventies and eighties and was committed by men and women who were constantly changing their names.

Sarafina said she was troubled by Ricky's inability to stop blaming himself for what happened to other children in The Family. He was talking more and more about how he'd like to see his mother dead. At Sarafina's suggestion, he talked to Daniel Roselle, who had emerged as a leader among second-generation defectors. They hoped to find justice through the courts, and a woman agent at the FBI office in San Diego had started looking into the abuse allegations. "I e-mailed Ricky and said, 'If you want to act, this is the most concrete thing I've heard so far.' I didn't hear back from him," Roselle recalled. "Then he called me from Seattle. He asked about the FBI lady, and I told him she hadn't got back in touch with me. I had nothing to offer him."[29]

Ricky and Roselle went over a list of second-generation Family members who had committed suicide in recent years. "We're dropping like flies," he told Ricky.

Then Ricky said, "Is there any way you can help me find my mother?"

Roselle was dumbfounded. Why find Zerby unless you have a subpoena for her? There had been some rumors that top Family leaders were in New Mexico, but Roselle told Ricky he had no idea where his mother was.

Then Ricky said, "She needs to die."

Roselle says he tried to change the subject. Maybe they could get justice through the courts.

"Right," Ricky said. "Nothing ever happens with that."

Then Ricky said, "Sometimes I think my mission is just to end them and me."

Roselle paused.

"What do you say when someone tells you that? It's not like Ricky and I were bosom buddies. Maybe we talked four times over a period of three months.

"During our last conversation," Roselle said, "he said the thing to do is take them out and then take myself out."

That was it for Roselle. Ricky called him two more times, but Roselle did not return the calls. He was scared. "I didn't call him back," he said, his eyes tearing up. "I don't agree with what he did, but maybe I could have helped him."

Ricky had grown tired of the second-generation defector community. He complained to one of his confidants that it was turning into a cult of its own. He had discovered something that often happens in the anticult movement. Former members simply turn their fanaticism against their former prophet or guru or cult leader. Ricky was sick of that scene. He wanted revenge.

Ricky called Aunt Rosemary and told her he wanted to visit her in Tucson. She and her parents were the only family he had outside The Family. Tucson was also the most likely place Ricky could get the information he wanted as to the whereabouts of his despised mother.

13

Into the Desert

TUCSON, ARIZONA
December 25, 2004 – Elderhaven Care Home

IT SEEMED STRANGE to Rosemary Kanspedos. Why would that woman be calling *here* on Christmas Day? This was *family* time, not *The Family* time. Rosemary never really trusted Sue Kauten, or Joy, or

Ricky outside Aunt Rosemary's home in Tucson.

Angela or whatever she was calling herself this year. Rosemary and her family had come over to celebrate Christmas with her parents. Her sister, Jeannie, was there with her family, and so was Ricky.

Ricky had been in Tucson for about three months. He'd gotten his own apartment, but still spent a lot of time with his Aunt Rosemary and her family. He'd split up with Elixcia and was on his own. It was only natural for him to be here with his grandparents on Christmas Day, Rosemary thought. Ricky was family. Sue Kauten was *not* family.

Jeannie talked to Sue for a while and then handed the phone to her husband. He wished Sue a Merry Christmas, then handed the phone to Rosemary, who did not want to talk to that woman. "We are having our family Christmas together," Rosemary said, curtly. "This is not an appropriate time for you to call."[1]

Rosemary Kanspedos handed the phone back to Jeannie, who then handed it to Ricky. He walked into the next room and had a private conversation with the woman who had once been one of his four childhood nannies. They talked for a while, then Ricky came back into the room. Nobody said another word about it.

For most of Ricky's life in The Family, Sue Kauten had been his mother's personal secretary. Ricky hadn't revealed his exact plans to his Aunt Rosemary, but he had come to Arizona to find his mother and kill her. There were rumors that his mother was back in the states. If anyone knew the whereabouts of Karen Zerby, it would be Sue Kauten.

Rosemary was never sure what to make of Sue. At first she was just a voice on the phone. She was the go-between for Karen Zerby and their parents. Sue would tell Rosemary's parents how Karen was, and relay news back to Karen about her parents. In the mid-nineties, Sue started showing up in Tucson and helping out at Elderhaven, getting to know Rosemary's sister, Jeannie, and her husband, Bill. They put Sue on the board of directors at Elderhaven, and Rosemary watched as Sue "became very friendly with Jeannie and Bill."

Ricky knew his Aunt Jeannie was closer to his mother than to his Aunt Rosemary, perhaps too close. Rosemary was his natural ally. Four months earlier, in August 2004, he had called Rosemary and asked if he could come and visit for the weekend.

"Of course," his aunt replied. "When can you get here? What do you want me to cook for you? What do you want to eat? Oh, you know you'll have to sleep on the living room floor. Is that OK?"

Ricky arrived the next day from San Diego. He was going to leave Tucson to go home to San Diego on Sunday, then on Monday. Then he asked if he could stay with Rosemary and her family for a few weeks. He'd decided to stay in Tucson and look for a job.

"You are more than welcome," said Rosemary, who'd been dropping hints all weekend that she'd love for him to stay.

Over the weekend, Ricky had helped Rosemary's husband, Tom, haul some stuff out to the dump outside Tucson. They talked during the drive, and Ricky didn't hide his intense anger toward his mother. He didn't tell Tom his exact plan, but it was clear that he had come to Arizona with revenge on his mind.

On Monday, Ricky saw a truck go by his aunt's house with "Flynn's Electric" written on the side. Ricky called the number and arranged to meet with Mark Flynn that evening. He was hired that night.

Tom and Rosemary hoped Ricky would settle into his new job, get on with this life, and get over the hatred. "He tried, but the resentment just grew against his mother," Tom said over dinner one night at their home in Tucson. "He just couldn't put it behind him."

They were at the table with their daughter, Rachel, who was the same age as Ricky, and son, Ben, who was three years younger. It was the week before Christmas, 2005, almost a year after that surprise phone call from Sue Kauten. This was not an easy after-dinner conversation with the Kanspedos family. They are deeply religious people, and they were getting into some deep family secrets.

Rosemary said Ricky mentioned the incest to her, but couldn't really talk about it. He told his aunt "it would be too much for you."

"He knew I had problems with depression and he was trying to protect me," Rosemary said.

One of the things Ricky wanted to understand was what had happened to his mother to turn her into the person he so despised. She had the same upbringing as Aunt Rosemary and Aunt Jeannie. What happened to Karen?

"Ricky said he could see it with Berg and all the history with his mother [Virginia Berg]. But with his mother [Karen Zerby], there didn't seem to be a reason," Tom said. "That troubled him."

Ironically, Tom Kanspedos had almost joined The Family back in the early seventies—years before he ever met Rosemary Zerby, his future wife. He first encountered the cult in 1972 in Brownsville, Texas. Tom was twenty-one years old and in the Army, stationed at Ft. Hood. "They were on the street," he recalled. "Preaching the gospel. Then they starting talking about these 'Mo letters' like they were the word of God. That gave me the idea that something was up. I struggled with it. I kind of wanted to stay with them. It was intense. It was a spiritual battle."

He ran into the sect again when he was back home in Tucson, in the summer of 1973. "I went to one of their meetings," Tom said. "They were down on Fourth Avenue, where the hippies would hang out. But there was this one guy with this look in his eyes—like he wasn't in his right mind. I'd just gotten out of the military, and I was not into that communal-type thing. I had a car, and they'd make you sell your car. I had my freedom. It kind of seemed like going back into the military. I was working for the post office at the time, and I remember feeling guilty that these guys were out preaching the gospel, and I was just this guy going to work."

In the fall of 2004, Ricky stayed with Tom and Rosemary for about a month. Every night he would study his electrician's manual. "He was not one to sit around and do nothing. He decided he was going to get a job, and then he got one," his aunt said. "He studied everything. He decided he wanted to be better at math and got this textbook from my daughter, who was going through college and living here. Pretty soon, he was telling her the answer to math problems. There was this draw in him for knowledge, to be learning something all the time.

"You'd have a conversation, and he'd say: 'What are you thinking? Why are you thinking that way? Why did you say that?'

"It would be very disconcerting. I'd say, 'Well, I said what I meant.'

'No, what did you mean by it?' Ricky would ask.

"I'd have to stop and think. He was interested in how real people functioned and thought. It was all learning to him."

Aunt Rosemary knew Ricky had been soured on religion by his upbringing in The Family, but she nevertheless told him that she would be happy to take him to their church. She would be proud to introduce him as her nephew.

There was another reason for Ricky to visit the church. There was a little of his mother's history at the church. It turned out that Karen Zerby was the one who had introduced Rosemary Zerby to this congregation back in 1968. "It was really small then," she said. "Just patches of carpet on the floor."

Sunday came around, and to her surprise, Ricky said, "I'm going to church with you."

"Are you going for me?" Rosemary asked.

"Yeah."

"Then don't go. You are not to go for me."

"No," Ricky replied. "I want to go."

They went to church, a nondenominational evangelical church near the university. "They introduced him as my nephew, and people were very friendly, but I knew it upset him. It was so hard for him to sit there. Our church is different than most churches. We wear shorts, flip-flops. It's come as you are. Just come. We have street people because we live near that part of town. Everybody is welcome. But I could see he had a very, very rough time."

After about a month, Ricky rented his own apartment. It was too crowded at Aunt Rosemary's house, and the atmosphere was too religious for him. He couldn't even drink beer at his aunt's house. Ricky's new place wasn't located in the best part of town, but it was a decent apartment. Rosemary's husband helped him move what few belongings he had into the flat. Ricky bought a table and chairs at Ikea—the same table and chair that would appear a few months later in his final videotaped message to the world. "His apartment was unadorned," his aunt recalled. "He didn't have pictures all over the place. He was just a simple guy. When he lived here he slept on the floor in our living room. In the morning you'd have never known he was there. He'd be sitting on the couch. Everything would be put away. He didn't need a lot. It was one of the really cool things about him."

Ricky's only other close friends in Tucson were his boss, Mark Flynn, and Mark's wife, Denise. Mark was doing a remodeling job at a school near Rosemary's house the day Ricky saw his big utility van with "Flynn Electric" on the side.

"He called and wanted to know if Mark needed help," Denise recalled. "He came over and had a résumé. He interviewed very well. Very personable. He was meticulous neat, polite. He'd show up early for work. He'd always said, 'You don't have to pay me overtime.' I'd say, 'I have to pay you. It's the law, Ricky. Stop with that.'"[2]

Ricky got his electrician's license in Seattle and had his own set of tools. Ron and Anneke Schieberl had found him to be a great worker in San Diego and so did his new boss in Tucson. "He was the perfect employee—a journeyman," Mark said. "Everybody that I work with—general contractors, suppliers—everybody liked him. He was an incredibly personable kid."

Ricky soon became a regular visitor at the Flynn's home in Tucson. Denise would often make him breakfast before work and dinner in the evening. "He attached to Mark. He liked Mark. He wanted to hang out around him."

Over the next four months, Mark spent a lot of time talking with Ricky during drives to work sites around Tucson and Phoenix. It soon became clear that Ricky had traveled a lot as a child. One day, Mark asked him what his parents did for a living.

"My parents were missionaries," Ricky replied.

"Interesting," Mark said. "You know, I don't care what religion you are, but I don't want to hear about it on the job site. I used to work with a Jehovah's Witness, and man, it was brutal."

"No. No. Don't worry about that," Ricky answered. "I'm totally unreligious."

Ricky rarely talked about his family, but one night he was having dinner at the Flynn's, and the subject of teenage pregnancy came up.

"My sister had a baby when she was sixteen," said Ricky, referring to Techi.

"Wow," Denise replied. "That must have been very difficult for your family."

"It was," Ricky replied.

Denise thought that seemed a bit strange for a nice missionary family, but sensed that was really all Ricky wanted to say about his family.

As they spent more time with Ricky, the Flynns realized how little they knew about him. He had a wife in Seattle, and they had separated but still talked all the time on the phone. "His story brought up a lot of questions," said Denise. "He was too traveled, too intelligent, too handsome to have no story and have nothing to say about himself. The fact that he was saying nothing spoke loudly. But I didn't want to corner him. I felt like there was a huge thing there, and if I started asking questions, he'd run."

Ricky did confide in his Aunt Rosemary. Before they split up, Ricky had brought Elixcia to Tucson for a couple visits. "They were trying to get it together," Rosemary recalled. "They told us about the difficulties that they had not knowing how to do anything. I just wanted to try to help with their lives and get it as normal as it could be. We can't choose our parents, but it's in our blood to want a parent. Most of the kids in the family never had real parents. When they left The Family they had no parents. I could be there for Ricky. He was needy. It was nothing to do with being for or against Karen."

Rosemary has trouble believing that Ricky moved to Tucson for one purpose and only one purpose—to track down his mother and kill her. "I've heard people say he came down here to kill Sue or to find his mother," Rosemary said. "Perhaps, but my husband and I are pretty good judges of character. People who grew up in The Family are good at portraying what they want to portray, but the length of time he stayed with us, my husband and I had a feeling he wanted to change his life. He wanted to be normal. I really truly believe that even if he had those things planned, he could have been changed."

Ricky's aunt started to cry again, sobbing between her words.

"I always feel like we didn't help him enough," she said. "If he could have found what he was looking for, he could have changed."

Perhaps, but on that Christmas Day in 2004, Ricky was just looking for one thing—information as to the whereabouts of Karen Zerby and Peter Amsterdam. He had reason to believe they might show up at his grandparent's place for the holidays. They had come here before, and so had Techi, the little sister he so desperately wanted to save.

Ricky's first visit to Tucson—his first meeting with Aunt Rosemary and Aunt Jeannie and his grandparents—was when he was just sixteen or seventeen. It was before he'd met Elixcia. Rosemary and her family had not seen Karen since she disappeared that day in 1969 in the van with Jane Berg and the Teens for Christ. There had been letters, some phone calls, but Karen was gone.

"It was like she died," her sister said.

Over the years, it became clear that Karen was not just an ordinary member of The Family. Former members and anticult movement leaders had established contact with Rosemary, and she had become well aware that her sister was practically running The Family.

The first emissary Zerby sent back to her family in Tucson was her son. It was the first time Ricky met his grandparents, aunts, and cousins.

His shepherds shadowed Ricky on his visit. Rosemary called them "his wardens."

It was the early nineties, and Ricky was still loyal to his mother. His escorts had a computer and were in constant contact with The Family. Ricky would talk for a while, and then someone would go into another room to call Family leaders. "He was still a young kid under the influence of his mother and the group. Everything he said was how wonderful his mother was and all that kind of thing—things that he was supposed to say. He was told to visit. He was told to go visit his grandparents."

Ricky did, however, get a glimpse at another world. Rosemary's daughter, Rachel, was the same age as Ricky and took him into Tucson to experience something called "Downtown Saturday Night," a gathering of the punk rock, pierced, and tattooed subculture of the early nineties. "She was just being friendly and wanted to take him somewhere," Rosemary said. "She thought he ought to go out and see the world." Ricky's "wardens" went along on the outing. Within a couple of days, the family visitation was over and Ricky was gone.

Two years later Zerby sent Ricky's sixteen-year-old sister, Techi, to Tucson to meet his grandparents. She seemed less comfortable out in the real world than her big brother. "I don't think it was something she wanted. She had been told to go visit her grandparents," Rosemary said. "It was the same drill, but Techi was different than Ricky. She was introverted. The women who were with her gave her comfort. She wasn't used to being away from the group and being introduced to these new people who came up and hugged her.

"It had been all very hush-hush about when they would get here. I'm not sure why they did it, but I knew my sister never does anything without a reason. After Techi left I told my sister that Karen would be coming. She had sent her kids here, and they were safe. Nobody pounced on them and now she feels that she can come."

Rosemary was right.

Karen came to Tucson in 1999. It was the same as the two previous visits. They said they were coming at one time, then they came at another time. Security was very tight. Everything was top secret.

Karen was most worried about Rosemary. She had publicly spoken out against The Family. One time, Rosemary was in the Kmart parking lot in Tucson when a couple of Family missionaries came up to her and handed her a tract. "I asked them, 'Do you have any clue who I am?' They didn't. I said, 'Don't even give me one of those. I'm Maria's sister, and I'm totally against all this.' They didn't react much. It didn't look like I made an impression, but my parents got a call a few days later telling me to keep quiet. My parents said, 'You better not tell us to tell Rosemary to be quiet. Number one, we're not going to do it. And number two, it wouldn't matter if we did.'"

Karen appeared at her parents' place for the big reunion. By now, her parents had started Elderhaven, a board and care home on the edge of Tucson, and were living there themselves. Karen's other sister, Jeannie, who is much closer to Zerby, was running the place with her husband, Bill.

After a day or two, Rosemary went up to Elderhaven to see her long-lost sister for the first time in three decades. "She was Karen, but she wasn't my sister. I had no idea who she was. She looked like my sister. She put her arm around me and said, 'Oh, my little sister!' I was like, 'Please, don't do that!' I didn't say that but I was thinking, 'I'm not your little sister. You have no clue *who* I am. Don't treat me like that.' I didn't say it, but it's what I thought."

Rosemary tried to be civil—for the sake of her aging parents. They could at least pretend to be a family for a day or two. They all went down to the historic "Old Tucson" neighborhood for dinner one night. Sue Kauten tagged along. Karen wore oversized sunglasses, like she had something to hide or something to fear.

Six years later, when Ricky returned to Tucson, Rosemary finally realized all that her sister had to hide. Rodriguez never liked to talk about his childhood, but he told his aunt all about it on his second visit, spewing out the story as fast as he could. Then he said he didn't want to talk about it anymore. He didn't want to dwell on it. He wanted to move on, or at least that's what Rosemary thought.

During one of their last conversations, his aunt gently suggested that he might want to talk to a therapist about his childhood trauma. Ricky wanted none of that. "He'd talked about how depressed he was. I have a problem with depression and can see it. Mine was a drop in the bucket compared to him. His was so deep and full of pain."

Rosemary started crying.

"When I talked to him about going to a therapist, he said, 'I can't. There's too much. I can't tell everything. I will die if I try to say everything that is in me. It will overflow. I won't be able to handle it. They won't be able to handle it. Everything in me will be gone.'"

14

Last Date

SCOTTSDALE, ARIZONA
January 2, 2005 – Apartment of Alisia Arvizu

RICKY RODRIGUEZ WAS leading a double life. Aunt Rosemary was getting the real story, but Mark and Denise Flynn had no idea what this seemingly well-adjusted guy had gone through growing up in The Family or that he was about to embark on a murderous rampage. Neither did Alisia Arvizu, but she did get a disturbing glimpse of a young man about to emotionally implode.

Ricky Rodriguez.

Alisia was one of Denise Flynn's old friends. She needed some temporary work, so Mark hired her on at Flynn's Electric as a simple laborer. "Ricky had already started," Alisia said. "Right away, he started teaching me things, like electrical wiring. He was always trying to make the job easier for me. Taking things and doing it himself."[1]

Ricky was quiet at first, but it didn't take long for him to start flirting with Alisia. She flirted back, but didn't think anything would come of it. After all, she was fifty-one years old, and he was this strong, good-looking guy in his twenties.

Alisia would pick him up and take him to various job sites. "He was a moody person. One day I picked him up and noticed he was angry. He'd get in the truck and wouldn't say anything. The silence was too much, and then he'd snap out of it. We'd talk about relationships. I asked him if he had kids, and he said he didn't want kids. He would say things about his wife—that he was mad at her or something. One time I asked him if he wanted to meet anyone new."

Alisia was thinking about some of her younger friends, not herself, but Ricky didn't seem interested. She stopped working as a day laborer in November and thought that was the last she'd see of Ricky Rodriguez.

"Then one Sunday, out of the blue, he called me and said he wanted to see me," Alisia recalled. "At first I didn't recognize his voice. I said, 'Sure, it would be nice to see you.' Within an hour, he was here."

Ricky had told Denise that he would pick up a few things for her at the Ikea store near Scottsdale. Alisia offered to go over there with him. "He seemed really happy," Alisia said. "He talked a lot about his martial arts and about having this gun. I asked if he expected someone to jump him, or what. He said he'd never use it on anyone—only in self-defense. We walked around at Ikea. We talked about fixing up his apartment. He liked the colors at Denise's house. He almost took this red rug. He picked it up and then said, 'No, I guess I don't need it.'"

They went for a bite to eat at a sports bar—beer and chicken wings. Ricky started flirting with her. "He seemed really young," she said. "At one point, he reached over to take my hand just as I happened to take it away. Later on, we held hands."

When they were back in the car, Alisia asked Ricky if he'd seen his mother over the Christmas holidays.

"Hell, no!"

It was a natural question. Alisia was exactly the same age as Karen Zerby.

"What do you mean?"

"I hate my mother," Ricky said. "My mother and dad, too. I hate them. All they are about is their religion. Have you ever heard of The Family, the Children of God?'

"No," Alisia replied.

"They use kids to impress people—to make points."

Alisia didn't really get what Ricky was trying to say, but she could see that he was suddenly burning with anger.

"Forget it," he said. "Fuck my mother!"

Ricky started cussing out his mother, slamming his fist on the steering wheel so hard that he almost lost control of his car.

"Ricky," Alisia said. "Be careful. Feeling so much hate isn't good for you."

"I'm going to hate her all my life," he said.

Alisia decided it was time to change the subject. She was taking care of a friend's cat, so they went over to her friend's place to check on the pet. Suddenly, Ricky was back in a good mood.

"We just drove around. I was listening to a country station. He liked the music. We were laughing, talking about Mark and Denise. He was talking about how much he liked them. He asked me if I wanted to go see a movie, but we wound up buying a six pack of Heineken and going back to my apartment."

It was a bit chilly that January afternoon—at least for Arizona. Alisia lit the fireplace in her apartment.

Here's how she remembers the conversation:

"Alisia," Ricky said. "We should make love."

"Ricky! I'm probably your mother's age. Why would you want to do that?"

"I've been with older women—ever since I was twelve."

"Twelve!" Alisia said, laughing. "You're a little pervert!"

"No, really Alisia," Ricky said. "I'm used to older women."

"Ricky. I have a son older than you."

"Come on. It's been a long time."

Ricky took Alisia by the hand and led her over to a blanket by the fireplace. At first, Ricky had a nice touch. Very smooth. They talked some more. Ricky told her the hearth reminded him of a fireplace at a place where he and his sister had lived in Russia.

"Wow," Alisia said. "You've been to so many places."

"It was nothing," he replied. "I wasn't trying to impress you or anything. It was just cold there."

As soon as Ricky and Alisia started to have intercourse, the entire mood changed. Up to then, he had been very gentle, very smooth. Not anymore. "He was doing it really hard," Alisia recalled. "He looked really angry. Had his eyes open with this strange look. It was like he was thinking of someone else. When he was done, he just sat there. It was like he was in a daze."

"I'm sorry," Ricky said.

"Why were you so rough?"

"I'm sorry. I didn't mean it."

Ricky laid his head on Alisia's breast.

"It felt like he was a little boy," Alisia told me. "I just held him, talking about how we have to find peace within ourselves. He said he wished he could have that. I said you have to forgive and forget. He said. 'I can't do that. I can't forgive anymore.'"

"What is it? What bothers you?" Alisia asked.

"Alisia," Ricky said. "There is so much … I can't even begin to tell you."

Then Ricky started talking about suicide.

"Don't say that," Alisia said. "That's a coward's way of going out of the world.…"

"That depends," Ricky replied.

They talked some more. It was getting late. Alisia tried to get Ricky to spend the night. It was a long drive back to Tucson.

"You can stay if you want."

"No. I gotta get going. I can drive."

Ricky kissed Alisia good-bye and walked out the door.

"I felt really bad for him," Alisia said. "To see him walk away with his head down. It was so sad."

Ricky and his prized K-bar knife.

15

Lost

SANTA FE, NEW MEXICO
January 8, 2005 – Tiago's
house

IT WAS TWO in the morning. Tiago had been talking to his brother on the phone and was ready to crash. Then the phone rang again. This time it was Ricky.

"Dude! I've been trying to call you all night long. What's goin' on?"

Tiago wasn't surprised it was Ricky, but he was surprised by his old friend's tone of voice. Tiago always felt there was a kind of eternal sadness with Ricky. In recent weeks, that sadness seemed to deepen every time they spoke. Not tonight.

"Dude! You sound really happy."

Ricky practically yelled into the phone. "That's because I'm drunk!"

There was music playing in the background. Loud music.

"Dude! You havin' a party? You have a girlfriend over?"

"No, I don't have a girlfriend. It's just me."[1]

From the moment he answered the phone, Tiago knew something was up. The last few times they spoke it was more talk about how Ricky had to find his mom, how he had to find her before he ran out of steam. To Tiago, it all seemed like a warped science fiction movie. This guy is running out of juice but had to accomplish his mission first. But tonight, Ricky sounded happy. Not drunk. Happy. Tiago drives a cab in Santa Fe. He knows the difference between happy and drunk.

"Dude! What's going on?"

"I found the solution!"

It was the latest clue. Ricky had been dropping little hints all week, starting with his encounter with Alisia the previous weekend.

On Wednesday, two nights before he called Tiago, Ricky had dinner with Mark and Denise Flynn. Denise sensed there was something different about him that night.

"One of the things I love about you, Denise, is you're so Zen," Ricky told her. "If I was going to be anything, I'd be a Buddhist. I'd be Zen. But I have too much anger."

"You? Anger? I have trouble putting you and anger together in my head," Denise said.

On Thursday, Ricky went over to Rosemary's house for a visit. They were sitting at the kitchen table. At one point, Ricky said:

"You know, I don't think I can handle it anymore."

Ricky visited Rosemary one last time on Friday evening, the same night he set up the video camera in his apartment on the other side of town, the same night he called Tiago. "He gave me this huge hug," Aunt Rosemary recalled. "We always hugged, but I usually gave the bigger hug. He really hugged me that night. I didn't think about this until after everything happened. But it ran through my mind. *Boy is he hugging me tight.*"

Later that night, Ricky called Sarafina in San Diego. She was sleeping and didn't hear the phone, but called him back in the morning. They had planned to get together later that month in San Diego at a memorial service for Abe Braaten, a twenty-seven-year-old defector who had just committed suicide by leaping off the roof of a building in Kobe, Japan. Ricky told Sarafina he wasn't going to be able to make it to Abe's memorial. Something important had come up.

Ricky told Sarafina he was sending her a videotape and hoped she could show it to people they knew. He was evasive when she asked him what was on the tape. "Just getting a few things off my chest," he said, changing the subject.[2]

On Friday, just hours before he shot his video, Ricky got a phone call from Sue Kauten, who was in Tucson, confirming their plans to meet for dinner on Saturday night. Ricky had to hold his temper and play nice. Ricky reveals on the tape that Sarafina's uncle, Gabe Martin, and his wife, two longtime Berg insiders and sect leaders, had helped arrange his meeting with Sue. During his phone conversation with Sue that night, Ricky could barely control his rage when she started telling him how wonderful Techi was doing in The Family. As he explained on the video he shot that night:

> It started with Gabe and [his wife]. Man, they have so much blood on their hands. It's not even fucking funny. Hope some-body takes 'em out. I don't think it's gonna be me. I definitely don't think I'm gonna get that far. But somebody's gotta take them out, those fuckers. Anyway, yeah, I talked to them on the phone, ya know, tell 'em all about myself, try to be nice, then, you know, Joy, Trust, Angela, Lusty Trusty, whatever her fuck-ing name is, she calls me, and you know I have to do the whole thing with her again. So, anyway. She tells me my sister's do-ing good. Yeah right. I can only imagine what my sister goes through.... That's been actually one of the hardest things lately for me—is to have to—you know, pretend like I'm mak-ing peace with these fucking perverts. You know you just want to grab 'em and rip their throat out.

Did Ricky tell anyone about his plans to torture Sue Kauten to get information as to the whereabouts of his mother? Did he tell the three people who got copies of the video—Sarafina, Tiago, or Elixcia? Sara-fina said he was evasive. Ricky was apparently replaying the video he just shot in his apartment when he called Tiago early Saturday morn-ing. That was the loud music in the background.

"Ricky lost the will to live," Tiago replied. "There was almost no point in trying to salvage him. He'd always talk about his need for vengeance and his mom. We talked about lots of things. Eventually, he wanted to stop The Family. We both felt they'd done a great injus-tice to us, to the kids. There were many ways to go about this. I'd say, 'We can become attorneys, or go into the FBI and set up an FBI cult division.' He just didn't have the patience, even though he was known for his patience.... At one point I said, 'Let's join the Marines, or the

Foreign Legion.' He liked the idea, but eventually he didn't have the willpower to live more than a couple weeks, more than a day or two at a time. Ricky had a plan of what he wanted to do. Ricky was not an idiot. He was very careful as to what he said and whom he said it to. Eventually, he quit talking to everyone. But those who knew him put two and two together."

At one point in that conversation early Saturday morning, Tiago and Ricky knew it might be the last time they spoke. Tiago said something about how he wished all his conversations with Ricky had been on tape. "At least you'll have the videotape I'm sending," Ricky said.

"And I know you'll keep it, and you'll get it into the right hands," he added.

"What video?" Tiago replied. "What are you talking about?"

Ricky wouldn't say, Tiago said. They talked for an hour that night. They talked about all kinds of things. At one point, Hinduism came up.

"We were talking about when you leave [The Family], you tend to reject God and reject everything," Tiago said. "But then you start to piece things back together as far as your belief system. One of my roommates is a Sikh from India, and he was telling me about Hinduism. They believe that you just keep on living and living and living, and how you live your life now affects your next life. Reincarnation and karma and all that stuff. We were talking about how we can't necessarily ignore religion. We both claimed to be atheists, but we know there has to be some truth in some of this—in some religion. We were trying to decide which religion was right.

"It really slowed him down when I said, 'How you live and how you die is really going to affect the way you live again.' Not because I believe that. I was just repeating what I heard. He got real quiet for a long time and then he said:

'That's an interesting concept. I'm going to have to think about that.'

"I told him. 'I don't know. It's really disturbing. You leave The Family having grown up in their version of Christianity. You don't want to have anything to do with religion anymore, and then you realize that Christianity is only one of many religions out there. Everybody has a different theory. It's kind of mind-boggling. We rejected Christianity out of hand because we knew everything there is to know in a way. We've memorized the Bible. But how can you reject Buddhism when you don't know a thing about it?' Anyway, that's kind of how the conversation went."

At the end, Ricky reminded him about the video.

"OK," Tiago said. "Just don't do anything stupid."

"You know me," Ricky replied.

Tiago, an aspiring writer, thinks one reason he got the tape is that he was supposed to write something about Ricky. What *would* he write about all this?

"Most of what I write is, you know, stuff about Generation X. Where are we going? What's going on? You know, the reaction you have when the world you thought you knew isn't the world you find. About how we're all lost."

16

"Come Die with Me"

TUCSON, ARIZONA
January 8, 2005 – Ricky's apartment

RICKY LEFT THE APARTMENT exhausted and exhilarated, adrenaline pumping, mind racing. Sue's body was left behind, draining blood into the thick brown shag of the living room carpet. He'd stabbed her five times, then he slit her throat.

Undressing.......for Sue!

Ricky with Sue Kauten in The Story of Davidito.

There had been a struggle. Sue raised her arms up to her face to defend herself against the blows of the knife. Blood splattered across the floor of the kitchenette, next to the table where Ricky had videotaped his manifesto the night before. There were stab wounds in Sue's right arm and left hand, and one of her shoes had been thrown across the room.

Ricky stuck the knife into Sue's right breast, and then into her stomach. She had been wearing black pants and a light gray sweater, which was pulled up just enough to reveal a white bra reddened with blood. She died in a fetal position with her fists clenched tight—raised up to her eyes like she could not believe what was happening to her.

It had been nearly three decades since she first walked into Davidito's life back on the island of Tenerife. In *The Story of Davidito*, there's a picture of Sue laying in bed with two-year-old Ricky, unbuttoning his shirt and seductively smiling down on him. Ricky is also smiling, ready for "love up" time. There's a caption under the photo explaining that the Prophet Prince was "Undressing .... for Sue!"

Ricky had learned on Christmas Day that she was going to be in Tucson over the first weekend in January of 2005. Sue had agreed to go out to dinner, to catch up on old times. Ricky knew his date was his mother's eyes and ears. She would know how to find Karen Zerby and her husband, Peter Amsterdam. He finally had his chance for revenge.

Ricky picked her up early Saturday evening. They never made it to dinner. Instead, Ricky took her back to his small one-bedroom flat at Los Altos Village, a large apartment complex not far from the Tucson gun shop and firing range where Ricky learned to use his Glock 23, the forty-caliber semiautomatic pistol he'd loaded the night before with hollow-point Golden Saber bullets.

None of Ricky's neighbors remembered seeing him or Sue enter or leave the apartment, which is tucked under a stairway on the ground floor of the two-story, chocolate-brown complex. The sprawling collection of flats is home to many Spanish-speaking immigrants and other people who—like Ricky—were newly arrived to the desert city.

No one knows exactly what Sue knew or what she told Ricky that night as to the whereabouts of his mother and other Family leaders. His knife assault was vicious, but police found no evidence that he had tortured his former nanny. After the murder, Ricky tossed his prized K-bar knife under the Ikea sofa in his living room. Then he walked out to his parking spot, climbed into his silver Chevy Cavalier, and drove off toward Interstate 10.

Before he reached the freeway on-ramp he pulled out his cell phone and called Elixcia. The phone in her Lakewood, Washington, apartment rang at 7:15 P.M.

"Don't let anyone ever tell you that taking someone else's life is easy. It's not," Ricky said. "It's the hardest thing I've ever done in my life."

His wife sobbed.

"I miss you so much," Ricky said. "Come die with me."

Listening to Rick that night, Elixcia felt like she *was* dying.

"He had just left the apartment," she said. "He told me he was sorry he failed me as a husband. But that's not true. It was just too hard for us to be together. There was so much pain."[1]

They talked several times that night as Ricky drove out of Tucson heading north on Interstate 10. They talked so much that Ricky had to pull off the freeway outside Phoenix and stop at a Target store to buy a car charger for his cell phone. Getting out of his car, Ricky noticed that Sue's blood was all over his jeans. He grabbed a clean pair of pants out of a bag in the trunk, jumped back into his car, and changed into the clean clothes, tossing the crumpled, bloodied trousers on the floor by the passenger seat.

Ricky called Elixcia back when he got on the freeway.

"He said he was afraid of dying," Elixcia said. "I told him I believed in angels and when he died he would feel love like he never got to experience in this world."

"Keep telling me nice stories," Ricky replied.

At one point in the conversation, Ricky saw road signs indicating that he was approaching a rest stop on freeway.

"I think I'll pull in here and kill myself," he told his estranged wife.

"I'm freaking out, yelling. 'What! What are you going to do?' He'd been awake for two days," Elixcia explained. "He was really tired, and just mumbling words."

Ricky decided there was too much light at the rest stop. It wasn't the right place to kill himself, so he pushed on to the California border.

"I'm so tired," he told his wife. "I'm so tired of thinking. I have to go now."[2]

Ricky hung up. He crossed the California state line and pulled into the Blythe Holiday Inn Express at 11:18 P.M. He chose one of the better-looking motels strung along Interstate 10. It's a two-story stucco building, pinkish in color, and adorned with arches meant to convey the traditional Spanish Mission architecture of the American Southwest. Ricky paid the clerk cash—$119.90, including tax—and was given a ground-level smoking room with two queen-sized beds. He walked into Room 109 and turned on the television set. He felt like he was in a movie. He was exhausted and wired at the same time. If it was a movie, there'd be a bulletin on the news: "Police across two states are searching tonight for a Tucson electrician suspected in the brutal slaying of a California woman...."

Ricky told Elixcia to call the police and have them search his apartment back in Tucson, but there was nothing on the news. This was not a movie. Elixcia had not called the Tucson police.

Ricky had no intention of spending the night in Room 109. All he wanted was a few beers and a hot bath. Then he was going to kill himself. But first he needed a little liquid anesthesia. He popped open the first of five bottles of Heineken and started filling the tub with water. There was still some of Sue's blood on his clothes and on his body. Now he saw more blood as he pulled off his black sweater and ribbed muscle shirt. Ricky tossed his soiled clothes on the bed nearest the window and headed into the bathroom.

After his bath and his beers, Ricky walked back out to his car, climbed in, and started driving. He headed south, away from the commercial glare of the cheap motels and fast-food joints. It doesn't take long to get out of Blythe and into the desert. Ricky rumbled over some railroad tracks and swung the Chevy sedan into the deserted driveway of the Palo Verde Irrigation District. He parked along a tall chain link fence topped with razor wire. It was just after 2 A.M. when he raised the pistol to his head, rested the end of the barrel on his right temple, and squeezed the trigger. The last thing he saw when he turned off his headlights were two yellow and black warning signs hung on the locked gate of the parking lot. The signs read "END."

17

End of the Road

BLYTHE, CALIFORNIA
January 9, 2005 – Palo Verde Irrigation District

DANNY HOLLIS DOESN'T USUALLY work on Sundays, but they'd drained the irrigation canals the week before and were still making repairs. They needed to get the system up and running as soon as possible, so Danny and his crew had pulled a Sunday shift.

Hollis saw the four-door Chevy sedan with Washington plates parked outside the fence when he came to work at 6:30 A.M. He didn't

Danny Hollis stands in the driveway where Ricky's body was discovered.

think much of it at first. Weary motorists were known to pull off Interstate 10 and park in the wide driveway to take a nap.

Hollis headed out to the fields to check on the repairs. He returned ninety minutes later and noticed that the guy in the Chevy was still asleep. Walking up to the car, Danny saw that the driver was in a strange position, leaning way back and over to the right. Then he saw all the blood and the brain matter splattered over the seats. He turned away and hustled back to the office to call the cops.

Patrolman Troy Fabanich and Sgt. Robert Matthews were the first two officers to arrive. Fabanich saw a pistol between the driver's right leg and the center console of the Cavalier. He checked the subject's pulse. There was none, and the body was cold to the touch. A team of paramedics arrived and pronounced the subject dead at 8:11 A.M. Fabanich secured the crime scene with yellow police tape and awaited the arrival of Detective Sgt. Jeff Wade.

Sgt. Wade pulled up at 8:23 A.M. Evidence technician Valerie Hudson got there at 9:02 A.M. and began to photograph the scene and dust the car for prints. It looked like a routine suicide. Then Wade noticed a receipt from "The UPS Store" stuffed in the pocket of the driver's door. Someone by the name of "Ricky Rodriguez" had sent three video tapes to three different people—to a Sara Martin in San Diego, an Elixcia Munumel in Lakewood, Washington, and to a guy in Santa Fe, New Mexico, named "Tiago." He dropped them off at the UPS store at 515 E. Grant Street in Tucson the previous morning at 10:49 A.M.

Wrapped inside the paperwork was a key card from the nearby Holiday Inn Express. Wade sent Sgt. Matthews over to the hotel to investigate.

Deputy Coroner Mike Presley arrived at 9:49 A.M. Wade had just picked up a cell phone that was sitting on the front passenger seat and was starting to brief Presley when the phone rang.

"Hello," he said.

There was a short pause, then a female voice on the other end of the line asked, "Is he dead?"

"Can I ask you who you are?"

"Elixcia Munumel," the voice said. "I'm his wife!"

"Okay. Try to calm down. Who do you think is dead?"

"Richard Rodriguez."

"Okay. Here is the situation. My name is Sgt. Jeff Wade, and I am investigating a death of a male subject who has not yet been identified."

"Oh, my God!" Elixcia cried out, then wept into the phone, barely catching her breath between sobs.

It took Wade several minutes to calm Elixcia down and get some basic information. Her name was Elixcia Munumel. She lived in Lakewood, Washington. She had separated from her husband about six months ago. He moved to San Diego and lived with a friend named Sara. Then he moved to Tucson. He called last night and told her to call the police and tell them to go to his apartment. They would find a body there. Elixcia told Wade she did not know who the victim was. Her husband had been suffering from depression. That might have something to do with all this.

"Did you call the Tucson police?" Wade asked.

"No," Elixcia said. "I called the police here in Lakewood, but I don't know what they did."

Wade looked at the receipt from the UPS store.

"Okay. Can you confirm for me that the address of your husband's apartment in Tucson is 2525 North Los Altos. Number 343."

"Yes," Elixcia said. "That's it."

"Okay, Elixcia. Now try to calm down. I will call you back as soon as we confirm the identity of this man."[1]

Wade finished up the call with Elixcia. Then he called the Tucson Police Department, gave them the address, and informed the dispatcher of a report that there might be a body in the apartment. It was the first call the Tucson police had gotten about a possible homicide at that address.

Valerie Hudson, the evidence technician working with Wade, found a spent shell casing in the backseat of the Cavalier. Wade picked up the pistol next to Ricky's right leg and pulled out the magazine. It held ten live rounds of ammunition. Wade placed the magazine in a handgun evidence box that Hudson had brought to the crime scene. The next step was to check to see if there was another live round in the chamber. Wade slid the side of the pistol open and was startled when a large amount of blood and brain tissue gushed out of the gun and poured into the evidence box. He ejected the final round into the metal box and handed the mess back over to Hudson.

Wade was then authorized by the deputy coroner on the scene to remove a brown wallet from the deceased's left rear pocket. It contained the Arizona driver's license of Richard Peter Rodriguez, confirming the subject's identity. Ricky's wallet also contained an Arizona concealed weapon's permit and a membership card for Jensen's shooting range in Tucson, the gun shop not far from his apartment.

Elixcia told Wade to check for a second wallet Ricky had taped to his leg. It was there, and just as Elixcia said, it contained Ricky's passport and $3300 in cash. "She told me the money was for his cremation," Wade said, "and to get the car back to her."

Shortly before noon, the deputy coroner removed the body from the car and transported it to the Frye Mortuary Chapel in Blythe. By then, the Tucson police department had called Sgt. Wade back to inform him that they had, indeed, found a body in the apartment of Richard Peter Rodriguez.

Tucson Police Detective Ben Jimenez had arrived at Ricky's apartment at 12:45 P.M. and was brought up to speed by two officers who already checked out the apartment and found the remains of Angela Marilyn Smith, a.k.a. Susan Joy Kauten. Like his counterpart in California, Jimenez initially thought he had pulled a routine murder/suicide.

Jimenez was standing outside Ricky's apartment when Rosemary and Tom Kanspedos walked up. Rosemary told Jimenez she was looking for someone named "Joy," a friend of the family who had been in town and staying with her sister, Jeannie Deyo. Rosemary explained that she and Jeannie were Ricky's aunts.

Jimenez decided to interview the couple separately, so he took Tom aside for a few questions. He explained that Joy was a good friend of his wife's sister, Jeannie, and her husband, Bill Deyo. They ran an elderly board and care home on the edge of town called Elderhaven. Sue was on the Elderhaven board of directors and was in Tucson for a meeting. Tom told Jimenez about The Family and how Ricky had been raised in the cult and sexually abused as a child by his nannies, including Sue. Ricky's mother, Karen, was now a leader in the cult. Two weeks ago, on Christmas Day, Sue had called and talked to Ricky and apparently arranged at that time to meet him last night for dinner. Tom told Jimenez what Sue looked like, and the detective told him the description matched that of the dead woman on the living room floor.

Jeannie later told police that she was first alarmed when Sue failed to return home late Saturday night. In the morning, Jeannie knew something was wrong. It was time to take Sue to the airport, and she hadn't even come back to collect her things. Jeannie called Rosemary to tell her that Sue had disappeared. The call prompted Rosemary and her husband to rush down to Ricky's apartment, where they found the place roped off as a crime scene.

It didn't take long for Detective Jimenez to close the Sue Kauten murder case. Yet several mysteries remain. What did Sue Kauten know about Ricky's mother, and what did she tell Ricky before she died? Why did Ricky head out toward California right after the slaying? Was he on his way to The Family Care Foundation offices in San Diego to extract more information or get more revenge? Was his next victim going to be Gabe Martin, Sarafina's uncle and a Family insider one step closer to Karen Zerby. Or was he planning on heading up Interstate 5 to reunite with Elixcia? Or was he just looking for a quiet spot to kill himself and stop the pain?

If anyone knows Ricky's state of mind that night, it's Elixcia Munumel.

"None of us were surprised he killed himself. It was only a matter of time," she said. "But I really didn't think he was capable of killing someone else. Berg lured [Sue] into this. Karen Zerby and David Berg are the ones responsible for this. They had the audacity to publish pictures of women sucking on a little baby's thingie. Ricky had to deal with that as a man. It was stabbing him in the back for the rest of his life."[2]

Sue just happened to be the first person who came along. She was the first opportunity he had to execute his plan. "Nothing that Ricky did was not planned out," Elixcia said. "He hated Sue, but Ricky was good at putting on a good face. He was able to make her believe that it was OK to meet with him."

Ricky had obsessed over planning his mission. He had spent months working out the details for his revenge, tracking down leads.

He passed untold hours assembling and disassembling the Glock and practicing at the shooting range near his Tucson apartment. He studied martial arts. He devoted himself to getting the sharpest possible edge on his K-bar knife. But he had never actually used that knife or that gun to kill anyone. Not until that night.

"He wanted to get somebody else," Elixcia said. "He wanted to get to people who were closer to his mother, but [Sue] came along, and then he was just too tired, too exhausted to go on. But he wanted to get other people."

Tiago agreed.

"Ricky had hoped his mother would show up over Christmas. He had been pretending to reconcile with The Family. But his mother was very careful. Ricky was able to convince his mom to allow the meeting with [Sue]. They [Zerby and Amsterdam] had gotten good reports from Gabe [Sarafina's uncle] in San Diego. They were thinking 'Ricky seems to be missing home. Ricky seems nicer—not as vengeful. He's willing to make amends. After all, he is our son. Why doesn't Angela drop by and see him?' All this was planned out."[3]

Sue's phone call on Christmas Day was his big break—not the one he expected, but a chance he could not afford to miss. Two weeks later, the meeting was about to happen. "At that point, he had totally run out of energy," Tiago said. "You can tell on the video that he is tired. He couldn't make it another day. Here was an opportunity. He wanted to go out with a bang. He deeply believed that was the only way things would change. He deeply believed that it was his responsibility to fix things. He was always apologizing for his mother—for the way she ran The Family, for all the indoctrination we suffered. He somehow felt like he was responsible because he was her son."

What really angered Ricky—and what still infuriates many in the second generation—is that their parents still don't get it. Nothing angered Ricky more than people putting down Merry or telling him that his little sister was doing fine in The Family. That is exactly what Sue told Ricky, but the most maddening thing she said turned out to be Sue's final words.

On the phone that last night of his life, Ricky told Elixcia that the hardest thing for him to handle was the fact that Sue didn't understand why he was so angry. Even as she lay bleeding to death on his living room floor, she didn't understand why he was killing her.

"Oh," Elixcia said softly into the phone to Ricky. "She didn't get it."

"That's right," her husband replied. "She didn't get it! You know, I wasn't expecting that answer. I don't understand *how* they can't see what they've done to us."

18

Ricky.com

CYBERSPACE
March 2007 and beyond

WITHIN WEEKS of his January 9 suicide, the warring forces of The Family International and its alienated second generation each tried to claim Ricky as their martyr. Each faction set up its own memorial Web site. Even in death, Ricky was still leading a double life.

Sue Kauten's murder and Ricky's suicide unleashed a torrent of media interest in the crime and the cult. There have been waves of

Karen Zerby and Peter Amsterdam in the mid-nineties.

journalistic attention paid toward The Family over the past three decades, but this one was a tidal wave of sensationalism. Sex, murder, suicide, cult, child abuse, incest, pornography, hypocrisy. After the story broke in the January 11 editions of the *San Francisco Chronicle* and the *Arizona Daily Star*, it was picked up and ran in print media ranging from the sleaziest tabloids to the front page of the *New York Times*.

Over the next year, the television newsmagazine shows on CBS, ABC, NBC, and CNN broadcast segments on Ricky and The Family. One documentary film on Ricky was produced and at least one other was pitched. TV movies were proposed. Montel Williams, the daytime TV talk-show host, interviewed Don Irwin (Shula's son and Merry Berg's brother). Dr. Phil televised an emotional family therapy session between Jim LaMattery (the guy who joined The Family in San Diego in 1971) and his angry daughter, Kristianity. The popular NBC police/prosecutor series, *Law and Order,* ran a thinly veiled dramatization where the Karen Zerby character gets tried and convicted. Ricky would have loved that show.

Media controversies around The Family continued more than two years after the murder-suicide. On January 23, 2007—just two days before Ricky would have celebrated his thirty-second birthday—a melee erupted at the Slamdance film festival in Park City, Utah, during the premier showing of *Children of God.*[1]

Protesters from The Family began the ruckus following the screening of the documentary film directed by Noah Thomson, a young Hollywood filmmaker who grew up in the sect. A confrontation between the protesters and one of the film's co-producers spilled out into the street when it was discovered that Family members had apparently made an audiotape during the screening. HBO planned to broadcast the movie later that year.

Thomson grew up in South America, where his parents did missionary work for The Family, and worked in the sect's video ministry before he left the fold at age twenty-one. He had already begun working on the film before Ricky went on his rampage. In an interview with the *San Francisco Chronicle* just days after the murder-suicide, Thomson said he had tried to get Ricky to participate in his project.

"We spoke about a month ago," Thomson said. "He was interested in doing an interview, then declined. The last time we talked he was speaking about the prophecies that he would be a martyr for the group. He said, 'I don't intend to be a martyr.' He joked about it."[2]

There were also heated arguments within the close-knit circle of second-generation defectors and former members over whether to participate in various media projects—including this book. Several insiders were writing their own books about their experiences and memories of Ricky. Arguments in the circle of defectors were conducted both in private and online via at least six different Web sites run by former members of The Family or the children of members. Thousands of pages of internal Family documents—many of them incriminating—have been posted over the past two years on Web sites like exfamily.org and movingon.org.

Ricky hoped his mission would put the public spotlight on the current leadership of The Family International. Although he succeeded in that effort, he would still be enraged by the fact that none of the top leaders, including his mother, have yet had to defend themselves in an American court of law.

Karen Elba Zerby declined to be interviewed for this book. But writing under the name Maria David, Ricky's mother prepared a eulogy for her son and posted it on www.Rickyrodriquez.com. She refers to her son as "Pete" in that testimony:

> Nothing and no one could fill the place Pete occupied in my heart while he was here on Earth. He lived with me for nearly 25 years, something I was very happy about, as I loved him dearly. Pete was a joy to me, a happy child, an exceptional teenager, and an intelligent and charming young man....
>
> Although he made some decisions in the last portion of his life that have greatly saddened me and those he loved, I know that he is now in a place where he can find rest and peace.

In her eulogy, Zerby went on to say that her son can only find forgiveness if he repents and goes through "the time of learning and rehabilitation that takes place in Heaven for those in need of it." Zerby also says that she has heard directly from Jesus Christ about Ricky, the child who was supposed to join her to battle the forces of evil on the eve of the Second Coming. Jesus Christ told Zerby that he has "erased the anger, the pain, and confusion Pete felt. Now he is discovering what he has desired all along. Now he is in a position where he can learn and grow and further develop the gifts and talents that I gave him from the beginning."

As for the incest allegations against her, Zerby issued a separate statement through her spokeswoman, Claire Borowik, in which she vigorously denied that she ever had sexual relations with her son. Borowik said the "recently hatched apostate tales of Maria engaging in incestuous relations with Ricky" were "absolutely false."

"This is an absolute lie! Even Ricky himself never accused Maria of such things in his video or his Internet rants about The Family," she said. "Not only did her son never accuse her of this, neither did any former member until just recently, eight months after Ricky's death, when this absurd story surfaced. Of course, given that Ricky is dead and never alleged that this happened, there is no evidence to support this story."

Karen Zerby's husband, Peter Amsterdam, said in another statement released by The Family that Ricky only turned against them after he left the fold and "started having a lot of contact with some very vindictive apostates."

> Ricky started coming out with accusations against us, complaints about his upbringing, and demands for money. As his contact with these apostates grew, so did his complaints. This is the cycle of apostasy, which is well documented in scholarly writings. Eventually he told us that he didn't want to be in contact with us at all, and to please stop writing him. Some time later, he came out with a physical threat in a post on a Web site, saying he wanted to find us and kill us.
>
> Some of Ricky's associates apparently were aware of the seriousness of Ricky's threats. They had heard him talk about his desire to kill his mother and they knew he had a penchant for knives. We can only assume that they tried, unsuccessfully, to convince him that this was wrong.

Others are now trying to make Ricky look like an innocent victim, and even a hero and role model, ignoring the fact that he murdered someone. He claimed that it was his deserved "revenge" because of alleged abuses. No matter what his motives might have been, and no matter how overcome by "darkness" he was at the time, that does not justify his killing someone. He was not the victim; *Angela* was the victim. She was a wonderful woman who suffered a cruel and violent death.

Sue Kauten's slaying and Ricky's suicide forced The Family to respond to reams of written evidence that David Berg saw nothing morally wrong with sexual activity between adults and minors. It forced them to respond to allegations by at least three women—including his granddaughter—that Berg had sexually molested them as children. While The Family statement does not address those specific allegations, it concedes:

> In the late '70s The Family's founder, David Berg, published some articles in regards to sex being a God-created natural activity, which could be engaged in without inhibition or sin. This opened the door for sexual experimentation between adults and adults, and minors with minors. However, unfortunately in some cases the lines blurred. In 1986, David Berg and [Zerby], realizing that stringent safeguards hadn't been put in place to protect minors, banned such conduct involving minors and put those safeguards in place. In 1988, David Berg renounced all literature, including his own, that indicated in any way that sexual activity with minors was permissible. All such literature was expunged from our communities. He clearly stated that any sexual activity between an adult and a minor was *not* to be tolerated. It was from that time forward that The Family made this grounds for immediate excommunication from our fellowship.

Another voice yet to be heard is that of Christina Teresa Zerby, also known as "Techi." Born March 19, 1979, Techi is the daughter of Karen Zerby and the late Michael Sweeney, a devotee known in the family as Timothy Concerned. Of the four children who got the closest look at "Life With Grandpa," including Ricky, Davida, and Merry Berg, Techi was the only one who has remained loyal to The Family. In 1987, the year before The Family says it instituted a firm policy against child molestation, The Family produced a comic book for children, entitled "Heaven's Children," in which David Berg fantasizes about having sex with Techi as a young teenage girl.

Techi herself gave birth to a son, Trevor, when she was just sixteen years old. Several former members close to the Unit said the child was fathered by an older Swiss devotee who has since left The Family. Techi herself vigorously denied that claim in an e-mail in January 2005: "I am married to my husband of nearly ten years, and my nine-year-old son is his," she wrote. "I am a grown woman living my own life. I think it's childish to even bring up things like this, which can serve no good purpose and only cause pain."[3]

Those making the allegation, including Don Irwin, say the issue is important because it shows that there was still sexual activity between adults and underage girls in the inner circle of The Family well into the nineties.

"Techi arrived in Vancouver, British Columbia [from Portugal] pregnant with a child," Don Irwin said. "The cult leadership lied to their membership saying that she got pregnant from a teenage boy in Vancouver. That was not what happened."

Irwin said he knows the real father of Trevor. On top of that, Irwin said that his own father, Ralph Keeler Irwin, legally changed his name to "Robert William Zerby" to make it easier for him to bring the pregnant Techi back to Canada.

"They encouraged the boys in that location [Vancouver] to have sex with her immediately upon her arrival. Trevor was born very quickly after and not a full nine months after her arrival."

Irwin also said Techi told him that she thought "there was nothing wrong" with "a fourteen-year-old having sex with adult men."

"Having the child made Techi dependent on the group," Irwin said. "She is not allowed to travel alone with the child. When she visits relatives, the child does not come with her. That is how they control her."

Techi declined to be interviewed for this book. But in the after-math of Sue's slaying and Ricky's suicide, she issued a prepared state-ment through The Family International. Watching the angry video her brother made before killing Sue Kauten and himself, Techi said, "made me physically sick to my stomach."

It was unbearable to hear the way he talked about my mother, and her husband, Peter—two of the most wonderful people on Earth, I think. Our mother! Our mother who loved us so deeply, who showed us that love at every possible opportunity, who did her best to make sure we had the best upbringing she could pro-vide for us. It's so horrible. And, I imagine, even more horrible for her to have to listen to it. So sad. Such unbelievable hatred, darkness and evil came out of his mouth.

We were close, and I know that when I knew him, he never ever felt any of the things he stated in his video. After Ricky left The Family, it's not like Mom stopped loving him, either, and she did all that she could to try to show him that. I don't under-stand why he refused to believe her. And for the record, I was never once in all my life in The Family abused.

Techi's statement, issued January 28, 2005, says Ricky "had no reason to think that either I or my son needed to be 'rescued.'

"In closing, I would like to say that I loved my brother. I love him now, and I forgive him, and I know that God loves him and for-gives him, and that I will see him again some day in a much better place."

Zerby, Amsterdam, and Techi were not the only current members of The Family to enter the media fray following Sue's slaying and Ricky's suicide. Borowik complained that early news reports only quoted a few alienated second-generation members who had left the movement and ignored the voices of the majority of second-generation adults who loved The Family and were still members.

Borowik pointed to a series of statements from second-generation members The Family compiled following the murder/suicide and put on the Web site www.myconclusion.com—another example of the ongoing Internet war over what happened to Ricky and his peers. Maria, twenty-five and a mother of one, wrote:

> It baffles me that some of you who are attacking us so vehemently do not get the point or have completely forgotten what the scriptures have to say about persecution, not to speak of the numerous times we've come out on top and that the Lord has delivered us from attacks such as these. But then again, when I think about it, you are helping to fulfill scripture....
>
> Those who think that you will weaken and frighten us and cause us to run are fools. We are not wimps! We will not take this lying down. No sir! You should know better than that. You think you can destroy us? Finish us off? Defeat us? Do you really think you'll win? You're gonna have hell to pay....
>
> Do yourselves a favor and let us live our lives, and go on and live yours. Really, move on! If you don't believe in what we're doing fine, don't. But it's useless to spend the rest of your lives trying to fight us and get us to believe the same as you do, because we never will....
>
> For the record, I've been living in [World Services] 6½ years, and I've had the privilege of meeting Mama, Peter and many other wonderful people whom you say are some of the so-called "evil abusers." Sorry, you are so wrong. May God help you for criticizing and accusing them of such terrible deeds!

Emmanuel Thomas, twenty-two, lives in a Brazil, and is a second-generation of The Family International. He wrote:

> I have lived in The Family my whole life, just about all of which has been in Brazil being a missionary. I'm married to the most wonderful woman in the world named Rafaela, and I have a son, Calvin who will be turning one very soon. I know beyond a shadow of a doubt that The Family International is where I want to live for the rest of my life. I would consider it an honor to live and work for Jesus in The Family for the rest of my life. This is where I want to bring up my son "in the nurture and ad-

monition of the Lord." I know that this is a safe place because it has been a safe place for me. I never suffered abuse or mistreatment of any kind! This is the best place Calvin could grow up in! I am sure of that.

Over the next year, more than 450 Family members would post their testimonies at www.myconclusion.com. They would paint a markedly different picture of what life was like growing up in The Family. Much of this is understandable. Those suffering the worst abuse were the older members of the second-generation—those born between 1972 and 1980. Even The Family's toughest critics will admit that minors living in the sect now are much less likely to experience sexual abuse than those in the late seventies and eighties. It also mattered where children grew up and under what level of leadership. Some Family colonies were loving homes—love in the best sense of the word. Others were ruled over by serial child predators.

Perhaps the main factor in the child abuse equation was simply this—how close one was to David Berg. Ricky was close. Davida was close. Merry Berg was close. One of Peter Amsterdam's sons, Jon-A, did not spend that much time around the Endtime Prophet, or even his own father. But he was Ricky's age and did spend time at the infamous Victor Camp in Macao. He wrote:

I knew both [Sue] and Ricky, and still cannot quite comprehend the needless death that took place. It's not every day someone you knew well was murdered, and rarer still, someone you knew who just four years earlier seemed like a normal individual, change to the point where he'd be willing to take the life of someone as sweet and harmless as [Sue]. I'm telling you, everyone reading this has done more harm to others through unloving acts than [Sue]. She was truly an angel.

I would say that my life was not that typical of a young person in The Family. Because of who my parents were, much was expected of me, and as a kid, naturally I resented that fact. I recognize now that it was to be expected. Any child with prominent parents, in any walk of life, has more expected of him than others....

I also went through my share of disciplinary type programs, such as the "Victor programs"—one in Japan and one in Peru. Both of those were typical of the types of programs used by The Family in some parts of the world in those days. In my opinion, these programs were no more harsh then their counterparts in secular society. There was silence restriction, extra labor and some corporal punishment—all to be expected from that type of system. These programs have not been used in The Family for many years—most likely for good reasons. However, considering that disciplinary boot-camp type programs are still actively used throughout the secular and Christian world today, I fail to see how one could be so up in arms about their previous use in The Family. . . .

The one program I was in that I would consider excessive by way of corporal punishment and hard labor, was the DT [detention teen] program in Macao during the late '80s. There were under ten young people admitted to that program, so its use was certainly not widespread, nor was this program duplicated elsewhere. I know for a fact that half of the participants are still in The Family, and the other half have left. Those who were negatively affected by this program, I personally feel sorry for. I don't think some of the things that went on were justified or necessary, and I consider it a failed experiment at best. It's something I feel was unfortunate, but I lived through it, and I've put it behind me. And most importantly, I forgave those who I feel wronged me. That's what I consider the bottom line here: it's about forgiveness! In life, you have to forgive people, just as you need to be forgiven.[4]

One problem with relying on e-mail postings and the Internet to tell "the other side" of Ricky's story was that one can't be certain who actually authored those statements and under what circumstances they were written. Shepherds could be telling rank-and-file members what to write. Nevertheless, it is important to hear those voices. What happens inside a religious cult often lies somewhere between the horror stories of apostates and the happy tales of current devotees.

In the weeks following the slaying of Sue Kauten and the suicide of Ricky Rodriguez, five second-generation members sat down for interviews at a Mexican restaurant in Old Town San Diego.[5]

Justin Paone, twenty-eight, was one of the five. He was born to Family missionaries in Venezuela and grew up in communal homes across South America. "My upbringing was different, but I'm very proud of my parents and my upbringing," Paone said. "I know a lot of these people who are bitter and are fighting against us now. A lot of times it's situations in their personal families. They get all worked up about it and generalize it over the whole Family. It makes us all suffer."

John Orcutt, twenty-six, was born in Italy, the third of nine children. Growing up, he lived in Argentina, India, Thailand, Puerto Rico, and the United States before going out on his own as a Family missionary in Hungary. He was not surprised by the post-Ricky wave of negative news coverage about his religious movement. "Persecution is part of our lives," he said. "You read news articles and meet people who don't like you, but in a way it motivates me more."

"They said Jesus hung out with whores," he added. "If they said those things about Jesus, they are definitely going to say those things about his followers."

Orcutt, Paone, and the others around the table worked for Activated Ministries in Escondido, which produces books, periodicals, and musical products sold by Family missionaries around the world. They were accompanied by Cassandra Mooney, fifty-two, one of the directors of Activated Ministries and a member of The Family for thirty-three years.

Mooney raised two daughters in the movement, both of whom now serve as missionaries in Mexico. "I love my girls and would never let anyone touch them," she said. "I was in The Family five and a half years until I had sex—and that was with my husband. We were prudish in a sense. I was a very wild hippie before I joined The Family, so that was a big change for me."

Mooney concedes that changed in the late seventies, when Berg directed his female followers to practice flirty fishing. Asked whether she ever engaged in flirty fishing (or FFing), Mooney replied, "Very little."

"When it first started happening, we were in Beirut, Lebanon, which was a difficult place to do it," Mooney said. "FFing was going out and meeting lonely people and witnessing to them. If it happened that we had an attraction or wanted to have sex, our religion did not forbid that. It wasn't prostitution. It was witnessing."

Several of the younger Family members around the table defended the sect's ongoing practice of sexual sharing among adult members, arguing that sex is just a small part of the equation and blown out of proportion by the news media and their critics.

"Why can't the law of love expand to all of your life? What's wrong with God and sex mixing?" asked Grace Galambos, who at age twenty was the youngest member at the interview session. "God created sex."

Paula Braaten, twenty-four, also defended the teachings.

"Do we live the Law of Love? Yes. The core of the Law of Love is to love the Lord thy God with all thy heart and to love your neighbor as yourself," she said. "If you want to have sex with other people, you can do whatever you want."

Just a couple weeks before Paula Braaten and her coworkers gathered in that Mexican restaurant, a larger group of second-generation Family folks—most of them apostates—joined together in San Diego for a memorial service for another one of the brethren who had killed himself.[6]

His name was Abe Braaten, and he was Paula Braaten's brother-in-law.

He died on December 14, 2004—three weeks before the deaths of Ricky and Sue—after falling from the roof of a building in Kobe, Japan. Abe was twenty-seven. Some of his family and friends, including one who saw him moments before the fall, say his death was another suicide of an abused child.

At the memorial, Daniel Roselle produced a list of twenty-five second-generation members of The Family who had allegedly committed suicide during the past ten years. "We're dropping like flies," said Roselle, repeating a line Ricky quoted in his video. "There is a lot of anger out there. I'm not worried about more violence against others. But I am worried about more suicides."

Ricky's profanity-laced video was still fresh in people's minds—as was his call to arms to the second generation.

"It's a war now between us and our parents," said John LaMattery, twenty-seven, who met Braaten in Japan when both boys were fourteen years old. He is also Jim LaMattery's nephew. "This is the cream of the crop coming back to get them."

Abe Braaten's Japanese-born mother, Yumiko "Phoenix" Taniguchi, is one of the top leaders in The Family International.

On the night of December 14, 2004, Braaten and a friend, Sam McNair, were kicking back in McNair's apartment in Kobe, Japan. Their wives were at Braaten's place with the kids, just a five-minute drive away.

Sam and Abe had knocked back a beer or two and were watching a movie on TV.

"All of a sudden," McNair said, "he was like 'Sam, um, I'm not feeling so good. My heart is pumping real fast.' And I felt his heart and, swear to God, I never felt anything like that before. It was beating super fast. It was that quick. At that point, I thought he was having a panic attack."[7]

Abe's mother, Phoenix Taniguchi, says it is not clear whether or not her son committed suicide. "Since no one was with him at the very moment when this happened, we were not sure exactly how it happened, whether he actually jumped or fell. We heard that shortly before he fell he'd drunk quite a bit, which seemed to affect him heavily," she wrote in a eulogy for her son.

The eulogy, entitled "Notice of my son Abe's Graduation" was originally posted on a members-only Family Web site. It ended with a purported message from Jesus, which read in part:

Abe is asking that his death be a testimony to those who will hear, that it's very dangerous to be foolish and light-hearted and take risks. He asks that this message be spread so that his death be not in vain. Abe did many things in his life that he regretted and he did many things that he didn't really plan to do but he just slipped. Well, this was the biggest slip yet and it cost him his life. It's such a sad thing that his earthly life had to be cut short, prematurely, because of the consequences of his actions, but please look on the other side of the tapestry and see the beauty and the wonders of eternal life that awaited Abe the minute his physical life was finished. He had a crown waiting for him and he had a reward waiting for him, for all the good things that he did in his life, all the times he was a testimony of My love and salvation, all the times he gave love sacrificially and tried to follow My ways.[8]

Other close relatives to Abe blame The Family for his death. Like many young people who grew up in The Family, Braaten had trouble adjusting to life in the real world.

"Yeah, he talked about suicide when he was living with us," said Braaten's sister, China Taniguchi. "This is the thing about Abe—every time it came close to his birthday, he would get supernegative. Just like, 'Oh my God, I'm already at this age, and I'm still doing nothing.... What am I going to do with my life?'"

China (pronounced Chee-na) said her brother—who left The Family in 2000—was seen as an especially rebellious teenager and was sent off to The Family's Victor Program for re-education. "I mean, I barely saw my brother because he was always shipped off to some other place to learn some lessons—to get 'victory' over some problem he had. It makes me so mad. I think that had a lot to do with the problems with self-esteem."[9]

On that December night in Kobe, Braaten was really flipping out, McNair recalled. He got tense. Then cold. McNair gave him a blanket, and Braaten curled up into it. "He started getting more and more negative, and then started saying, 'I gotta go. I gotta go.' He was getting incoherent and mumbling 'Moses ... David ... mind control.'

"I said, 'Abe. Don't be talking about that now. Let's do something else.' I turned on the lights and tried to make him comfortable. I didn't know what was going on. I was just doing my best not to freak out."

McNair blocked the door so that his panicking friend couldn't get out of his apartment, but Braaten jumped out the first-floor window and ran down the street. Minutes later, he climbed to the top of a four-story building a few blocks away and leapt to his death.

China Taniguchi said her brother's death, followed so closely by Rodriguez's suicide, was a wake-up call for the second generation.

"Ricky was the poster child for us kids," she said.

There were other tragedies on other continents—other suicides that fit the pattern.

Josh was eighteen years old when he left The Family. Three years later, he sat down at his brother's desk in Show Low, Arizona, and shot himself in the head. His brother, Chris, found the body. There was still color in Josh's cheeks and the smell of gunpowder in the air.

Josh left two handwritten notes, one addressed to his young sons and one to his siblings. "He did not leave a note for our parents, and I'm sure there was a reason for this," Chris wrote in a remembrance of his brother. "Sometimes I wonder what they think about at night.... But they have their God, and their religion to cling to—the same God and religious beliefs that they placed above their children."

Chris asked that his and his brother's last name not be used. But he told me that Josh—like Ricky—had a hard time adjusting to life outside The Family and that may have contributed to his death on January 26, 1999.

Adding to Josh's troubles, his brother said, was Josh's participation in the Victor Program. "Josh was part of a detention and retraining program involving sleep deprivation, food deprivation, manual labor, silence restriction, and isolation," Chris said.

Other family members cite different reasons for Josh's suicide. In an e-mail sent to Family spokeswoman Claire Borowik, Josh's father wrote, "As is normal when such a thing happens, there are countless questions of why. Why didn't we see it coming? What could we have done to prevent it? Who is to blame for it?"

Josh's father says his son was depressed following a fight with his wife, adding that Josh's history of drug use contributed to his troubles. "Josh was facing the pressures of parenthood, supporting his family, and a new move all at once," his father wrote. "It was a lot of pressure, and he started using drugs again at this time."

Second-generation members of The Family were not the only ones taking their own lives.

Rick Dupuy was seventeen when he joined The Family in Tucson in 1969. He left the sect in 1992 and died of an intentional drug overdose in Loa, Utah, on June 2, 1996. He was forty-four.

Dupuy was not born into the sect, and his name is not on a list of suicides provided by defectors. But in many ways, his story is the same.

"He had three severe suicide attempts," said Marina Sarran, a friend and lover who was fifteen years old when she joined The Family in Italy in 1977. "He felt like a freak. He couldn't think straight," she said of the period after he defected. "He'd say 'my life is over.' He was a lot like Ricky Rodriguez. He had fantasies about getting an AK–47 and taking out Karen Zerby and Peter Amsterdam."

In 1993, Dupuy emerged as a leading defector and source of information about abusive practices inside The Family. At the time, Dupuy revealed that many young cult members had been sent to the Victor Program. He called the retraining center an "oppressive and brutal system of thought reform" subjecting inmates to "mental, psychological, and even physical abuse."

Dupuy appeared on *Larry King Live* in 1993 to debate officials of the sect. At one point, the officials denied that there were policies and doctrines that encourage molestation of children. Asked by King how he knew there were such policies, Dupuy replied, "because I was ordered in the group to have sex with a ten-year-old by the leadership of the group."

"Did you?" King asked.

"Yes," Dupuy replied. "It was to get me in so deep that I would be afraid to ever come out and speak against the group."

Dupuy later testified before Justice Ward in the British child-custody case. He told the judge that he and another adult man had been asked by the child-care directors at a Family home in the Dominican Republic in November 1983 to allow two girls to masturbate them.

In his 1995 court decision, Lord Justice Alan Ward concluded that Dupuy had, in fact, been "asked to share with girls who were only ten and eleven years old. The little girl presented herself in a sarong with no panties. She masturbated him."

Ward identified the two girls as the daughters of two high-ranking leaders of The Family.

Sarran said Dupuy had been haunted for the last three years of his life by the abuse he committed, his confession on the Larry King show, and the years of his life wasted in The Family.

Before killing himself in 1996, Dupuy made the following entry on the last page of his journal: "What have I done with my life? Wasted it in the insanity of some maniacal bunch of pathological deviates.... Some things are worse than death, and my continued existence in this unspeakable state is one of them."

They say the truth will set you free, but Marina Sarran isn't so sure.

"Telling the truth," she said, "can destroy you."[10]

Borowik, The Family spokeswoman, questioned whether there are really that many suicides in the second generation. "We have examined the list posted of supposed suicides and have found several instances where the deaths were definitely not suicides, or were unconfirmed as police could not ascertain if the death was accidental or not."

In a written statement, Borowik said The Family was aware of only ten suicides among former members over the past thirteen years. She said that 32,000 people had been in The Family over the past thirty-five years and that its full-time membership in early 2005 stood at around 8,000. "We have even been accused of causing River Phoenix's death," Borowik said, "even though he had left The Family at five and been involved in a world of drugs."

Phoenix, a promising actor and perhaps the most famous person born into The Family, died in 1993 of a drug overdose. He was twenty-three.

One year earlier, Ben Farnsworth, a teenager who was raised in The Family and sent to one of the sect's re-education camps, jumped to his death from a building in Hong Kong. His suicide inspired Zerby to write a letter to Farnsworth's father. His death, The Family leader insisted, would be a wake-up call that would keep other second-generation members from committing suicide. "Even in his death, Ben is going to have a very good effect on The Family," Zerby wrote. "I think it's going to have wonderful repercussions with our teens being very greatly strengthened by this."

Conclusion

Family recruits pray at their Los Angeles mission in the late seventies.

NEARLY THIRTEEN YEARS after Karen Zerby wrote that letter to Ben Farnsworth's father, telling him how his son's suicide would only strengthen other teens in The Family, Zerby's own son wrote a letter about his own suicide. It was not addressed to Zerby. Ricky sent his suicide note to Mark and Denise Flynn, the Tucson couple who gave him a job and welcomed him into their lives. Ricky's handwritten letter thanked them for all they did for him in the last few months of his life. He apologized for never telling them who he really was and how hard he was struggling with his past. "My one regret," he wrote, "is deserting you or hurting you in any way.

"I come from an extremely abusive cult and have tried in the four years I've been out to figure out what 'normal' life is like, and how I can be a part of it.... I guess I haven't done that bad. But that's on the surface. Emotionally, it's gotten harder every day I've been out. I've become more and more angry at all the sick perverts who to this day are not the least bit sorry for the thousands of little kids that they have repeatedly raped, molested, and methodically tortured for many years. To me, these people are the worst of the worst, and unfortunately, my evil mother is the head of it!"

Ricky went on to tell the Flynns how he had been "hunting down some of the leadership for some time now in the hopes of getting ahold of my mother, because as with most cults, you cut off the head and the body dies. I have been trying to run from my past for years, but now it's time for me to take a stand against this evil."

In the end, Ricky could neither run from his past nor escape his destiny. He could never escape the twisted prophecies of David Berg and his own mother.

Six months after Ricky killed Sue Kauten and took his own life, Karen Zerby issued another letter to The Family about murder-suicide. It was entitled "Questions and Answers on Angela and Ricky's Death, Persecution, and Other Issues." It was published in the June 2005 edition of "Good News," The Family's internal newsletter sent out to trusted members. Zerby, writing as "Maria," took questions sent in from members and passed them on to Jesus. In other words, Zerby's answers were the Lord's answers.

"Regarding what Ricky did," one question began. "It really leaves me·wondering why he embraced the dark side so completely. Was there something dark in his past that made him go that far?"[1]

This may have been a real question from a real member of The Family, or it may have been a question Zerby and Amsterdam thought they had to address. Either way, it's a good question to ask a woman accused of having sex with her suicidal son.

Was there something dark in his past?

Jesus, speaking through Zerby, said there was not.

"No, there was nothing dark in his past that made him go as far as he did. It was not Ricky's early years or some hidden thing in his past that drove him to do what he did. It was his 'present' that drove him. It was his choice to hold onto his pride and rebellion and follow the dark, evil voices."

"Ricky had a great calling," Jesus/Zerby said. "He struggled with accepting it, not necessarily because he didn't want to accomplish the great things that were awaiting him, but because he didn't want to pay the price that came with the calling. He didn't mind the crown, but he *did* mind the '*cross*'—the sacrifice. Surrendering to My will, yielding, humbling yourself, and following My Word is not easy for any of you, but it is possible."

Karen Zerby declined to be interviewed for this book, as did Peter Amsterdam, Sara Kelley, Christina "Techi" Zerby, and several other key Family loyalists. They were firsthand witnesses to the childhood events described in this book by other firsthand witnesses, including Davida Kelley, Elixcia Munumel, Merry Berg, and her mother, Shula. No doubt, Zerby's memories and interpretation as to what happened to Ricky, Davida, and Merry would be very different.

When she declined my interview requests, Family spokeswoman Claire Borowik suggested I talk instead to Gary Shepherd, the sympathetic sociologist who interviewed the nineteen-year-old version of Ricky. Shepherd is the Oakland University scholar who authored the 1994 assessment with psychologist Lawrence Lilliston, the report that found Ricky suffered "no evidence of long-term negative effects" from child sexual abuse. Borowik sent me a partial transcript from an interview The Family had conducted with Shepherd a few months after the murder/suicide. Not surprisingly, the sociologist's interpretation of Ricky's actions are much like those expressed by Karen Zerby and Peter Amsterdam—that Ricky was fine until he came under the influence of angry and alienated defectors from the second generation.

"My guess is that Ricky, or Davidito, was very depressed," Shepherd said. "I think he did fall in with bad company who clearly influenced a lot of his ideas and feelings towards The Family. He seemed to have a strong sense of having been wronged growing up in The Family. He clearly stated that he was seeking revenge. That was his motive. He wanted revenge for what he had perceived as mistreatment growing up. Now I wasn't there when he was growing up. I have had conversations with many people who knew Davidito at various points in his life within The Family, some growing up right in World Services with him. And their accounts of him are that he was a sweet kid then, and he certainly never outwardly manifested to them the kind of hostility and the kind of anger that he was expressing as an adult."[2]

In my interview, I asked Shepherd if he still believed that Ricky was not sexually abused when he grew up in The Family. After all, we now have the accounts and pictures of adult-children sex play in *The Story of Davidito*. We have testimony from Merry Berg and Davida Kelley. We have Ricky's own account of what happened inside the Unit.

So I asked Shepherd:

"Was Ricky sexually abused? What explanation do you have for the events of January 2005?"

"Remember that there is very little that I concretely know about his experience, but I don't believe that he was the target of any abuse," Shepherd replied. "During his time growing up in The Family, I don't think he sensed that anything was going wrong. My guess is that he began to reassess his experience later—to reinterpret what was going on after the fact. But at the time he didn't have a sense he was living in some depraved environment. There's an assumption that merely being exposed to things has this corrosive effect. But if sexual activity is seen as normal and enjoyable then that doesn't have an independent effect to create emotional disturbance. You *reinterpret* that experience, and then you become upset. Now you are defining that experience with another set of norms."

That may be so, I replied. But doesn't *our* society consider sexual activity between adults and children outside *our* set of norms?

"There are societies all over the world where girls are married and have sex at twelve," Shepherd replied. "There are states where girls can marry at fourteen with parental consent. If a child's experience of sex is that it is brutal or demeaning, it will have immediate negative effects. But sex in and of itself does not produce psychological harm to young people. There are young people in The Family today who had those experiences who did not leave The Family and who are still committed and devoted. They may have the same experience, but they have a completely different interpretation of that experience."

Of course, Ricky was not a typical young person growing up in The Family. Some of his childhood abuse *was* sexual, but it may just be that the greater burden placed on him was *prophetic abuse*. Many parents have high expectations for their children, but David Berg and Karen Zerby asked Ricky—playing the role of Davidito—to save the world and die doing it.

Among the second generation, *that* was a cross only Ricky had to bear. What made Ricky's experience different—though not unique—was his intimate knowledge of the real David Berg. That knowledge was shared with Berg's daughter, Deborah, his granddaughter, Merry, and the Endtime Prophet's sexual playmate, Davida. They grew up with the wretchedly flawed man behind the Endtime Prophet myth. Most members of The Family never saw David Berg. Until recent years, they never even saw a picture of him. They saw his teachings, but they never saw him.

It's not hard to understand what drew disciples into The Family in the late sixties and seventies. It was an era of political rebellion, sexual liberation, and evangelical revival. Berg's radical critique of the church's traditional view of sexuality and the human body was the right message at the right time delivered to the right audience. It was also a time of seeking. Many of those who joined The Family were people in need. They were vulnerable. They were at crossroads in their lives. They were looking for alternatives—for a purpose. They wanted to believe in something with all their hearts. Berg offered certainty. He and his shepherds made them feel loved. They felt special.

David Berg was a deeply flawed human being, as were many of those close to his throne. Berg picked true believers and hung onto those who showed unquestioning loyalty. That boosted their egos—at least for a time. Berg would raise leaders up, then knock them down. He would promise them everything and leave them nothing. He was a believer in his own myth *and* a master manipulator of those around him. "Like many gurus, Berg found something very bewitching about developing absolute control over people" said David Millikan, the Australian minister and authority on new religious movements. "But this weird thing happens with leaders and followers. You convince someone to crawl across the floor and kiss your feet, but before long you begin to despise that person."

Berg's law of love was not his own creation, nor were the words he would chant while he walked around naked at his sexual sharing parties. *To the pure, all things are pure.* That line does not carry a Berg copyright. He borrowed it from the Apostle Paul, but Berg didn't finish the quote. "To the pure, all things are pure," Paul says, "but to the corrupt and unbelieving, nothing is pure. Their very minds and consciences are corrupted. They profess to know God, but they deny him by their actions. They are detestable, disobedient, unfit for any good work."[3]

To the pure, all things may indeed be pure, but David Berg was not pure. What corrupted Berg and those around him was not his *theology* of sexual liberation. What destroyed the people in the inner circle were the prophet's own sexual demons. "There is great irony in Berg's story," Millikan said. "When he was working for Fred Jordan in the fifties, going around the country buying airtime on radio stations, he would spend a lot of time with hookers. Later on, he talks about going to strip clubs and masturbating under the table. After the late sixties, he had trouble getting it up. He actually had this visceral distaste for female sexuality. After sex he would get out of bed and compulsively wash himself five times. This is not the behavior of a liberated sexual being."[4]

Millikan is one of several scholars The Family considers sympathetic to their cause. Another authority—one The Family places in the hostile camp—is Stephen Kent, a sociologist at the University of Alberta in Edmonton, Canada. Kent has done extensive interviews with abused and alienated young people from the second generation. Over the years, Millikan has been given unique access to top Family leaders. These two experts have very different perspectives on The Family, but they agree that Berg's overbearing mother and childhood sexual trauma are key to understanding the rise and fall of the Endtime Prophet.

Berg's rise began with the death of his mother—the same woman who threatened to castrate him as a child and called him to Huntington Beach at age fifty to save the hippies. "When he reached his fifties he suddenly found himself leading hundreds, then thousands, of hippies whose ideas of sex were very different from the ones with which he had been reared," Kent writes. "Berg would 'work out' his childhood sexual traumas through the deviant policies and practices that he initiated in the name of God."[5]

David Berg has been dead well over a decade, but his sexual obsessions and twisted prophecy still haunt the lives of those who grew up in his shadow. Ricky's suicide and Sue Kauten's slaying are fading memories, footnotes in the story of a band of Jesus freaks that went dangerously awry. Even before the events of January 2005, The Family was a religious movement facing a steady decline in membership. Since the death of its founder, it has been a cult looking for a reason to exist. It claimed 8,000 full-time members in January 2005 and conveniently changed the way it calculates its membership in the months following the murder/suicide. But even if The Family never recruited another convert or made another baby, there are still thousands of people living in the shadow of David Berg. According to their own statistics, more than 13,000 babies were born into The Family between 1971 and 2001. Of course, when they were born and where they were raised determine the darkness of that shadow.

The Family was a machine built to spread the message of David Berg. But this enterprise was not just about the reproduction of religious tracts. It was the reproduction of *human beings* to embody and spread the word. It's not hard to find women in The Family with six, eight, ten, thirteen children. What did they call babies produced from "flirty fishing"? What did they call them when the biological fathers would disappear? They called them "Jesus babies." David Berg was the fisherman. His sacred whores were the bait. The babies were the harvest.

Central to David Berg's arrogance was his willingness to use people as means to an end. This was especially true for his own children and grandchildren. Berg sexually abused two generations of his own progeny, but that was not the worst of it. He used them—he engineered them—to fulfill his own self-serving prophecy.

It happened to Ricky. It also happened to Merry Berg.

In the summer of 2005, Merry was locked up at the Las Colinas Detention Facility in Santee, a town east of San Diego, where she was being held on charges of driving while intoxicated. According to her brother and her mother, Merry was addicted to speed and working as a prostitute in southern California.

It had been eighteen years since Berg terrorized his granddaughter during those exorcism sessions in the Philippines. If she tried to leave The Family, Berg warned her then, "the only way you could make it is to be a whore!

"You wouldn't even be a FFer. You wouldn't even be doing it for God. You'd just be doing it for a living. You'd probably end up on drugs—a drug demon possessed, alcoholic, diseased whore and soon dead! Now is that what you want!"

"No sir!" Merry replied.[6]

In a letter from jail, and in a series of phone conversations after her release, Merry told me she was trying to forget her childhood in The Family. Merry wanted to live in the moment, not dwell on the past. "I am so not in the mood to discuss that shit," she said in her letter. "I'm much more interested in life in the present and making the most of it and new experiences, despite the down times. I love real life in America, especially nonreligious, open minded life in San Diego, CA. I have a kick-ass life now."

Later, on the phone after her release from jail, Merry delivered a series of speedy, stream-of-consciousness monologues about how she had lost her wallet or lost her cell phone or was worried that her relationship with her boyfriend might be over. One night she called me at 1 A.M. to see if I would drive from San Francisco to San Diego (a ten-hour drive) that morning·and take her to the jail where her boyfriend was incarcerated. Another night she called to hold the phone up to some stereo speakers to play songs that would explain her feelings. One song was "American Life" by Madonna: "I tried to be a mess, I tried to be the best, I guess I did it wrong, That's why I wrote this song."

Over the course of two or three hours on the phone with Merry, the subject of David Berg only came up once. "Grandpa," she said. "I used to idolize him, but I'd kill him now too. Taking out his ridiculous style on everybody. That poor kid [Ricky] never had a chance. He was supposed to be this and that and ended up nothing."

As for her memories of being sexually involved with Ricky in the Philippines, Merry said, "He was too young. We were having some good sex, and then they told me that he was old enough to get me pregnant. And that was it for me."

Then there's Davida. She left The Family in 1996, when she was twenty years old and working as a missionary in Russia. That was also where she reunited with Ricky for the first time in nearly ten years. They hadn't seen each other since back in the Philippines.

"We both got very disillusioned in Russia," Davida told me. "This was the first time Ricky was really in the field. In Russia, the circumstances were so extreme. We were in this home in the middle of winter. It was ten below zero, and we had to hoof it to raise support. I was nineteen and he was twenty. We were in Odessa, the most godforsaken, crime-ridden city. It was Sodom and frickin' Gomorrah—the most evil spot in all of Russia where all the gangsters and crime lords and drug lords hang out. We are stuck in this home with six young people, including a pregnant woman.

"We are supposed to be giving out humanitarian aid to orphanages and hospitals, but we are so broke we are eating boiled beets and hard bread and potatoes for weeks at a time. For a while there was no electricity and the apartment was freezing cold. We'd try to raise support, but in Russia there is no middle class. There are the crime lords and the poor."

It was the first time Ricky really got a sense of what it was like to be a rank-and-file member of The Family, working countless hours to raise money—and then sending ten percent of it back to "World Services" to support Berg, Zerby, and their staff.

"We had lived in luxury and seclusion in the Unit, but we were living off these people and their tithes. These people in The Family are on the streets ten hours a day begging and singing and are barely getting by."

They were both fed up with Russia, but Ricky had the option of moving back to the comfort and safety of the Unit, which at the time was located at a beachfront mansion on the coast of Portugal. Davida didn't have that choice, but she was young, attractive, and knew how to sexually please members of the opposite sex. "I met some rich guy who was very cool in Russia. I had somebody to look out for me. Rick had nowhere to go. He couldn't just live on the streets there."

Davida stayed a few months in Russia, then headed to London to stay with another second-generation defector. Her new roommate was working in gentlemen's clubs in London. She taught Davida how to strip. When her British visa expired, Davida took her new trade to the Big Apple. She arrived with $2,000. She got a room at the YMCA, went for an audition, and was hired on the spot. Perhaps it was Davida's "destiny." She had been an erotic dancer since she was born.

When we last spoke, Davida told me she'd had it with the exotic dance business. She wanted to do something else with her life. "I'm trying to go to school," she said. "I'd love to go and study culinary arts. But I can't afford to take time off to go to school. I got to pay my rent. It's like I'm stuck in a vicious cycle. Imagine being molested your whole life by adults—taught that you have to be submissive to every adult man. That is your only experience with adult men. Then ending up on the streets in Russia. I wake up in the morning and ask myself, 'What am I doing?' I have no life. I can't find the happy ending."

This has been a dark story. There are no heroes or heroines. I've struggled to find someone who rose above it all and found justice and redemption. Then I got a phone call from a woman who grew up in The Family. She is not in the book. She never knew Ricky Rodriguez or David Berg, but she suffered horrible sexual abuse as a young girl and teenager. I hadn't heard from her in many months. For a while, I had thought she could be my example of someone who overcame the horrors of the past and found redemption. She had nothing when she left The Family and returned to the United States. She wound up with an advanced degree and a satisfying, well-paying job. We never had a formal interview, but I talked to her enough to realize she was still an emotionally damaged woman. Then late one night, out of the blue, she called me as I was working on this conclusion.

At first, I wasn't sure why she called. She sounded very depressed—and perhaps drunk. We talked for about twenty minutes. Ricky was right, she said. There is no justice. Right before she hung up, she told me she was going to die soon. I asked her what she meant. She told me she was thinking about killing herself. Then she hung up.

This is not an unusual event in the circle of Family survivors, but it was a bit unsettling for me. I called a few people who knew the woman much better than I did and told them to give her a call. One of them was Don Irwin, the brother of Merry Berg, another second-generation source with whom I had not spoken to for many months.

Researching a book like this involves the collection of thousands of pieces of paper and bits of information. After getting off the phone with Don Irwin, and being assured that someone would check up on the woman who called me that night, I remembered that I had saved a text of the eulogy Don Irwin gave at a memorial service held for Ricky in San Diego.

"Many of us grew up hearing constant lip service to love," Irwin said to the congregation of second-generation survivors. "We all learn to love in different ways.... Allow me to tell you how all of *you* have taught me about love.... When there were young people who you did not even know, but you knew of their pain because some of it was your own, *you* showed love. You provided a place for them to meet and know that they were not alone."[7]

Around the time Ricky was born, Berg began calling his flock The Family of Love. Irwin's eulogy reminded me that none of us ever really leave our families, including the second generation of this Family. All we can do is find new ways to be a family. In a story as dark as this one, we have to take our hope and find our redemption wherever we can. Someone who grew up in The Family reached out that night and comforted the suicidal woman who called me. She got some help. She survived. In the end, there was still a little love and still a little family in The Family of Love.

Acknowledgments

MANY OF THE CHARACTERS in this story initially did not want to be interviewed. Some of them had something to hide, but most were simply people who did not want to resurrect the pain that comes with reliving their past. Others thought they should be paid for their stories. They felt like they had already been exploited in life. Why should they allow someone writing a book or making a movie to use them again? Their families and their church had raised them as spiritual commodities. Why should they put themselves through *that* again?

No one in this book was paid to tell their story, but there are people in all of the above categories who—in the end—agreed to be interviewed, as well as people who chose not to talk to me. I respect the decisions of those who declined to cooperate, and I thank all of those who made a leap of faith and chose to trust me with their stories. High on the latter list are Shula Berg, Don Irwin, Davida Kelley, Rosemary Kanspedos, Elixcia Munumel, and Tiago Rugely.

Most of the current leaders in The Family International declined to be interviewed, but I would like to thank Family spokeswoman Claire Borowik for obtaining the organization's permission to publish many of the photographs in the book. Many of the source documents used to tell the story were unearthed by the diligent work of the people behind the screen at the Web sites www.exfamily.org, www.xfamily.org, and www.movingon.org.

I also thank my editor at HarperOne, Eric Brandt, for his light touch and deep insight; his colleague, Kris Ashley, who does her job with patience and grace; copyeditor Laurie Dunne; and Deputy Publisher Mark Tauber, whose friendship and longtime support of my work is greatly appreciated. I also thank my former editors and colleagues at the *San Francisco Chronicle,* who saw the potential in this story from the very beginning and gave me the time and space to tell it while it was still news.

Special thanks to Steve Proctor, George Csicsery, Richard Brzustowicz, Ginny McPartland, Cheryl Daniels Shohan, and to my literary agent, Amy Rennert, all of whom read early drafts of the manuscript and made helpful suggestions.

Final thanks go to my wife, Laura Thomas, who tempers the critical eye of a journalist with the loving support of a life partner.

Author's Note on the "Mo Letters"

DAVID "MOSES" BERG released hundreds of missives known as "Mo Letters" between 1969 and his death in 1994. Many of them were based on edited audiotapes of lectures and conversations with his leading disciples. Berg continued to issue communiqués from the grave via Family members who purported to receive posthumous revelations from the Endtime Prophet. Some of the Mo Letters were secret, private communiqués only meant to be seen by top leaders in The Family. Others were intended for distribution to the general public. They were published and reprinted both individually and in various formats and collections over the years.

Family leaders later attempted to destroy all copies of certain controversial letters or expunge objectionable material from them. Early letters were not numbered, and the numbering system in later years was not always consistent.

My research was based on original Mo Letters saved by early devotees, reprints issued by The Family, and a bound collection of original letters found in the rare books collection of the Graduate Theological Union library in Berkeley, California. (The volume containing the most controversial letters had been stolen from the library.)

In recent years, many Mo Letters have been posted on various Web sites run by The Family (www.thefamily.org/ourfounder/ourfounder.htm) and critics of The Family (www.xfamily.org/index.php/Mo_Letters). Whenever possible, I attempted to check the text against the earliest available version of the letter.

Notes

INTRODUCTION
1. David Brandt Berg, 22 December 1973, Mo Letter #286.
2. Berg, 20 May 1980, Mo Letter #999.
3. Berg, Mo Letter #999.
4. Berg, 27 March 1973, Mo Letter #258.
5. Jonathan Kirsch, *A History of the End of the World* (2006), 245.
6. Spencer Klaw, *Without Sin* (1993), 11, 16, 58.
7. Berg, December 1982, Mo Letter #1357.
8. Jon Krakauer, *Under the Banner of Heaven* (2003), xxiii.
9. Todd Compton, *In Sacred Loneliness* (1997), 11.
10. Richard and Joan Ostling, *Mormon America* (1999), 14–18.
11. Don Lattin, *Following Our Bliss* (2003).
12. Don Lattin, "Children of a Lesser God," *San Francisco Chronicle*, February 11–14, 2001, A1.

CHAPTER 1: REVENGE OF THE SAVIOR
1. *Boondock Saints*, directed by Troy Duffy (Indican, 1999).
2. Ricky Rodriguez, videotape, 7 January 2005, Tucson, Arizona.

CHAPTER 2: MAMA BERG
1. David Berg, 12 January 1982, Mo Letter #1350.
2. Virginia Brandt Berg, "From Deathbed to Pulpit," in Deborah Davis with Bill Davis, *The Children of God* (1984).
3. Virginia Brandt Berg, Letter to Clara Duncan (Spring 1919; reprint 1980, Mo Letter #884).
4. "Stuns Woman Preacher: Missile Thrown Through Window in Miami, Hits Mrs. Berg," *New York Times*, July 25, 1926.
5. Berg, 28 June 1977, Mo Letter #779.
6. Berg, Mo Letter #779.
7. Berg, 6 December 1980, Mo Letter #958.
8. Berg, 6 November 1982, Mo Letter #1535.
9. Berg, Diary (1941; reprint *Good News!* and Mo Letter #1716).
10. Reverend Charlie Dale, interview by the author, 2005.
11. Berg, Christmas 1948, Fundraising letter.
12. Betty Findley, interview by the author, 2005.
13. Berg, Fundraising letter.
14. Deborah Davis with Bill Davis, *The Children of God* (1984), 24.
15. Davis and Davis, *Children of God*, 28.
16. Davis and Davis, *Children of God*, 29.

17. Lord Justice Alan Ward, "The Judgement of Lord Justice Ward on the 26th May 1995" (October 1995), 33.
18. Davis and Davis, *Children of God*, 24.

CHAPTER 3: JESUS FREAKS
1. Kent Philpott, interview by the author, 2006.
2. Ronald M. Enroth, Edward E. Ericson Jr, and C. Breckinridge Peters, *The Story of the Jesus People* (1972), 103.
3. Chuck Smith, "History of Calvary Chapel," *Last Times* (Fall 1981).
4. Smith, "History of Calvary Chapel."
5. David Berg officiated at the marriage of his daughter, Faithy, to Arnold "Joshua" Dietrich in Orlando, Florida on February 28, 1967. Later that year, on November 26, Berg performed a double marriage ceremony at the Texas Soul Clinic ranch joining his son, Aaron, to Sara, the fifteen-year-old daughter of Mary Glassford, an early Berg supporter. In that same service, Art "Caleb" Dietrich was betrothed to Claudia, one of the first members of the Teens for Christ. By then, Deborah Berg was already married to John "Jethro" Treadwell.
6. David Hoyt, interview by the author, 2005.

CHAPTER 4: GOSPEL OF REBELLION
1. Christian and Missionary Alliance, *Alliance Witness* (April 14, 1968), 18.
2. Berg, "Hear the Teens for Christ," Handbill, 1967.
3. Berg, 8 March, 1970, Mo Letter "E."
4. Pamela Powell, "Hippies 'See the Light.' Huntington Ceremony 'As Good as Marriage,'" *Daily Pilot* (1968).
5. Thomas Edwards, "Hippies Suffer Sermon for Feed-In," *Huntington Beach Haven*, (1968).
6. Berg, 29 December 1979, Mo Letter #897.
7. Shula Berg, interview by the author, 2006.
8. Berg, 4 January 1978, Mo Letter #1358.
9. Berg, Mo Letter "E."
10. Berg, Mo Letter #1358.
11. Rosemary Kanspedos, interview by the author, 2006.
12. Berg, Mo Letter #1358.
13. Berg, Mo Letter #1358.
14. Kanspedos, interview.
15. Berg, Mo Letter #1358.
16. Berg, Mo Letter #1358.
17. Berg, August 1969, Mo Letter #89.
18. Berg, 11 April 1975, Mo Letter #381.
19. Anonymous, interview by the author, 2005.
20. David Hoyt, interview by the author, 2006.
21. Philpott, interview.
22. Virginia Brandt Berg, "A Sample, Not a Sermon" (reprinted in Letters from a Shepherd, 1972), 1.
23. Ted Patrick, *Let Our Children Go!* (1976).
24. Berg, 1 November 1971, Mo Letter #125.

CHAPTER 5: FAMILY CIRCUS

1. Shula Berg, interview.
2. Shula Berg, interview.
3. Hosea Berg, "The Pioneering of North America," Book of Remembrance (1983).
4. Herbert J. Wallenstein, *Final Report on the Activities of the Children of God* (1974).
5. Thomas Moore, "Where Have All the Children of God Gone?" *New Times*, October 4, 1974.
6. Moore, "Where Have All the Children of God Gone?"
7. Shula Berg, interview.
8. For much of his life, the Endtime Prophet was known as Mo (short for "Moses") Berg. Later in the seventies, his letters were used as an initial recruitment tactic, but only some of them were made available to the general public. Others—including some of the most shocking letters—were marked "D.O.," meaning they were to be seen by trusted "disciples only." Eventually, The Family would publish and distribute more than 3,000 Mo Letters.
9. Jim LaMattery, *Stealing God* (unpublished novel).
10. Shula Berg, interview.
11. Berg, May 1973, Mo Letter #234.

CHAPTER 6: MY LITTLE FISH

1. Sara Davidito, *The Story of Davidito* (1982), 25.
2. Rev. 11:3–13.
3. Davidito, *The Story of Davidito*, 47.
4. Davidito, *The Story of Davidito*, 33.
5. Berg, 5 June 1978, Mo Letter #699.
6. Anonymous, interview by the author, 2005.
7. Lattin, "Children of a Lesser God."
8. Davidito, *The Story of Davidito*, 57.
9. Davidito, *The Story of Davidito*, 38.
10. Davidito, *The Story of Davidito*, 108.
11. Davidito, *The Story of Davidito*, 138.
12. Davidito, *The Story of Davidito*, 335.
13. Davidito, *The Story of Davidito*, 200.
14. Davidito, *The Story of Davidito*, 302.
15. Berg, 27 March 1973, Mo Letter #258.
16. Berg, Mo Letter #258.
17. Bernd Doerler, "*Sie betteln und beten für einen Mann den sie nicht kennen,*" *Stern* no. 287 (July 1977), 14–21.
18. Doerler, "*Sie betteln und beten für einen Mann den sie nicht kennen,*" 14–21.
19. Davidito, *The Story of Davidito*, 393.
20. Davidito, *The Story of Davidito*, 411.
21. Davidito, *The Story of Davidito*, 426.
22. Davidito, *The Story of Davidito*, 426.
23. Anonymous, interview by the author, 2006.
24. Anonymous, interview, 2006.
25. Davida Kelley, interview by the author, 2005.

26. Davidito, *The Story of Davidito,* 709.
27. Davida Kelley, interview.

CHAPTER 7: TEEN TERROR
1. Daniel 5:25.
2. Sweeney was known in The Family as "Timothy Concerned." He died of cancer in the early nineties.
3. Joseph Hopkins, "Children of God Cult Records Higher Numbers," *Christianity Today* (November 26, 1982).
4. Ricky Rodriguez, 4 June 2002, "Life with Grandpa—the Mene Story."
5. Ward, "The Judgement of Lord Justice Ward" (October 1995), 48.
6. Don Irwin, interview by the author, 2005.
7. Berg, March 1987, Mo Letter #2306.
8. Ward, "The Judgement of Lord Justice Ward," 51.
9. Ward, "The Judgement of Lord Justice Ward," 66.
10. Ward, "The Judgement of Lord Justice Ward," 67.
11. Ward, "The Judgement of Lord Justice Ward," 68.
12. Karen Zerby, "False Accusers in the Last Days!" 1992.
13. James Penn, "No Regrets, Why I Left The Family—February 2000."
14. Davida Kelley, interview.
15. Davida Kelley, interview.
16. Davida Kelley, interview.
17. Daniel Roselle, interview by the author, 2005.
18. Roselle, interview.
19. Celeste Jones, interview by the author, 2005.
20. Berg, 1988, Mo Letter #2525.
21. Irwin, interview.
22. Rodriguez, "Life with Grandpa—the Mene Story."

CHAPTER 8: JOY
1. Angela Smith, Memorial Web Site, 2005.
2. John Kauten, interview by author, 2005.
3. Anneke Schieberl, interview by author, 2006.
4. Berg, 18 November 1978, Mo Letter #1673.
5. Berg, Mo Letter #1673.
6. Berg, 30 October 1981, Mo Letter #1841.
7. Anonymous, interview by the author, 2005.
8. Berg, 3 February 1977, Mo Letter #619.
9. Berg, Mo Letter #1673.
10. Davidito, *The Story of Davidito,* 681.
11. Rodriguez, "Life with Grandpa—the Mene Story."
12. Kauten, interview.

CHAPTER 9: EXPERT WITNESS
1. David Millikan, interview by the author, 2006.
2. James R. Lewis and J. Gordon Melton, *Sex, Slander, and Salvation* (1994), 246–47.
3. Ed Priebe, "My Apology and Accounting," 4 April 2004.
4. Gary Shepherd, interview by the author, 2006.

5. Lewis and Melton, *Sex, Slander, and Salvation* (1994), 50.
6. Carol Buening, "Critical Commentary on 'Psychological Assessment of Children in The Family'" (December 2003).
7. Melton, interview by the author, 2005.
8. Lewis and Melton, *Sex, Slander, and Salvation*, 4.
9. Lewis and Melton, *Sex, Slander, and Salvation*, 25.
10. Ward, "The Judgement of Lord Justice Ward," 118, 122.
11. Peter Amsterdam, *Good News!* #653 (October 1995).
12. Amsterdam, *Good News!* #653.
13. Amsterdam, *Good News!* #653.
14. The Family, "Our Founder: David Brandt Berg," http://www.thefamily.org/about/davidberg.php.

CHAPTER 10: ELIXCIA
1. Elixcia Munumel, interview by the author, 2005.
2. Michael "Tiago" Rugely, interview by the author, 2005.

CHAPTER 11: LOVING JESUS
1. Amsterdam, *Good News!* #653.
2. Karen Zerby, June 2005, *Good News!* #1137.
3. Penn, "No Regrets," 18.
4. Zerby, *Good News!* #1137.
5. Karen Zerby, 5 July 1995, Maria Letters #306 and #307.
6. Millikan, interview.

CHAPTER 12: MOVING ON
1. Jonathan Thompson, interview by the author, 2005.
2. Don Lattin, "IRS Documents Show Ties Between Charity, Sex Cult," *San Francisco Chronicle*, February 6, 2005.
3. Lattin, "IRS Documents Show Ties Between Charity, Sex Cult."
4. Lattin, "IRS Documents Show Ties Between Charity, Sex Cult."
5. Millikan, interview.
6. Karen Martin, Juvenile Dependency Petition, San Diego County Superior Court, March 5, 1998.
7. Jim LaMattery, interview by the author, 2005.
8. Don Lattin, "Mixed Memories of 'The Family,'" *San Francisco Chronicle*, February 27, 2005, A1.
9. Lattin, "Mixed Memories of 'The Family.'"
10. Karen Martin, Juvenile Dependency Petition, 5 March 1998.
11. Celeste Jones, interview by the author, 2006.
12. Rodriguez, 14 August 2004, "Still Around."
13. Rodriguez, 29 May 2000, Letter to Karen Zerby and Peter Amsterdam.
14. Rodriguez, 26 November 2000, Letter to Gabe Martin.
15. Rodriguez, 22 December 2000, Letter to James Penn.
16. Rodriguez, 16 January 2002, Letter to Mom and Peter.
17. Rodriguez, Letter to Mom and Peter.
18. Rodriguez, 25 May 2002, "Gospel of Rebellion."
19. Rodriguez, "Life with Grandpa—the Mene Story."
20. Anonymous, interview by the author, 2005.

21. Irwin, interview.
22. Sara Martin, interview by the author, 2005.
23. Rodriguez, May 2002, "E-mail to Johnny."
24. Martin, interview.
25. Jennifer Schroeder, interview by the author, 2005.
26. Rodriguez, "Life with Grandpa—the Mene Story."
27. Rodriguez, "Still Around."
28. Anneke Schieberl, interview by the author, 2006.
29. Roselle, interview.

CHAPTER 13: INTO THE DESERT
1. Rosemary Kanspedos, interview by the author, 2005.
2. Denise Flynn, interview by the author, 2005.

CHAPTER 14: LAST DATE
1. Alisia Arvizu, interview by the author, 2005.

CHAPTER 15: LOST
1. Rugely, interview.
2. Sarafina Martin, 15 January 2005, "Ricky's Last Days."

CHAPTER 16: "COME DIE WITH ME"
1. Don Lattin, "Rage Turns to Vengeance Against 'Family,'" *San Francisco Chronicle*, January, 15, 2005, A1.
2. Nick Godwin and Sorrel May, "Cult Killer," British television documentary, August 2006.

CHAPTER 17: END OF THE ROAD
1. Jeff Wade, interview by the author, 2005.
2. Munumel, interview.
3. Rugely, interview.

CHAPTER 18: RICKY.COM
1. Steve Zeitchik, "Slamdance Screening Ends in Melee: Fracas Follows Cult Film 'Children of God,'" *Variety* (January 24, 2007).
2. Noah Thomson, interview by the author, 2005.
3. Christina "Techi" Sweeney, e-mail correspondence to the author, 2005.
4. Jon A., "Peter Amsterdam's Son Speaks Out," myconclusion.com, January 28, 2005.
5. Lattin, "Mixed Memories of 'The Family," A1.
6. Don Lattin, "Deaths in The Family," *San Francisco Chronicle*, January 27, 2005, A1.
7. Lattin, "Deaths in The Family," A1.
8. Yumiko Taniguchi, "Notice of My Son Abe's Graduation," 2006.
9. Lattin, "Deaths in The Family," A1.
10. Lattin, "Deaths in The Family," A1.

CONCLUSION

1. Zerby, June 2005, *Good News!* #1137.
2. Gary Shepherd, interview transcript from The Family, 2005.
3. Titus 1:15
4. Millikan, interview.
5. Stephen A. Kent, "Lustful Prophet: A Psychosexual Historical Study of the Children of God's Leader, David Berg," *Cultic Studies Journal* 11, no. 2 (1994; reprint 2000): 135–188.
6. Berg, March 1987, Mo Letter #2306.
7. Don Irwin, 26 March, 2005, Eulogy for Ricky Rodriguez.

Bibliography

Amsterdam, Peter. *Good News!* #653. Zurich: The Family, October 1995.

Bainbridge, William Sims. *The Endtime Family: Children of God.* Albany: State Univ. of New York Press, 2002.

Berg, David Brandt. Diary. 1941. Reprinted as "The War Year? A Turning Point!" Mo Letter #1716. The Family, 1998.

———. "Joyous New Year's Greeting to You in His Name!" Fundraising letter. Christmas 1948.

———. "Hear the Teens for Christ." Handbill. 1967.

———. "Prophecy at Laurentide." Mo Letter #89. The Children of God, August 1969.

———. "The Old Church and the New Church—A Prophecy of God-Mo." The Children of God, 16 August 1969.

———. "Who Are the Rebels?" Mo Letter "E," 8 March 1970.

———. "Persecution." Mo Letter #125, 1 November 1971.

———. "Revolutionary Sex." Mo Letter #258, 27 March 1973.

———. "Aaron on the Mountain." Mo Letter #234, May 1973.

———. "Come On Ma! Burn Your Bra!" Mo Letter #286, 22 December 1973.

———. "The Last American Nightmare." Mo Letter #381, 11 April 1975.

———. "My Childhood Sex! Doin' What Comes Naturally." Mo Letter #779, 28 June 1977.

———. "Prophecy for Davidito. Two Years Old." Mo Letter #619, 3 February 1977.

———. "Our Love Story!" Mo Letter #1358, 4 January 1978.

———. "The End-Time Witnesses!" Mo Letter #707, 2 May 1978.

———. "You Are the Love of God." Mo Letter #699, 5 June 1978.

———. "Bigger Jobs! Dad Talks to His Staff." Mo Letter #1673, 18 November 1978.

———. "Millions of Miles of Miracles." Mo Letter #897, 29 December 1979.

———. "The Devil Hates Sex!—But God Loves It!" Mo Letter #999, 20 May 1980.

———. "Happy Daze!" Mo Letter #958, 6 December 1980.

———. "Daily Might." Booklet. Zurich: World Services, 1981.

———. "Church Fire Dream." Mo Letter #1841, 30 October 1981.

———. "Faith of Our Fathers." Mo Letter #1350, 12 January 1982.

———. "Sex with Grandmother." Mo Letter #1535, 11 June 1982.

———. "Influences! In My Life!" Mo Letter #1357, December 1982.

———. "The Last State? The Dangers of Demonism." Mo Letter #2306, March 1987.

———. "Our Teens—The Devil's Target." Mo Letter #2525, 1988.

Berg, Hosea. "The Pioneering of North America." Book of Remembrance. The Family, 1983.

Berg, Virginia Brandt. Letter to Clara Duncan. Spring 1919. Reprinted in Mo Letter #884, 1980.

———. "A Sample, Not a Sermon." Reprinted in David Brandt Berg, Letters from a Shepherd. Children of God, 1972, 1.

Buening, Carol. "Critical Commentary on 'Psychological Assessment of Children in The Family.'" Ohio State Univ. College of Social Work, December 2003.

Chancellor, James D. Life in The Family: An Oral History of the Children of God. New York: Syracuse Univ. Press, 2000.

Christian and Missionary Alliance. Alliance Witness (April 14, 1968), 18.

Compton, Todd. In Sacred Loneliness: The Plural Wives of Joseph Smith. Salt Lake City: Signature Books, 1997.

Davidito, Sara. The Story of Davidito. Zurich: World Services, 1982.

Davis, Deborah (Linda Berg), with Bill Davis. The Children of God: The Inside Story. Grand Rapids, MI: Zondervan, 1984.

Doerler, Bernd. "Sie betteln und beten für einen Mann den sie nicht kennen," Stern no. 287 (July 1977), 14–21.

Edwards, Thomas. "Hippies suffer sermon for feed-in." Huntington Beach Haven, 1968.

Ellwood, Robert S., Jr. One Way: The Jesus Movement and Its Meaning. Englewood Cliffs, NJ: Prentice-Hall, 1973.

Enroth, Ronald M., Edward E. Ericson, Jr., and C. Breckinridge Peters. The Story of the Jesus People: A Factual Survey. Exeter, U.K.: Paternoster Press, 1972.

Godwin, Nick, and Sorrel May. "Cult Killer." British television documentary, WagTV, August 2006.

Hopkins, Joseph. "Children of God Cult Records Higher Numbers," Christianity Today (November 26, 1982).

Irwin, Don. Eulogy for Ricky Rodriguez. Delivered 26 March 2005. www.xfamily.org/index.php/Ricky_Rodriguez _Memorial/Eulogies_and_Dedications.

Kent, Stephen A. "Lustful prophet: A psychosexual historical study of the Children of Gods' leader, David Berg," Cultic Studies Journal 11, no. 2 (1994): 135–188.

Kirsch, Jonathan. A History of the End of the World: How the Most Controversial Book in the Bible Changed the Course of Western Civilization. San Francisco: HarperSanFrancisco, 2006.

Klaw, Spencer. Without Sin: The Life and Death of the Oneida Community. New York: Penquin, 1993.

Krakauer, Jon. Under the Banner of Heaven: A Story of Violent Faith. New York: Doubleday, 2003.

Lattin, Don. "Children of a lesser God." San Francisco Chronicle, February 11–14, 2001, A1.

———. Following Our Bliss: How the Spiritual Ideals of the Sixties Shape Our Lives Today. San Francisco: HarperSanFrancisco, 2003.

———. "Rage turns to vengeance against 'Family.'" *San Francisco Chronicle*, January 15, 2005, A1.

———. "Deaths in The Family." *San Francisco Chronicle*, January 27, 2005, A1.

———. "IRS documents show ties between charity, sex cult," *San Francisco Chronicle*, February 6, 2005, A1.

———. "Mixed memories of 'The Family,'" *San Francisco Chronicle*, February 27, 2005, A1.

Lattin, Don, and Todd Wallack. "Hewlett grant went to cult-linked charity." *San Francisco Chronicle,* February 12, 2005.

Lelyveld, Nita, Paul Pringle, and Larry Stammer. "A young 'prophet' cannot defeat the demons of his past," *Los Angeles Times*, March 13, 2005.

Levine, Judith. *Harmful to Minors: The Perils of Protecting Children from Sex*. Minneapolis: Univ. of Minnesota Press, 2002.

Lewis, James R., and J. Gordon Melton, eds. *Sex, Slander, and Salvation: Investigating The Family/Children of God*. Stanford, CA: Center for Academic Publications, 1994.

Marconi, John. *Children of God, Family of Love.* Downers Grove, IL: InterVarsity Press, 1980.

Martin, Karen. Juvenile Dependency Petition, Superior Court, San Diego County, CA. Filed 5 March 1998.

Martin, Sarafina. "Ricky's Last Days." 15 January 2005. www.movingon.org.

McManus, Una, and John Charles Cooper. *Not for a Million Dollars*. Nashville: Impact Books, 1980.

Melton, J. Gordon. *The Children of God, "The Family.* Signature Books, 1997.

Moore, Thomas. "Where have all the Children of God gone?" *New Times*, October 4, 1974.

Ostling, Richard, and Joan Ostling. *Mormon America: The Power and the Promise*. San Francisco: HarperSanFrancisco, 1999.

Patrick, Ted. *Let Our Children Go!* New York: E.P. Dutton, 1976.

Penn, James. "No Regrets—Why I Left The Family, February 2000." www.xfamily.org.

Powell, Pamela. "Hippies 'see the light.' Huntington ceremony 'as good as marriage.'" *Daily Pilot*, 1968.

Priebe, Ed. "My Apology and Accounting." 2004. www.movingon.org.

Rodriguez, Ricky. Letter to Karen Zerby and Peter Amsterdam. 29 May 2000.

———. Letter to Gabe Martin. 26 November 2000.

———. Letter to James Penn. 22 December 2000.

———. Letter to Mom and Peter. 16 January 2001.

———. E-mail to Johnny. May 2002.

———. "Gospel of Rebellion." 25 May 2002. www.movingon.org.

———. "Life with Grandpa—the Mene Story." 4 June 2002. www.movingon.org.

———. "Still Around." 14 August 2004. www.movingon.org.

———. Farewell Video. 7 January 2005.

Singer, Margaret Thaler. *Cults in Our Midst: The Hidden Menace in Our Everyday Lives*. San Francisco: Jossey-Bass Publishers, 1995.

Smith, Angela. Memorial Web Site. 2005. www.angela-smith.org.

Smith, Chuck. "History of Calvary Chapel." *Last Times*, Fall 1981. www.calvary-chapelcostamesa.org.

Sparks, Jack. *The Mind Benders: A Look at Current Cults*. Nashville: Thomas Nelson Publishers, 1977.

Streiker, Lowell D. *The Cults Are Coming*. Nashville: Abingdon, 1978.

Taniguchi, Yumiko. "Notice of My Son Abe's Graduation." 2006. www.xfamily.org.

Van Zandt, David E. *Living in the Children of God*. Princeton, NJ: Princeton Univ. Press, 1991.

Wallenstein, Herbert J. Final Report on the Activities of the Children of God. New York: Attorney General of the State of New York, 1974.

Ward, Lord Justice Alan. "The Judgement of Lord Justice Ward on the 26th May 1995." London: High Court of Justice, Family Division, October 1995.

Wilkinson, Peter. "The life and death of the chosen ones," *Rolling Stone* (June 30, 2005), 162.

Williams, Miriam. *Heaven's Harlots—My Fifteen Years in a Sex Cult*. New York: Eagle Brook/Morrow, 1998.

Zerby, Karen. "False Accusers in the Last Days!" Maria Letters #174, 1992.

———. "Loving Jesus! Part 1, Part 2," Maria Letters #306 and #307, 5 July 1995.

———. "Questions & Answers on Angela and Ricky's Deaths, Persecution and Other Issues." *Good News!* #1137. The Family International, June 2005.

Index

Page references followed by *p* indicate photographs.

Activated Ministries (Escondido), 193
Alan, 137
Alliance Weekly (Valley Farms), 21–22, 35–36
American Soul Clinic, 25
Amsterdam, Jon-A, 191–92
Amsterdam, Peter ("King Peter," Steven Douglas Kelly): denial of Ricky's accusations by, 186–87; early Family work by, 88, 92; "Marriage of the Generations" campaign promoted by, 128–30; photograph of, 183*p*; Ricky's mission against, 6; as Zerby's new consort, 105, 125
Amy, 108
Antichrist government, 47
anticult movement (1970s), 52
Arizona Daily Star, 184
"The Ark" (Berg's mobile headquarters), 44
Arvizu, Alisia, 161–64
Assemblies of God, 36
Azusa Street revival, 15

Berg, Aaron: depression and accidental death of, 61–62; early ministry participation by, 36, 38; marriage with Shula, 55–59; photograph of, 35*p*
Berg, David Brandt (Endtime Prophet): on Aaron's death, 62–63; childhood sexual experiences of, 16–17, 18–19; childhood sexuality theories (Law of Love) of, 74–75, 78–80, 89, 114–15, 127–30, 187–88, 206; death of, 115, 125, 126; family background of, 11–19; The Family Web site on, 115–16; on his childhood, 16–19; incestuous misconduct by, 24–25; influence and legacy of, 205–11; move to Huntington Beach

Light Club ministry by, 33, 35–40; ordained to ministry, 19–20; photographs of, 35*p*, 65*p*, 105*p*, 125*p*; on relationship with his mother, 17–19; relationship with Karen Zerby, 40–45; "Revolutionary Sex" written by, 74; Ricky's desire to punish, 2, 6; sexual obsessions of, 50–51, 57–58, 206–7; Valley Farms ministry of, 20–24; work with Fred Jordan, 25–26, 207. *See also* The Family; The Family's abuse practices
Berg, Deborah. *See* Davis, Deborah Berg
Berg Evangelistic Dramatic Company, 15–16, 19, 20
Berg, Faithy: on "betrothal ceremonies," 37; incestuous relationship with father, 25; introduction to Karen, 41–42; marriage of, 33; photographs of, 27*p*, 35*p*
"Berg Family Singers," 26, 33
Berg, Hjalmer, 13, 14–15, 19
Berg, Hjalmer, Jr., 13, 36
Berg, Hosea, 35*p*, 36, 38–39, 54, 55
Berg, Jane (Miller), 20, 21, 35*p*, 42, 44, 45, 62
Berg, Merry: early childhood sexual abuse of, 83–84; early life of, 58, 61, 62, 63; Family attacks against, 93; forced sexual relationship of Ricky and, 84, 209; mock marriage ceremony with Berg, 84; photograph of, 81*p*; post-Family life of, 207–9; public denunciations of The Family by, 87–88, 112, 113, 125; rebellion against The Family by, 84–88; returned to the Unit, 80, 81–83; Ricky's memories of, 82–83, 94–95; sent to Macao "Victor Camp," 86–87

"Psychological Assessment of Children in The Family" study, 109–12

Queen Rachel, 65p, 70, 101

Reedus, Norman, 3
Resettlement Administration, 20
"Revolutionary Sex" (Berg), 74
Right On (underground Christian newspaper), 31
Rodriguez, Ricky Peter ("Davidito"): begins to leave The Family, 139–41; biological father (Carlos) of, 70–71, 72; birth and early childhood of, 65–74; commits suicide, 175–78, 183–84, 201–2; early childhood sexual abuse of, 72–73, 77–80; early meetings with his mother's family, 158–59; early relationship with Elixcia, 117–20, 122–23; emotional damage and anger of, 8, 102, 141, 144–50, 161–64, 179–81, 201–2; forced sexual relationship of Merry and, 84, 209; "Gospel of Rebellion" by, 142–43; on lack of understanding by abusers, 180–81; legal name changes by, 103; life after leaving the cult, 6–7, 151–70; marriage to Elixcia, 146; meeting between Millikan and, 105–8; memories of Merry by, 82–83, 94–95; moves in with his Aunt Rosemary, 151–60; as one of the "two witnesses," 66, 101; photographs of, 1p, 105p, 117p, 131p, 151p, 161p, 165p, 171p; placed in the Heavenly City as student, 91–93; "Psychological Assessment of Children in The Family" study interviews with, 109–12; relationship with Alisia Arvizu, 161–64; search for mother by, 2, 6, 149–50, 157; Sue Kauten's murder and escape by, 1–2, 10, 171–74, 183–84; Sue's Christmas Day call to, 151–52, 178–79, 180; videotape on his mission of revenge, 4–10, 166–67, 176, 180, 189, 195
Roosevelt, Franklin D., 20, 22

Roselle, Daniel, 149, 150, 194
Rugely, Michael ("Tiago"), 121–22, 165–68

San Francisco Chronicle, 184
Sarafina, 146, 149, 166
Sarran, Marina, 198, 199
Schieberl, Anneke, 98–99, 148, 156
Schieberl, Ron, 148, 156
Schroeder, Jennifer, 146–47
second-generation Family defectors: Davida on her post-Family life as, 209–10; The Family Web site testimonies attacking, 189–92; Merry Berg as, 87–88, 112, 113, 125; Ricky's "Life with Grandpa" supporting, 143; suicides by second-generation, 149, 166, 194–97, 210–11; testimonies on child sexual abuse by, 72–75, 77–80, 81–95, 89–90, 134–40, 143; testimonies on damage done to second-generation, 143–44; Web sites for second-generation, 143, 185. *See also* The Family
second-generation Family members: Old Town San Diego interviews with, 193–99; Web site testimonies by, 189–92
"The Second Letter to the Christians" (tract), 31
"Secret Rapture" vision, 47
Sex, Slander, and Salvation: Investigating The Family/Children of God (anthology), 110–12
sexual abuse. *See* childhood sexual abuse; The Family's abuse practices
"the shakeout" (Heavenly City School), 92
Shepherd, Gary, 109–12, 203–4
Show Me!: A Picture Book on Sex for Children and Parents (1974), 74
Simpson, Rev. Albert Benjamin, 22
Slown, Phillip, 134, 135, 136–37, 138
Smecker, Paul, 10
Smith, Chuck, 31, 32
Sparks, Jack, 31
Spencer, Jeremy, 49

Zerby, Karen Elva (*continued*)
accusations by, 186; disapproval
of Ricky and Elixcia's relationship,
122–23; early life of, 40–41; eulogy
written for Ricky by, 185–86; letter to Ben Farnsworth on his son's
suicide, 199, 201; "Marriage of the
Generations" campaign promoted by,
128–30; as one of the "two witnesses," 66, 101; photographs of, 65p,
183p; relationship with David Berg,
40–45; response to Ricky's suicide by,
185–86, 202–3; Ricky's search for, 2,
6, 149–50, 157; sexual relationship
with Carlos by, 70–71; Sue's assistant
position with, 100; Techi on character of, 189
Zerby, Rosemary. *See* Kanspedos, Rosemary (Zerby)
Zerby, Trevor, 188